THE CELTS AND THE RENAISSANCE
TRADITION AND INNOVATION

THE CELTS AND THE RENAISSANCE

TRADITION AND INNOVATION

*Proceedings of the Eighth International Congress
of Celtic Studies*

1987

Held at Swansea, 19–24 July, 1987

EDITED BY

GLANMOR WILLIAMS AND ROBERT OWEN JONES

CARDIFF
UNIVERSITY OF WALES PRESS
1990

British Library Cataloguing in Publication Data

International Congress of Celtic Studies (*8th: 1987*).
   The Celts and the renaissance: tradition and
   innovation: proceedings of the Eighth International
   Congress of Celtic Studies 1987.
   1. Celtic civilization, history
   I. Title   II. Williams, Glanmor, *1920–*   III. Jones,
Robert Owen, *1941–*
940′.04916

   ISBN 0–7083–1054–0

Printed in Great Britain by The Bath Press, Bath

Llywydd y Gyngres/President of the Congress

Yr Arglwydd/Lord Cledwyn

Is-lywyddion/Vice-Presidents

Y Prifathro/Principal B. L. Clarkson
Dr D. W. Dykes
Y Prifathro/Principal G. Owen
Dr B. F. Roberts

Noddwyr/Patrons

Y Gwir Anrhydeddus/Rt. Hon. Peter Walker
Ysgrifennydd Gwladol/Secretary of State for Wales

Cynghorwr/Councillor H. W. Ayres
Arglwydd Faer Abertawe/Lord Mayor of Swansea

Yr Arglwydd/Lord Callaghan KG
Llywydd Coleg Prifysgol Abertawe/
President, University College of Swansea

Pwyllgor Ymgynghorol/Advisory Committee

Yr Athro D. Simon Evans (Cadeirydd/Chairman)
Dr R. O. Jones (Ysgrifennydd/Secretary)
Yr Athro Ceri Lewis
Dr B. F. Roberts
Dr H. N. Savory
Yr Athro Glanmor Williams
Yr Athro J. E. Caerwyn Williams

Pwyllgor Trefnu/Organizing Committee

Yr Athro Glanmor Williams (Cadeirydd/Chairman)
Alun Evans (Trysorydd/Treasurer)
Dr R. O. Jones (Ysgrifennydd/Secretary)
Dr F. G. Cowley
Yr Athro R. A. Griffiths
W. G. Harries
Dr N. Lloyd
Dr Prys T. J. Morgan
R. G. Rhys
I. Rowlands

CONTENTS

FIGURES

PLATES

PREFACE

In 1987 it became the turn of Wales to act as host to the International Congress of Celtic Studies for the second time—the first occasion had been in 1963. The venue chosen by the Board of Celtic Studies of the University of Wales was the University College, Singleton Park, Swansea, where the Eighth Congress was held on 19-24 July 1987. The central theme of the proceedings was 'Tradition and Innovation', and some ninety papers were delivered on a wide variety of topics in the sectional sessions. At the plenary sessions, six speakers were invited to deliver lectures to illustrate the central theme by reference to the impact of the Renaissance on individual Celtic-speaking countries. These have been brought together and published in full in this volume of the Proceedings of the Conference, together with summaries of the sectional papers.

We should like to take this opportunity of expressing our sincere gratitude to all those who so readily helped to make the Congress such a success. First and foremost, our thanks go to the large number of friendly and enthusiastic participants from a wide range of countries and institutions, and particularly to those who delivered papers. We acknowledge gratefully the generous patronage of the Secretary of State for Wales (Rt. Hon. Peter Walker, MP) and other members of the Welsh Office and CADW, the Lord Mayor of Swansea (Councillor H. W. Ayres) and the City Council, the National Library of Wales (Dr B. F. Roberts, Librarian), and the National Museum of Wales (Dr D. W. Dykes, Director). We should also wish to thank the University of Wales for the sustained help and interest rendered by the Pro-Chancellor (Lord Cledwyn), the Registrar (Dr Alan Kemp), and many others, and especially the Director of the University of Wales Press (Mr John Rhys) and his colleague Mrs Ceinwen Jones for expertly seeing this volume through the press. Finally, we acknowledge our deep indebtedness to the President (Lord Callaghan, KG), to the Principal (Professor B. F. Clarkson), and to many of our colleagues among the staff of the University College of Swansea, and particularly to Mrs G. Miles (Secretary, Department of Welsh), Miss M. Jacobs (Accommodation Officer), and Mr A. Capel (Catering Officer), for all their support and co-operation.

Glanmor Williams
Robert Owen Jones

CHAPTER I

THE RENAISSANCE[1]

by Glanmor Williams

THERE are widely used, even indispensable, terms like 'classical antiquity', 'Dark Ages', or 'Industrial Revolution', which were not the labels given by contemporaries to those developments which they describe but were subsequently applied to them by historians. This is not true of the name, 'the Renaissance'. It was first given to the phenomenon it categorizes by those who were responsible for bringing it into being. The Italian word, *rinascita*—renaissance or rebirth—it is true, was not first used until 1550, when the Italian art historian, Giorgio Vasari, employed it in his famous book on *Lives of the Most Eminent Painters, Sculptors, and Architects*.[2] But the associated metaphors of 'awakening', 'renewal', 'restoration', or 'revival', may be traced right back to what is usually regarded as the dawn of the Renaissance in the fourteenth century; to the man who can be conceived of, more positively than anyone else, as the first true Renaissance figure, Francesco Petrarch (1304-74).[3] He himself referred to the revival of classical literature in terms of images like the coming of light after darkness, or the return of spring following winter. A little later, his fellow-Florentine, Giovanni Boccaccio (1317-75), acclaimed what he saw as the new dawn of poetry associated with Dante and Petrarch, and of painting with Giotto. After nearly a century, in 1442, Lorenzo Valla in the foreword to his *De Elegantiis Linguae Latinae* similarly observed how 'those arts that are closest to the liberal arts, to wit, painting, sculpture, and architecture, were first so long and so greatly degenerated, and almost perished with letters themselves, and are now being reawakened and revived, and there is such a flowering of fine artists and lettered men'.[4] Eventually, by the sixteenth century, Vasari had developed the whole concept of the birth, growth, age, and death of the arts in classical times, the barbarism of the age that followed, and the 'renaissance (*rinascita*) of the arts and the perfection to which they have attained in our own time'.[5]

Those Italian humanists of the fourteenth to the sixteenth centuries were profoundly conscious of living through a seismic upheaval; but their conception of it was limited to classical literature and learning and the fine arts. Only in later centuries was the term 'Renaissance' broadened to cover a much wider span of social, and even political, change, some of it hotly debated and highly contentious. For the purposes of this chapter, I propose to steer well clear of such minefields. I shall be content to confine my remarks to the impact of the Renaissance on language, literature, and learning. In the process, I should like to look first at the nature of the Renaissance in Italy; then, to trace its diffusion to other parts of Europe; and, finally, to examine some of the implications of this for the Celtic countries.

I. The Renaissance in Italy

The Renaissance was not born in Petrarch's Italy like Minerva, fully armed and bursting unheralded on the scene. Early commentators on Dante had claimed that it was he who had revived dead poetry and recalled to men's minds those philosopher-poets of antiquity from the oblivion into which, for centuries, they had been shamefully allowed to fall. On a lower and more prosaic level, Italian universities, too, had long specialized in the *ars dictaminis*, the teaching of rhetoric, through the medium of classical authors, whom they had come to appreciate for their literary merit as well as their practical usefulness. Early in the fourteenth century, in Italian cities like Verona, Arezzo, and especially Padua, proto-humanism was firmly rooted among men like Lovato Lovati (1241–1309) and the poet laureate, Alberto Mussato (1261–1329).[6] But if, in its origins, the Renaissance manifested some of the characteristics of evolution, it also bore so many of the symptoms of revolution that Petrarch could conceive of it as a sudden, abrupt revival or renewal. This was due in large measure to his own genius. Long before Renan ever hailed him as the first modern man, he had rightly been adjudged the founding father of the Renaissance. His distinctive contribution to the understanding and appreciation of the classical authors was that he was the first man for centuries to meet them on their own terms as fellow-citizens. In this respect his re-evaluation of Cicero was crucial. To the Middle Ages Cicero had been a Stoic sage and a model of aloofness. Petrarch's discovery of Cicero's intimate letters in Verona Cathedral library awakened in him a new and overwhelming enthusiasm, not merely for the purity of the great man's Latin style but even more for his concept of civic virtue. The consequence was that Petrarch became aware, as no one else in the Middle Ages previously had been, of the huge gulf which separated classical civilization from the medieval world. It awakened in him an insatiable enthusiasm for classical literature, the city of Rome, and ancient republican virtue.

As a textual critic, he was unequalled before Lorenzo Valla. But he was more than a restorer of ancient literature; he was also the initiator of a new approach to it. Convinced that it contained indispensable moral values, he was sure that it had a central role to play in the formation of a truly virtuous man. He gave fresh relevance to Cicero's message that the proper object of education was the shaping of the *vir virtutis* through the mastery of rhetoric and moral philosophy, the combination of eloquence and wisdom. On such a basis he stood forth as the perfervid advocate of what he claimed to be the true aims and proper content of education, to enable man to fulfil his real nature, the extent of his capacities, and the rightful goals of his life. Men could, he contended, aspire to excellence; the due purpose and process of education should be to enable them to attain that end. Petrarch, it need hardly be added, was not just a student of literature; he was, in addition, a creative artist of the front rank, a poet laureate and an illustrious littérateur—in the *Volgare* and in Latin, though he himself expected to win undying fame as a Latin writer. Summing up Petrarch's achievements, Leonardo Bruni in 1436 portrayed him as the first 'who recognized and restored to light the ancient elegance of style which was lost and dead, and although in him it was not perfect, nevertheless by himself he saw and opened the way to this perfection'.[7]

Once Petrarch had thus so brilliantly blazed the trail, others followed where he had led. They energetically and persuasively adumbrated the concept of the sudden revival of classical letters and rejected medieval values and scholastic learning in favour of what the ancient world had to offer. Such revolutionary notions were, by the end of the fourteenth century and the beginning of the fifteenth, winning many eager disciples. Nowhere were they more active or numerous than in Florence, many of whose sons began to envisage themselves as the veritable heirs of republican Rome and their city as the counterpart in fifteenth-century Italy of fifth-century Athens.[8] But to trace, even in outline, the dissemination and flowering of the Renaissance at Florence and elsewhere in Italy during the fifteenth century would be impracticable. All that can be done, perhaps, is to agree with the verdict that 'there was more challenge and response and a greater concentration of personalities in Italy from 1390 to 1550 than perhaps since the fourth and fifth centuries BC in Attica'.[9]

What may be useful, however, is to try to summarize, no matter how inadequately, the main features characterizing the Italian Renaissance during that era.

Implicit, and indeed explicit, in much of what the Renaissance upheld were the rejection and abandonment of many of the values and criteria of the earlier medieval world. Out went the learning of the schoolmen, based as it was on corrupt texts and impure Latin, with its emphasis on logic and theology, and the priority it gave to asceticism and renunciation of earthly esteem and worldly possessions as the road to the highest human fulfilment. Such a marked change of intellectual and spiritual direction possibly came all the easier in Italy, where scholasticism had never taken so firm a grip as in northern Europe.

In place of medieval ideals and methods was enthroned a new and impassioned determination to return *ad fontes*; to the clear, unsullied sources of the original texts. Only through imbibing long and deep the pure waters of the unmuddied springs of ancient authors could the secrets of a full, beautiful, and virtuous life be acquired. Or, as Lorenzo Valla summed it up, the ancient Latin language had spread among the nations the noblest and truly divine fruit; food not of the body but the soul. Latin, he believed, had 'taught the best laws, prepared the way for all wisdom, and ... made it possible for them no longer to be called barbarians'.[10] Classical Latin literature reawakened on the part of its fifteenth-century devotees what has percipiently been described as a 'single-minded even militant dedication'[11] to its life-enhancing wisdom and elegance.

That enthusiasm embraced Greek as well as Latin. Greek literature had been eulogized as the source and inspiration of Latin wisdom by, among others, the idol of Renaissance *cognoscenti*, Cicero, who had acknowledged that the most perfect expression of *humanitas* was to be found in Greek. It took some time, nevertheless, for the language to become widely known in Italy. Warmly though Petrarch admired Greek, he never found it possible to learn the language in the circumstances of the mid-fourteenth century. The turning-point came with the appointment of the Greek scholar, Manuel

Chrysoloras, to a chair at the university in Florence in 1397. The movement to advance Greek studies then really took off—half a century before the fall of Constantinople in 1453, once thought to have been the main trigger of Greek studies in Italy. One of the consequences of the overrunning of the Eastern Empire's ancient capital by the Turks, nevertheless, was that it encouraged many more Greek scholars to flee from Constantinople to Italy, bringing their treasured manuscripts with them. Throughout the fifteenth century, therefore, interest and delight in, and study of, the Greek language, literature, and thought increased apace in Italy.

This thirst for the revival of Latin and Greek literature inspired an almost frenetic search for ancient manuscripts. Cathedral, monastic, and other libraries were minutely combed in pursuit of lost or neglected texts; discoveries of long-forgotten works were hailed with inordinate delight; manuscripts were avidly copied; and Greek works were translated into Latin. Collections of books were enthusiastically accumulated; and libraries—public and private—were built to house them. A single citizen of Florence, Niccolò Niccoli, was reputed to be the possessor of no fewer than 8,000 manuscripts; while Pope Nicholas V, pre-eminent humanist, founded in the mid-fifteenth century the Vatican Library, soon to become the largest public library in Europe, though Nicholas was only one among a number of distinguished patrons to set up such a collection.[12]

The recovery of manuscripts and the build-up of extensive holdings of them were but a part of the crusade. Scholars were also concerned to ensure that reconstituted texts would correctly represent what their authors had originally written. In their quest for authenticity, humanists exhibited a passion for accuracy and paid the most meticulous attention to ancient usage. They complained vociferously that medieval copyists had been culpably defective in their knowledge of Latin, and deplorably ignorant and slipshod in their copying. To arrive at a sound text, therefore, it was necessary to compare as many copies as possible, to emend mistaken readings, eliminate interpolations, and expose forgeries. Naturally, this required vastly higher standards of scholarship, a close study of the problems of palaeography, orthography, grammar, syntax, and usage—and all without the aids that the present generation takes for granted in the shape of printed texts, grammars, dictionaries, and the like. Gradually, however, Renaissance editors evolved the critical historical and philological methods which enabled them to arrive at accurate texts. They were greatly assisted in these labours by the discovery of printing in mid-century. The press gave them the means of conveniently producing edited texts, rationalizing and stabilizing orthography and grammar, and circulating uniform and accurate copies in large numbers at a relatively cheap price. By the end of the fifteenth century, humanists in all parts of Italy had mastered the art of writing and publishing fluent and correct Latin and Greek.

As a result of their efforts, scholars had not only brought back into circulation an extensive range of classical literature but had also reintroduced a number of literary forms which had dropped out of fashion in the Middle Ages; genres like the dialogue, the essay, the familiar epistle, or the drama, and the literary treatment of history, biography, moral philosophy, and political theory.

Central to this transformation of their approach to language, literature, and learning was the intellectual revolution wrought in their midst by the content of classical literature, the *studia humanitatis*. This humanism they embraced so ecstatically was the most exciting and pervasive current of thought in fifteenth-century Italy. The *studia humanitatis* were recognized as consisting of a clearly identified group of disciplines: grammar, rhetoric, poetry, history, and moral philosophy. Out of the absorption in them emerged a philosophy based on a new-found confidence in the dignity and creative powers of man, increased individualism in literature and the arts, rejection of the ascetic ideal of renunciation, and enhanced belief in the value of the active life. Such attitudes were closely linked to greater realism in the visual arts, enriched by the discovery of the laws of anatomy, optics, and perspective, knowledge of which was indispensable to express the new ideal. Emboldened by such enlargement of the range and nature of his resources, the *vir virtutis*, the new Renaissance man, might confidently and unashamedly embark on his quest for glory, honour, fame, and recognition.

The difference between the attitude of Renaissance humanists towards life and that of the medieval schoolmen came to be reflected plainly in education. In order to disseminate their ideals and ensure their transmission from one generation to another, humanists aimed at imparting a purely literary training; a liberal education not subordinated to philosophy or theology. They laid particular emphasis on the advantages of a thorough knowledge of the Greek and Latin classics, including the Christian Fathers. Instruction was to be based on the humanities, the *bonae litterae*, the liberal studies worthy of a free man; those disciplines through which virtue and wisdom were attained, which trained and developed the highest gifts of body and mind that ennobled men. Following the example of eminent fifteenth-century schoolmasters like Vittorino da Feltre and Guarino da Verona, Baldassare Castiglione could depict in detail his ideal portrait of *Il Cortegiano* (1528). Here was the rounded and versatile product of Renaissance education; the beau ideal of physical prowess, practical aptitude, ripe judgement, trained mind, and cultivated sensibilities, capable of exercising his talents to the full in public and private life. He was to be the supremely gifted individual who combined 'the courtier's, soldier's, scholar's eye, tongue and sword', as Ophelia characterized Hamlet in such admiring tones.[13]

All the intense adulation lavished on the classics might have been expected to lead to the overshadowing of the vernacular language. There was, without doubt, a genuine risk that Italian might become regarded with disfavour as an inferior and unworthy language during the first half of the fifteenth century, when a writer like Biondo could disdainfully dismiss the *Volgare* as an adulterated speech with an outlandish usage. But even at that stage the *Volgare* was not without its stout defenders. The illustrious precedents established in the native tongue by the three Florentine masters, Dante, Petrarch, and Boccaccio, were a source of immense and understandable pride. Bruni maintained that every language had its own perfection and Manetti insisted that Dante had ennobled Italian as Homer had Greek and Virgil Latin. Later, Lorenzo dei Medici ardently championed the language in which he expressed himself so felicitously and in 1504 Esaia da Este justified it on the grounds that, in printed form, an Italian

Bible could bring the whole of the sacred Scriptures (*tutta la sacratissima Bibbia*) to the knowledge of ordinary unlearned people—including women![14] We need hardly wonder, consequently, that, some twenty years later, Bembo had no hesitation in saluting Latin as the language of the past and hailing Italian as the language of the future, worthy to stand alongside Latin, just as the latter had once taken its own place alongside Greek. By that time, with the vernacular gaining the upper hand, it had already absorbed into itself all the typical achievements of classical humanism in matters of style, terminology, textual and philological scholarship, literary form, and subject matter. Similarly, in a number of other European languages, there would be writers willing to emulate the example set by the Italians in supplying the lessons learned from a study of the classical languages as guide-rails for the creation of a new literature in the midst of increasingly self-conscious nations groping towards greater unity.[15] Added to which, the printing-press exercised a decisive influence in precipitating the need for a commonly understood literary language, with uniform grammar and regularized spelling, as well as in diffusing literary publications more extensively than ever before.

So much for some of the principal achievements of the Renaissance in Italy. May I just add something very briefly about some of those features with which it has often been wrongly credited? Wonderfully integrated and persuasive as was Jakob Burckhardt's depiction of the Renaissance—a portrait whose ideal proportions and harmonious rhythms were themselves worthy of a Renaissance masterpiece—scholars have now had to query its rounded perfection. Nothing like as sharp or dramatic a contrast existed between the Middle Ages and the Renaissance as Burckhardt supposed. The Renaissance did not suddenly irradiate a benighted and barbaric Europe with dazzling shafts of celestial light. Medieval Europe had itself, in the course of the Renaissance of the Carolingian Age and that of the twelfth century, restored important aspects of classical literature and emphasized humanist values.[16] It had, moreover, created its own climate of art and thought worthy of the utmost respect and admiration. From the medieval world the Renaissance derived more than it was willing to recognize or admit. The Renaissance did not represent the first expression of individualism nor the beginnings of the modern world. But neither, on the other hand, was it as pagan or as irreligious as it has often been portrayed. Nevertheless, however much less the differences between it and the Middle Ages may have been, and whatever its own overestimations of its accomplishments and consequences, nothing is to be gained by trying to argue it away altogether or pouring the baby out with the bath-water. There certainly *was* such a phenomenon as the Italian Renaissance; it had an epoch-making impact on Italy; and its influence elsewhere was profound and enduring.

II. *The spread of the Italian Renaissance elsewhere in Europe*

To explain the migration of Renaissance influences further afield from Italy, we should first of all take account of how other European countries were becoming potentially much more receptive to them. By the fifteenth century the status of laymen and lay governments was noticeably more assured in relation to the Church and clerics than it had been. In kingdoms, principalities and cities, more powerful and centralized secular authority was being consolidated. Its agents were, in general, trained and educated lay lawyers and administrators. Equally visible was the rise (or should one say the recovery?) of capitalism, with the bodies of influential merchants, traders, and artisans inevitably associated with it. Everywhere, and among a variety of social groups, there was increasing emphasis on the need to educate the laity. Literacy spread relatively rapidly in their midst, especially among the urban classes, and the resultant increase in demand for reading materials was too steep to be met by the traditional means of manuscript-copying. It led to the evolution of the printing-press, first in Germany, whence it spread quickly to other countries. Called into being by increased literacy, the upsurge of religious devotion, and the growth of national consciousness, the press soon had the effect of fanning the flames of religious and patriotic sentiment. Alongside these developments, in more than one country, there unfolded a growing realism in art and letters, so much so that some scholars have been led to play down the influence of Italy and to argue that her humanism occupied a far less creative role in fashioning that of the north than used to be thought. We should, nevertheless, be wary of underestimating what other countries owed to Italy. Witness in this context the testimony of Erasmus, who was better fitted, perhaps, than anyone to appreciate what Italy had contributed to other lands. He complained—with typical Renaissance exaggeration, no doubt—how these less favoured regions had, in time past, suffered from the 'obstinate growth of barbarism' and lived through an era in which men 'turned their backs on the precepts of the ancients'. But now, a full knowledge of the humanities had been recovered, 'with admirable scholarly application' by 'our good Lorenzo Valla and his disciples in Italy', as a result of which it had at last become possible 'to bring back into use' all the neglected ancient authors and their works.[17]

How, then, had it been possible for Italy to enrich other regions with those innovations for which she had originally been responsible? In the first place, of all the countries in Europe, Italy was the one which had the most widely ramifying network of contacts of various kinds with other lands. The city of Rome alone had for centuries attracted a vast concourse of visitors from all quarters of Christendom in the form of petitioners, litigants, and pilgrims. When the headquarters of the Church itself became the most conspicuous centre of Renaissance art and learning, as it did late in the fifteenth century and early in the sixteenth, it could be expected to exercise a magnetic influence on the rest of Europe. Furthermore, Italy was the pioneer of European trade and still the most active and advanced participator in it. As such, its widespread and profitable commercial connections extended all over Europe—with Aragon and southern France within the Mediterranean, with southern Germany and central Europe along the great Alpine routes, with Switzerland, the Rhineland, France, and the Low Countries along the Rhine, and by sea with England. From 1494, also, the protracted wars in Italy attracted the predatory rulers and nobility of a number of European countries, tempted there by the prospect of plunder and profit held out by its Renaissance wealth and treasures.

Again, by the second half of the fifteenth century Italy had fallen under the rule of the *signori* or despots. As a result, Renaissance culture and patronage were firmly lodged in a milieu that was courtly and aristocratic and flourished in an ambience thoroughly congenial to the countries of northern Europe. Italian humanists were themselves well enough aware of the lucrative possibilities of employment open to them in other countries. Some went to teach their subjects at universities; just as Beroaldo went to Paris, where he proposed to lecture 'on the arts of poetry and the *studia humanitatis*', in order to show 'how closely this kind of study connects with philosophy' and 'how much the study of philosophy can benefit from this connection'.[18] Other Italian humanists, about the end of the fifteenth century, arrived in Oxford and Cambridge, where they attracted a considerable following. The growing enthusiasm kindled for the humanities was not long in promoting a two-way traffic, with scholars from outside Italy excitedly making the pilgrimage to its universities and libraries in a bid to extend and deepen their knowledge of the classical languages and literatures. One such was John Colet, who went from England to spend three very significant years in Italy between 1493 and 1496. So did Erasmus from 1506 to 1509; while the German savant, Conrad Celtis, spent even longer there from 1487 onwards and, in the course of his sojourn, worked at Venice, Padua, Florence, and Rome.[19] When scholars like these returned to their own countries, the Renaissance influences they radiated among their fellow-countrymen were even more philoprogenitive.

But it was not simply a matter of coming and going by men of learning on their own account as individuals. Just as important, if not more decisive, was the initiative taken by rulers like Francis I, Henry VIII, or the Emperor Maximilian, to entice artists and literati to their courts. Francis I earned himself the title of *Père des Lettres* on account of his patronage of humanists, translators, littérateurs, and poets. In 1530 he created chairs of Greek, Hebrew, Latin, and oriental languages, and many translations were carried out at his command, especially of Greek and Latin classics.

Perhaps the most momentous key of all to the spread of Renaissance culture was the discovery of the printing-press.[20] Humanists seized on the new invention with greater alacrity and delight than anyone else. And with good reason, when the press enabled them, for the first time, to rely on the uniform publication of hundreds if not thousands of copies of an accurate text, arrived at by a patient process of critical scholarship and careful proof-reading. They were further helped by the publication of teaching aids in the form of grammars and dictionaries, which made the learning of languages easier. Most important of all, possibly, was that classical texts could now be issued cheaply and conveniently, and circulated in large enough numbers and over an area sufficiently wide as to be able to defy the ravages of war, tumult, and insurrection. In any previous age, given the scarcity and vulnerability of manuscript copies, such disasters would have been deeply injurious, if not fatal, to any revival of scholarship. During the Twelfth-century Renaissance, for example, Otto of Freising (*c.* 1110–1158) had proved the Donation of Constantine to be a forgery; but all knowledge of his arguments was subsequently lost, so that it was left to Lorenzo Valla to prove it anew as one of the most sensational discoveries of the Renaissance.[21] Of all the differences between the Italian Renaissance and earlier renaissances, the most fundamental was that the advances it made were universally diffused and rendered permanent by the printing-press. The links between the press and the Renaissance are evident from the location of the printing industry in the year 1500. Presses were found in the largest numbers in those countries where the Renaissance had struck its deepest roots—at 45 places in France, 64 in Germany, and nearly 80 in Italy. Well might Louis XII of France refer to printing in 1513 as a divine rather than a human invention, or François Rabelais conclude that it was the press which had filled the world with learned men and extensive libraries and that the new learning itself had involved a restoration of 'every method of teaching' and the most fruitful intercourse with the unrivalled civilization of the ancient world.[22]

Finally, when the Renaissance reached other countries, it tended to develop along different lines, in accordance with the political, social, and cultural circumstances prevailing in each. In some of the leading monarchies, it was outstanding figures at court—rulers, aristocrats, or ministers—who tended to dominate; Francis I in France, Cardinal Ximenes in Spain, or Thomas Cromwell in England. But in countries without a centralized monarchy, like Germany, Switzerland, or the Low Countries, prosperous towns and cities, with their patrician merchants, civic officials, and men of the learned professions, including some of the clergy, often took the lead. Other characteristics, too, were common to most, if not all. Universities were usually the foci of these studies; the cult of classical languages (including Hebrew) was ecstatic; and the addiction to philological and historical criticism knew almost no bounds. One of the most universal traits was the efflorescence of Christian humanism. Classical and biblical scholarship became fused; the Scriptures were regarded as supreme among all the ancient sources, and their true understanding as holding out incomparably the sublimest and most lasting reward of all.

Outstanding among the Christian humanists was Erasmus,[23] whose reputation throughout western Europe ranked higher than that of any other scholar. Like many of his fellows, he was sharply critical of the corruptions of the clergy and the superstitions widely prevalent in the Church, made no secret of his deep antipathy to scholastic learning, and yearned to purify religion by a return to the teaching of Christ as interpreted in the light of the newly understood antiquity. 'Habemus fontes Salvatoris', he trustingly declared, secure in the belief that these sources were infinitely safer than the musings of theologians. By reconciling Christian and pagan antiquity he furnished many northern intellectuals with their nearest approach to full acceptance of both the forms and the norms of the classical era. Early in the sixteenth century he and his fellows were suffused with a buoyant optimism concerning the possibility of reforming religion through the medium of the revival of letters. Typical of them was the fine scholar and precursor of reform, Lefèvre d'Étaples. With unhesitating confidence he pronounced to the youthful Guillaume Farel in 1512, 'My son, God will renew the world and you will be a witness of it.'[24] Alas! in practice, the Protestant Reformation, though in some respects the culmination of earlier humanism, proved to be even more surely the ruination of its sanguine and unclouded hopes.

III. The Renaissance and the Celtic countries

In the third and final section of this chapter, I should like to consider very briefly some of the implications of what has earlier been written for the Celtic lands, their languages, and their cultures. Intriguingly enough, no less commanding a figure than Erasmus was at one point decidedly confident about the process by which 'public letters, which were almost extinct, are now cultivated by Scots . . . and Irishmen', when writing to his friend, Capito, in 1517.[25] Elsewhere, in 1516, he had expressed the hope that the Scriptures would be translated 'into all languages so that they could be read and understood not only by Scots and Irish but also by Turks and Saracens'.[26] Even so, just beneath the surface of his optimism, there was a broad hint that these Celtic peoples were on the outermost fringes of Europe. Those countries on its geographical periphery—Scandinavia in the north and the Celtic-speaking lands in the west— were predictably the ones to which the Renaissance spread very slowly. It could hardly be said to have reached Wales or Ireland by the end of the first quarter of the sixteenth century. Even in Scotland, in spite of the ancient universities there, it had made very little impression. Learning and education remained stiffly medieval in Scottish universities for the most part, and they showed little change in their curricula until the advent of the Reformation. One of the few Scottish academics really attracted to humanism was Hector Boece, friend of Erasmus and principal of King's College, Aberdeen.

The truth was that if the Renaissance was to flourish, it required favourable milieux in which to do so. That called for the patronage of kings, princes, or influential ministers, who needed the services of humanists with special skills in verbal manipulation and were prepared to reward them. Or else the interest of wealthy aristocrats prepared to acquire—or hire—as much of humanist culture as might be necessary to assist them in maintaining their political and military predominance. It was the languages of state and government which were encouraged and perfected and which tended to triumph. Language was, as the Spanish humanist Elio Antonio Nebrija percipiently informed his royal master, 'the perfect instrument of empire'.[27] No Celtic language, as you will not need to be reminded, was in so fortunate a position—not even in Scotland, still an independent kingdom. On the contrary, each was coming under steadily heavier pressure from powerful neighbouring languages, like French or English, partly as a result of deliberate governmental attempts to secure linguistic overlordship, and partly because of the inherent competitive strength of those languages themselves.

Nor, again, could Celtic languages look for encouragement among the wealthy population of large towns and cities, with a relatively numerous class interested in books and reading. Such phenomena existed only on a most restricted scale in Celtic countries, and, where they were present, were usually strongholds of alien speech and culture. Celtic-speaking communities tended to be rural, kin-based, and self-sufficient. Their culture could hope to survive best in such conditions. Among affluent urban groups elsewhere, the practice of reading with the eye was rapidly gaining ground at the expense of listening with the ear (see Chap. IV, pp. 64, 65, 70–1). Enjoyment of literature was thus becoming a more private and individual experience and far less of a public and social affair than it had customarily been in Celtic countries. Prose was increasing at the expense of poetry, hitherto so dominant. It depended, moreover, on a different style of education in schools that were likely to be in sharp competition with bardic schools with their traditional learning (see Chap. III, pp. 42–3). The latter had changed little over the centuries but were now faced with the possibility of drastic modifications and even extinction. Scotland and Ireland were cut off from that close and intimate cultural and educational contact they had long maintained. In Scotland the educational mores of the Lowland spread strongly and in Wales new-style grammar schools became more common.

Implicit in all that has gone before is the heavy dependence of the Renaissance on the printing-press (see Chap. II, p. 21; Chap. III, p. 42; Chap. IV, pp. 60, 70, 72). Printed books were far and away the most effective instrument for the speedy and widespread diffusion of the new learning—whether in the classical languages or the vernaculars. In Celtic regions, diffusion by word of mouth or by manuscript was usual and deep-rooted. Could existing traditions readily adapt to the new medium? In answering that question it is essential to bear in mind that printing books did not simply arise from aesthetic choice or intellectual decision. Printing was, first and foremost, a business, whose executants were primarily interested in making a profit out of satisfying the public demand. As a commercial enterprise it was capital-intensive; printers were obliged to have considerable financial resources in hand in order to acquire machinery, buy raw materials, and wait some years to recover their initial outlay and make a profit on it. It was necessary for them to plan their work ahead, often in close touch with authors and patrons, to establish far-flung business contacts, and to be favourably placed in relation to trading-routes and book fairs. They were normally the sort of hard-headed entrepreneurs who would not risk heavy losses in publishing books in languages which could command only a limited public. Printing-presses in the British Isles were all in the hands of English-speaking printers. In addition, if literary men wanted to be able to take advantage of the new medium, it generally meant availing themselves of a different kind of education, attitude, and expertise from those which had ordinarily been available to them in Celtic-speaking countries. They might well have to shift from being the quasi-hereditary medieval wordsmith to becoming a university-educated intellectual looking to a very different system of patronage and support.

The general upshot of these Renaissance changes significantly modified the attitude of those who adopted them. Renaissance culture by its very nature tended to be courtly, learned, and often snobbishly exclusive (see Chap. II, pp. 18–19, 35–6). The humanist ideals of education and attainment embodied in that complete and cultivated man, *il cortegiano*, exalted him as the highest exemplar of a different kind of nobility, clearly marked off from the earlier, more heroic, medieval type of social paragon. It was an achievement which served to admit an individual or social class to an élite group but could hardly fail seriously to erode the traditional values associated with leaders of society which had so long been admiringly promulgated in verse and prose characteristic of an earlier era. In such circumstances, the ruling groups who had always been looked to for patronage, in so far as they were influenced by Renaissance culture, might be less interested, since they were mentors of traditional genres, and their sponsorship would consequently be more difficult to win, especially when accompanied by far-reaching political and social change of a kind hostile to an older order.

It was true, of course, that the Renaissance provided a potent stimulus for many European vernacular literatures. The triumph of the *Volgare* in Italy and the arguments adduced on its behalf found echoes elsewhere. Other languages, too, began to cherish hopes that in due course they might stand side by side with Latin and Greek on the upper slopes of Mount Parnassus. To reach those heights, they must themselves acquire all the trappings of learning and elegance, must be correct in grammar and syntax, and uniform in orthography and practice, must possess an opulence and abundance of vocabulary, turns of phrase, and figures of speech (see Chap. II, pp. 24–6; Chap. IV, pp. 76–7). New aids to language development, such as grammars, dictionaries, or works on rhetoric, had to be produced so as to facilitate the coveted upward mobility of vernacular languages. Novel literary forms like the sonnet, the essay, drama, or history, were introduced. Prose works came more into their own, often at the expense of poetry. Authors and poets might aspire to more distinguished individual reputation and enhanced fame; the concept of the individual artist was emerging to take the place of the craftsman-member of a medieval guild. On the face of things, there was little reason why many of these trends could not be absorbed within the Celtic heritage. The age and validity of its literary traditions suggested they might be. Earlier cultural importations, such as the Twelfth-century Renaissance or the *amour courtois*, had been assimilated without any obvious difficulty. But one cannot escape observing how much had changed by the sixteenth century. The pace of social and cultural development was much faster; it was linked more closely to the rise of a commercial economy, an urban society, and the social forces dependent upon them, and was associated to a greater extent with political centralization and the emergence of a nation-state. There is reason to suppose that neither material circumstances nor cultural conditions in Celtic countries could keep pace with the march of the Renaissance. It was the bigger battalions among the literatures of faster-developing languages—Italian, French, Spanish, English, German—which stood to gain most. The temptations posed to authors of Breton, Scots, Irish, Welsh, or Cornish origins to publish in French or English should not be underestimated.[28]

Nor should we, either, overlook the seductions of Latin. The Renaissance breathed new life into Latin writing as well as giving a fillip to the vernaculars. Latin was as well known to the men of the Italian Renaissance as their own language and written as easily and fluently by them. Their ambition to express themselves in elegant Latin after the best classical models was shared by humanists elsewhere. The prestige of Latin was everywhere very high, and works composed in it were confined by no national boundaries. There had always been an enviable tradition of Latin authorship in Celtic countries, and, with Latin as the lingua franca of the literati, if a man of Celtic origin wanted to reach a wide audience, then he must write in Latin. Many did, even those with a keen interest in their own tongue. To name but a few, in Wales there were

Sir John Price and Drs John Davies of Brecon and Mallwyd, in Scotland, George Buchanan and Hector Boece, and in Ireland, Luke Wadding and Canice Mooney; all were accomplished Latin authors who found their way into print (see Chap. II, pp. 19, 21–2; Chap. III, pp. 44–6, 48–50; Chap. IV, pp. 78–9).

For the literatures of smaller European countries, the source which offered the most dramatic prospects of innovation was the association between the Renaissance and religion (see Chap. II, pp. 31–3; Chap. IV, pp. 70–1, 72–4). Northern humanists were at one with the Italians in rejecting scholastic learning. For men of Erasmus's outlook, it had been responsible for the deformation of Christianity and sound learning. The decisive achievement of these northern scholars, including the Hebraists among them, men like Reuchlin, had been to apply to the Scriptures the methods hitherto focused on classical literature. They believed that the most valuable service that scholarship could render to the age was to rescue the Scriptures from the hands of scholastic theologians and canon lawyers, who had torn them to shreds. Their supreme purpose was to return to the earliest sources of the Bible in all their original purity and, by careful translation, make them available to everyone. In the heady, hopeful days before 1517 it seemed as if their aspirations heralded a general move for the wholesale translation of the Bible and reform of the Church. But, after Luther's revolt, in the atmosphere of what Michel Suriano stigmatized as the curse of the sects, Europe became increasingly divided over religion. As time went on, the Celtic-speaking countries were pitted against one another as well as torn within themselves. Brittany, Ireland, and Gaelic Scotland were to remain mainly Catholic; while Cornwall and Wales became Protestantized as part of the kingdom of England. No attempt was made in either Catholic Brittany or Protestant Cornwall to furnish the inhabitants with a Bible or a service-book in their own language. Apart from the publication of the Psalms in Gaelic in 1659, the translation of the Bible into that language was a comparatively modern development. The Book of Common Prayer was, indeed, translated into Manx by Bishop John Phillips in 1610 and, though not printed at the time, was published in two volumes in the Manx Society's series in 1893–4.[29] The New Testament was translated into Irish and was published in 1602, to be followed by the Book of Common Prayer in Irish, published in 1608–9; although the loyalty of most of the Irish to the Catholic religion precluded any widespread use of either of these publications. That did not, however, prevent many devoted Irishmen and others affected to some extent by the Renaissance from producing a considerable body of Counter-Reformation literature in their own language. The only Celtic-speaking country where vigorous and successful efforts were made to translate the Bible and the Prayer Book at this time, to use them regularly in public and private devotions, and keep on reprinting them at regular intervals, was Wales.

Looking at the impact of the Renaissance on the Celtic countries overall, it may, in the light of what has been written in this chapter, seem meagre and disappointing— though let it be admitted, at once, that later chapters in this volume reveal stronger and more extensive influences than might have been anticipated. But even if the end-products are thought still to be slighter than might have been hoped, before too many tears are shed on that score, it would be as well to remember that even in those countries most deeply influenced by the Renaissance—and they include Italy—the old world of medieval cultural values and assumptions continued to survive strongly. At the end of the sixteenth century, Italian universities, like those of the rest of Europe, were still decidedly medieval in their attitude and the strength of Renaissance opinions lay rather in the Italian academies. 'In all fields of activity', Douglas Bush pointedly observed, 'men of the Renaissance were much less emancipated than they thought they were; most of them, even such heralds of modernity as Bacon and Descartes, were rooted in medieval tradition.'[30] Renaissance changes, where they took root at all, were those of an élite minority. The majority of the population continued in their old ways largely unaffected. Not surprisingly, therefore, amid languages and literatures with so ancient and conservative a tradition as those of the Celts, many of their older fashions still clung on, tenacious and unmodified.

Notes

1. Innumerable books and articles have been written on the Renaissance and continue to appear. Reference can be made here to only a tiny fraction of that vast literature; but among the works I have found particularly useful are the following:
Anglo, S., *Machiavelli: a Dissection* (London, 1969); Baldwin, C. S., *Renaissance Literary Theory and Practice* (Columbia, 1939); Baron, H., *The Crisis of the Early Italian Renaissance* (Princeton, 1966); Bolgar, R. R., *The Classical Heritage and its Beneficiaries* (Cambridge, 1954); Brucker, G. A., *Florentine Politics and Society, 1343–1378* (Cambridge, 1962); Burckhardt, J., *The Civilization of the Renaissance in Italy* (Phaidon ed., 1960); Burke, P., *Culture and Society in Renaissance Italy, 1420–1540* (London, 1972); *Cambridge History of the Bible*, Vols. II and III (1963); *New Cambridge Modern History*, Vols. I and II (1957, 1958); Caspari, F., *Humanism and the Social Order in Tudor England* (New York, 1968); Chabod, F., *Machiavelli and the Renaissance* (London, 1958); Cheyney, E. P., *The Dawn of a New Era, 1250–1453* (New York, 1936); Clark, D. L., *Rhetoric and Poetry in the Renaissance* (Columbia, 1922); Ferguson, W. K., *The Renaissance in Historical Thought* (New York, 1948); idem, *Europe in Transition, 1300–1520* (Boston, 1962); Gilbert, F., *Machiavelli and Guicciardini: Politics and History in Sixteenth-century Florence* (Princeton, 1965); Gilmore, M. P., *The World of Humanism, 1453–1517* (New York, 1952); Green, V. H. H., *Renaissance and Reformation* (London, 1964); Hale, J. R., *Machiavelli and Renaissance Italy* (London, 1961); idem, *Renaissance Europe, 1480–1520* (London, 1971); Hall, R. A., *The Italian Questione della Lingua* (Chapel Hill, 1947); Hall, V., *Renaissance Literary Criticism* (New York, 1945); Haskins, C. H., *The Renaissance of the Twelfth Century* (Cleveland, Ohio, 1951); Hay, D., *The Italian Renaissance in its Historical Background* (Cambridge, 1961); Herlihy, D., *Medieval and Renaissance Pistoia* (New Haven, 1967); Hexter, J. H., *The Vision of Politics on the Eve of the Reformation* (London, 1973); Holborn, H., *Ulrich von Hutten* (New Haven, 1937); Huizinga, J., *Erasmus of Rotterdam* (London, 1952); Jacob, E. F. (ed.), *Italian Renaissance Studies* (London, 1960); Jones, P. J., *The Malatesta of Rimini and the Papal States* (Cambridge, 1974); Jones, R. B., *The Old British Tongue* (Cardiff, 1970); Jones, R. F., *The Triumph of the English Language* (Stanford, 1951); Kristeller, P. O., *The Classics and Renaissance Thought* (Cambridge, Mass., 1955); idem, *Studies in Renaissance Thought and Letters* (Rome, 1956); idem, *Renaissance Thought* (2 vols., New York, 1961, 1965); Larner, J., *Culture and Society in Italy, 1290–1420* (London, 1971); McNeil, D. O., *Guillaume Budé and Humanism in the Reign of Francis I* (Geneva, 1975); Martines, L., *The Social World of Florentine Humanists, 1390–1460* (Princeton, 1963); Mazzeo, J. A., *Renaissance and Revolution: the Remaking of European Thought* (London, 1967); Panovsky, E., *Renaissance and Renascence in Western Art* (Stockholm, 1960); Plumb, J. H., *The Horizon Book of the Renaissance* (London, 1961); Phillips, M. M., *Erasmus and the Northern Renaissance* (London, 1949); Pullan, B., *A History of Early Renaissance Italy* (London, 1973); Renaudet, A., *Préréforme et humanisme à Paris pendant les premières guerres d'Italie (Paris, 1953); Ross, J. B. and McLaughlin, M. M.,

The Renaissance Reader (Penguin Books, 1977); Rubenstein, N., *The Government of Florence under the Medici* (Oxford, 1966); Schevill, F., *A History of Florence* (New York, 1936); Simore, F., *The French Renaissance* . . . (London, 1969); Skinner, Q., *The Foundations of Modern Political Thought* (2 vols., Cambridge, 1978); Spitz, L., *The Religious Renaissance of the German Humanists* (Cambridge, Mass., 1963); Staines, D. W. T., *Renaissance Dictionaries* (Texas, 1954); Waley, D., *The Italian City-Republics* (London, 1969); Weiss, R., *The Dawn of Humanism in Italy* (London, 1947); idem, *The Spread of Italian Humanism* (London, 1964); idem, *The Renaissance Discovery of Classical Antiquity* (Oxford, 1969); Whitfield, J. H., *Petrarch and the Renaissance* (Oxford, 1943); Woodward, W. H., *Studies in Education during the Age of the Renaissance* (Cambridge, 1906).

2. G. Vasari, *Lives of the Most Eminent Painters, Sculptors and Architects*, ed. W. Gaunt (4 vols., Everyman ed., London, 1927).

3. J. E. Seigel, *Rhetoric and Philosophy in Renaissance Humanism* (Princeton, 1968); cf. ' "Civic Humanism" or Ciceronian Rhetoric? The culture of Petrarch and Bruni', *Past and Present*, 34 (1966), 3-48.

4. L. Valla, *De elegantiis linguae Latinae* in F. A. Gragg, *Later Writings of the Italian Humanists* (New York, 1927), foreword.

5. Vasari, *Lives*, I, 18.

6. Skinner, *Foundations of Modern Political Thought*, I, 35-41.

7. L. Bruni, 'Vita di Messer Francesco Petrarca' in Ross and McLaughlin, *Renaissance Reader*, p. 128.

8. Baron, *Crisis of the Early Italian Renaissance, passim.*

9. Jacob, *Renaissance Studies*, p. 22.

10. Valla, loc. cit., note 4.

11. Baron, op. cit., p. 4.

12. Hay, *Italian Renaissance*, pp. 119ff.

13. *Hamlet*, III, i, 160.

14. *Cambridge History of the Bible*, III, 110.

15. Jones, *Old British Tongue*; Jones, *Triumph of English*.

16. Haskins, *Renaissance of the Twelfth Century*.

17. Skinner, *Foundations of Modern Political Thought*, I, 201.

18. Renaudet, *Préréforme à Paris*, p. 116.

19. Spitz, *German Humanists*.

20. S. H. Steinberg, *Five Hundred Years of Printing* (revised ed., Bristol, 1961); L. Febvre et H. J. Martin, *L'apparition du livre* (Paris, 1971); E. L. Eisenstein, *The Printing Press as an Agent of Change* (Cambridge, 1980).

21. E. L. Eisenstein, 'The advent of printing and the problem of the Renaissance', *Past and Present*, no. 45 (1969), 19-89, at p. 52.

22. F. Rabelais, *The Histories of Gargantua and Pantagruel*, trans. J. M. Cohen (Penguin Books, 1955), p. 194.

23. Phillips, *Erasmus and the Northern Renaissance*; Huizinga, *Erasmus of Rotterdam*.

24. *Cambridge History of the Bible*, III, 38.

25. Erasmus, *The Epistles*, trans. T. M. Nicholas (London, 1901), letter 522.

26. R. L. DeMolin, *Erasmus* (London, 1973), p. 92.

27. Hale, *Renaissance Europe*, p. 297.

28. G. Williams, 'Welsh authors and their Books, 1500-1642' in M. B. Line (ed.), *The World of Books and Information* (London, 1987).

29. I have to thank Dr R. L. Thomson for so kindly providing me with this information in a letter written after the Conference was over.

30. Quoted by Ferguson, *Renaissance in Historical Thought*, p. 355.

CHAPTER II

THE RENAISSANCE AND WELSH LITERATURE

by R. Geraint Gruffydd

MY task is to survey the effects of the Renaissance on Welsh literature.[1] It is made substantially lighter by the masterly conspectus of the Renaissance as a whole presented to us by Emeritus Professor Glanmor Williams (Chapter I), so that I need take up little time with preliminaries. I shall perforce be concentrating on Renaissance human-ism, and shall be following Professor Paul Oskar Kristeller in understanding that term to mean 'the study and imitation of classical, Greek and Latin literature'.[2] As we have seen, humanism became dominant in the intellectual life of Italy during the fourteenth and fifteenth centuries and thence spread to northern Europe in the sixteenth. Its natural habitat was the princely courts of Italy, sometimes with their attendant academies, and there is little wonder that there evolved in that milieu the new ideal of the cultured courtier, the scholar-gentleman, the doer who was also a thinker (and maker), an ideal most persuasively expounded by Baldassare Castiglione in his *Il Corte-giano* (1528). From the courts, humanism penetrated the universities, especially of course the arts faculties, particularly in the fields of grammar, rhetoric, poetry, history, and moral philosophy (here I am again following Kristeller, although I am aware that he has his critics);[3] and the new demands of the universities in turn brought into being a new kind of secondary schooling. The same or similar institutions were the bearers of humanism in northern Europe as well. In England, in particular, human-ism flourished in the royal court and noble households, both lay and ecclesiastical, in the universities of Oxford and Cambridge (although somewhat tardily), in the endowed grammar schools which multiplied exceedingly during the sixteenth century, and finally, in the Inns of Court and Chancery, the London law schools which now prospered as 'seminaries and nurseries wherein the gentry of this kingdom are bred and trained up', as a contemporary observer noted.

   In precisely the period when humanism began to take root in England, that is, the first half of the sixteenth century, Wales and England were brought into much closer contact than ever before. In particular, the newly emergent Welsh gentry class, which had been quietly forming under the surface chaos of late medieval administration, was finally won over to the side of the English Crown by the victory of a part-Welshman, Henry Tudor, at the Battle of Bosworth in 1485, and recruited for the service of that Crown by the so-called Acts of Union of 1536 and 1543, which reduced chaos to uniformity and created a need for such office-holders as justices of the peace, sheriffs, and Members of Parliament in Wales, although at the cost of outlawing Welsh as a language of administration. By means of the Acts of Union the English Reformation, which had already been set in train, was applied to Wales, and it, too, created a demand for intellectually trained personnel, although at a rather lower social level, generally speaking, than in the secular sphere.[4]

As a result of these social and political developments, Wales participated fully in what has been called the educational revolution of the sixteenth century. Even in the Middle Ages the more able of the Welsh clergy, and even a few of the gentry, were schooled at Oxford, although they were not always very well received there:

> In 1389 northerners in their turn were the aggressors against the Welsh: shouting 'war, war, war, sle, sle, sle the Walshe dogges and her [whelpes] and hoso loketh out of his hous shall be dede', they drove the Welshmen to the town gates, made them urinate upon the gates and kiss the gatepost, and then banged their heads upon the gate until their noses bled and the tears rolled from their eyes, looted Deep Hall, Neville's Inn and other halls [and] killed a number of their Welsh inmates.[5]

Such corporate experiences did not put the Welshmen off, however, and in the sixteenth century the trickle became, if not a flood, then certainly a stream. A recent comprehensive study, as yet unpublished, estimates that perhaps as many as 3,000 students from Wales entered Oxford, Cambridge and the Inns of Court between *c.* 1545 and 1642, which was a not inconsiderable achievement for a country with a total population of between 250,000 and 300,000.[6] Many of these students were by now laymen, and in the universities tended to follow arts courses. Of the two universities, Oxford was overwhelmingly the favourite, especially after Jesus College was founded in 1571; but Cambridge's contribution, particularly through St John's College, was, qualitatively if not quantitatively, of a very high order. I should add that a few Welsh Roman Catholic humanists, forced into exile by the persistence of Protestantism as the English state religion from 1559 onwards, took advantage of degree courses offered by Continental universities as well. In addition to the two universities and the Inns of Court, many Welsh pupils flocked to English endowed grammar schools, which could, of course, offer an excellent grounding in Latin together with some Greek, as those who have followed William Shakespeare's intellectual formation will know: Shrewsbury, Winchester, and Westminster were among the many patronized. In time, a crop of endowed grammar schools sprang up in Wales as well—some two dozen in the century following the Acts of Union—but the English schools continued to attract. Beyond these formal educational establishments there remained, as in Italy, the royal court and the noble households where, if the monarch or nobleman were so inclined, young men employed as retainers could assimilate humanistic values as well as genteel manners, and many young Welshmen were so employed during the later sixteenth and earlier seventeenth centuries. This happened not only in the case of noblemen with extensive Welsh landed interests, such as the Earls of Leicester, Arundel, Essex, and Pembroke, but also with those, such as the Earl of Dorset, Thomas Sackville, Lord Buckhurst, who had few if any Welsh lands. The first Earl of Pembroke of the second creation, William Herbert, although said by his enemies at court to be illiterate, was an extraordinarily discriminating and influential patron of early Welsh humanism:

he may, indeed, have been its midwife. William Herbert held court at Cardiff Castle as well as at Wilton, his principal seat; and his son Henry, as President of the Council of Wales and the Marches, added Ludlow Castle to these two. Minor Renaissance courts also appeared in Wales at a lower social level: notable examples were the episcopal palace at Abergwili when Richard Davies was Bishop of St David's, St Donat's Castle in the Vale of Glamorgan when Sir Edward Stradling was head of the family, and Llyweni in the Vale of Clwyd under the stimulating government of Sir John Salusbury, for whom Shakespeare wrote his 'Phoenix and the Turtle'.[7]

By frequenting such places as I have described, a number of young Welshmen became imbued with humanistic ideals. In almost all instances these ideals were combined with strong adherence either to Protestantism or to Roman Catholicism: it is, of course, a vulgar error to suppose that Renaissance humanism was in any sense opposed to religion (although that rule, too, has its exceptions). Apart from the religious division, the group was remarkably homogeneous. Socially, they tended to be sons of the lesser rather than the greater gentry, and they also included among their number sons of clergymen, yeomen, tenant farmers, and a few craftsmen; they themselves, by and large, were either minor gentry—not so minor in one or two cases—or professional people: clergymen, lawyers, physicians, schoolmasters, civil servants, and secretaries (at least two captained privateers). Geographically, they tended to concentrate in north-east Wales, the old Gwynedd Is Conwy, although there were other significant pockets in the Dyfi Valley, north Pembrokeshire, the Vale of Glamorgan, and what may be called the Middle March. Intellectually, they were by definition lovers of classical Latinity, which they practised whenever they could, often with notable success, as recent studies have clearly shown.[8] But their fiercest loyalty was reserved for their own language, and their chief desire was to see it remodelled and revivified so as to become comparable with Latin and Greek, and the peer of those modern languages which had already undergone that transforming process: Italian, French, Spanish, German, even English up to a point.[9] Basic to that desire was a shared vision of a glorious past, the realization that the present fell far short of that glory and the determination that the glory should be restored.

First, the vision of a glorious past; this was founded on four stories of very diverse origin which most Welsh humanists believed (although not all believed all four) and which we may conveniently label the myths of Samothes, Brutus, Joseph of Arimathea, and Ysgolan. The myth of Samothes was based on the pseudo-Berosus which John Annius of Viterbo published in Rome in 1498 and which deluded most of Europe for the better part of a century: according to Berosus, as interpreted by the English reformer and antiquary John Bale, Samothes was the son of Japhet (and therefore the grandson of Noah), who occupied the Celtic parts of Europe after the Flood and founded a long line of kings which included Druys and Bardus who—as you will have guessed—established the learned orders of Druids and Bards. The myth of Brutus is of course derived from Geoffrey of Monmouth's *Historia Regum Britanniae* of *c.* 1136: according to Geoffrey, Brutus was the great-grandson of Aeneas of Troy, and he led the remnants of the Trojans here to Britain *c.* 1170 BC, defeated the giants who then inhabited the island, renamed it after himself, and founded the line of kings who ruled the realm until the Romans came and after they left—pre-eminent among them, of course, were Brennus 500 years before Christ and Arthur 500 years after Christ.[10] The myth of Joseph of Arimathea was invented by the monks of Glastonbury in the early thirteenth century, together with the Grail legend, and was incorporated into a cunningly revised version of William of Malmesbury's *De Antiquitate Glastoniensis Ecclesiae* (it was, in fact, a monkish fable of the kind the Reformers normally held in high contempt, but which in this case was too useful to discard). Again, as adopted by John Bale, it related how St Joseph of Arimathea came to this country to preach the pure Gospel of Christ some thirty years after the Crucifixion. Rather more than a century later, the country became officially Christian through the conversion of King Lucius (this is in Geoffrey); it upheld the pure Faith until forced by the English to renounce it following the coming of St Augustine of Canterbury from Rome in 597. (That was the Protestant version of the myth, and it was naturally not accepted in that form by all Catholics.)[11] These three myths together furnished the Welsh language with an extraordinarily exalted lineage: through Samothes it could be connected with Hebrew, through Brutus with Greek, and through St Joseph (in a curious way) with Latin—the three learned languages. No wonder some of the humanists believed it had some special function reserved for it in God's providence. Moreover, the founding by the descendants of Samothes of the learned orders of Druids and Bards—which, as the King's Antiquary, John Leland, saw before Bale, are given honourable mention by various classical authors including Julius Caesar[12]—compelled the belief that there had once existed in Wales (and indeed in Britain) a vast deposit of high learning enshrined in books, including possibly an ancient version of the Scriptures in Welsh. Because these books could no longer be found it was necessary to have recourse to a fourth myth, that of Ysgolan: he seems to have figured in both Welsh and Breton stories (see Chapter V, p. 93) as a malefactor who had destroyed a book or books,[13] and he served well enough as an explanation of the present paucity of Welsh books, as contrasted with the richness that had once obtained, together with more normal explanations such as wars, conquests, rebellions, and the malice of enemies (some of them quite recent).

The Ysgolan myth already indicates that the Welsh humanists found the state of the language, as they perceived it in their day, far from satisfactory. There was little prose-writing of substance and eloquence: not only had the books of ancient learning disappeared, little had come to take their place except monkish fables and suchlike (actually there were two or three interesting prose-writers at work in the earlier sixteenth century but they do not seem to have been recognized by the humanists as kindred spirits). Secondly, the professional poets they saw plying their trade around them seemed to them unworthy of their distinguished ancestry: in this they were essentially correct, for there had already been a marked decline from the commanding heights achieved by such master-poets as Guto'r Glyn in the later fifteenth century and Tudur Aled in the first quarter of the sixteenth. Thirdly, the language itself needed attention: it was in dire danger of losing its learned status and becoming a patchwork of mutually incomprehensible dialects, if not of dying out altogether because of the readiness of its speakers (especially the gentry) to abandon it in favour of English; and the medieval grammar-books and vocabularies of the poets certainly failed to meet contemporary humanistic criteria. Finally, the cherished myths on which the total vision was based had to be defended—the myth of Brutus, in particular, came under fairly persistent attack.

So the humanists evolved a programme for the restoration of Welsh letters. They would create a new learned prose in place of the one that had been lost; in particular, they would translate (or, rather, retranslate) the Bible into Welsh. They would recall the poets to their ancient greatness and provide them with the means of achieving it, as well as making their art more easily accessible to cultured amateurs like themselves. They would reduce the language to regular order and record and amplify its vocabulary. They would defend the foundation myths to the best of their ability and also seek to elucidate later periods of Welsh history, all the time searching for the remains of the lost learning in ancient manuscripts. In doing all this they would, of course, seek to make the greatest possible use of the relatively new device of the printing-press, which (as you know) had been invented in Germany in the middle of the fifteenth century. It had been basic to the spread of humanism and Protestantism, and had been a powerful force for good in England ever since William Caxton set up business in Westminster in 1476. Unfortunately, printing remained confined by law to London and the two universities throughout the period of the Renaissance in Wales, and only a few Roman Catholic humanists managed to evade these restrictions. Such then was the humanist programme. It was an extraordinarily noble and ambitious one. With hindsight we can see that it was also quite unrealistic. Let us now consider briefly how the humanists attempted to carry it out and the extent to which they succeeded or failed.

First, in the realm of scholarship, interest was focused on two areas; the Welsh past and its records (real or imagined), and the Welsh language. With regard to the Welsh past the first priority (as I have suggested) was the defence of the foundation myths, particularly that of Brutus. Geoffrey of Monmouth had been attacked not long after his death by Gerald of Wales and William of Newburgh, but it was the Italian humanist resident at the Tudor court, Polydore Vergil, who delivered the most damaging onslaught in his *Anglica Historia* of 1534: his basic contention was that the story of Brutus was incredible because it was not known to Roman historians. His standpoint was cautiously and politely endorsed more than fifty years later by the young William Camden in the first edition of his great book *Britannia* (1586). (There was also a distinctive, and trenchant, Scottish contribution to the debate from such fine scholars as John Major (or Mair) and George Buchanan (Chapter IV, pp. 44–7). John Leland, the King's Antiquary, quickly sprang to Geoffrey's (or Brutus's) defence but it was the royal servant, Sir John Price of Breconshire, the earliest identifiable Welsh humanist, who produced what Sir Thomas Kendrick has called 'the first of the great books on the subject of the antiquity of the British', the *Historiae Brytannicae Defensio*:[14] this was in draft before 1545, was finished 1547–53, and was published by Price's son

Richard in 1573, eighteen years after his father's death (the father dedicated his book
to William Herbert, Earl of Pembroke, and King Edward VI; the son to William
Cecil, Lord Burghley). By appealing to Welsh evidence, real or supposed, Price seeks
to undermine Vergil's use of the silence of Roman historians concerning Brutus and
his descendants as a definitive negative criterion, and in so doing creates a glowing
picture of the British learned past and the records it created: given these records,
what reason was there for denying Geoffrey's assertion that he was a mere translator
rather than an author (especially since the man was also a bishop)? Price's lead was
followed by later Welsh humanists, of whom three achieved print, all in Latin: Humphrey Lhuyd of Denbigh in 1572, Dr David Powel of Ruabon in 1585, and Dr John
Davies of Mallwyd in 1632. A far more remarkable defence than any of these, written
in Welsh by Dr John Davies of Brecon (Siôn Dafydd Rhys) in 1597, remained in
manuscript: I shall be returning briefly to this later. Similarly, there remained in
manuscript form substantial treatises in English by the lawyer, John Lewis of Llynwene,
and the remarkably learned country gentlemen, Robert Vaughan of Hengwrt and
William Maurice of Llansilin; Lewis was writing between 1603 and 1612 (his work
was actually printed in 1729), Vaughan and Maurice some fifty years later.[15] In 1655
Vaughan wrote to his kinsman, Rowland Vaughan of Caer Gai, who in 1629 had
eloquently denounced Camden for 'putting Brutus to sleep in the cave of eternal oblivion', bitterly rebuking him for abandoning Geoffrey of Monmouth: 'I could here give
you the names of more ancient authors who write of Brutus long before Geoffrey,
but to what end, if you will deny all things?'[16] Rowland Vaughan's defection signifies
that the game was up, that Geoffrey was indefensible. The Welsh humanists were
indeed aware of the beginnings of scientific historiography as exemplified in the work
of such scholars as Francesco Guicciardini and Jean Bodin, but because of their fervent
patriotism they could not bring themselves to apply the new criteria to the study of
the remote Welsh and British past. It was one thing for Flavio Biondo, for example,
to say of Geoffrey, 'I have never come across anything so stuffed with lies and friv-
olities':[17] it was quite another matter for Robert Vaughan of Hengwrt—who in his
own way was no less learned—to force himself to say such a thing.

Not all the historical endeavours of the Welsh humanists were so ill-directed. The
more recent Welsh past presented fewer obstacles to objective investigation than did
the period from Brutus (or Samothes) to Arthur. Late in the thirteenth century an
anonymous monk of the Cistercian Abbey of Strata Florida had compiled in Latin
a chronicle of the Princes of Wales, from Cadwaladr in the late seventh century (with
whom Geoffrey's tale had ended) to the final conquest of Gwynedd in 1282–3: this
survived in several Welsh versions as 'Brut y Tywysogyon', which Sir John Edward
Lloyd described as 'the greatest monument of Welsh historiography in the Middle
Ages'.[18] In 1559 Humphrey Lhuyd, whom we have already met—he was an Oxford
graduate in the service of the Earl of Arundel[19]—decided to translate into English
a somewhat truncated version of the text, suitably embellished and annotated, and
this he did. In 1584 Dr David Powel of Ruabon published a revised and extended
version of Lhuyd's translation as *The History of Cambria now called Wales*—a kind of

supplement to Raphael Holinshed's slightly earlier *Chronicles of England, Scotland and Ireland* and employing (to bizarre effect) the same illustrations; the *History of Cambria* had been instigated by Sir Henry Sidney, President of the Council of Wales and the Marches at Ludlow, and was dedicated to Sir Henry's son Philip. The following year Powel put Gerald of Wales's *Itinerarium Kambriae* and *Descriptio Kambriae* (the complimentary part) into print for the first time, flanked by Ponticus of Virunnius's digest of Geoffrey and a letter to William Fleetwood in defence of Geoffrey: a judicious mixture of the backward-looking and forward-looking; both Sir Henry and Philip Sidney were dedicatees.[20] In Welsh, and in manuscript, two more erudite country gentlemen, Roger Morris of Coedytalwrn and Ifan Llwyd ap Dafydd of Nantymynach, recounted the early history of Britain for the benefit of their fellow-countrymen, without any dominant polemical intent although both treatises were soundly based on Geoffrey: Morris was a product of Oxford, but I am doubtful about the humanist credentials of Ifan Llwyd.[21] A new departure in Welsh historiography was chorography, that is (very broadly), the combination of history and geography. Sir John Price was again the pioneer with a brief 'Description of Wales' in Latin, which was translated and expanded by Humphrey Lhuyd and printed by Dr David Powel as a kind of introduction to the *History of Cambria*. At the instigation of the great Flemish geographer, Abraham Ortelius, Lhuyd in his last years went much further and produced a chorography of Anglesey and then, in outline, of the whole of Britain (with attendant maps): the one was published in Antwerp in 1570, the other in Cologne in 1572 and was to lead directly to Camden's *Britannia* fourteen years later. To the same genre essentially belongs the small crop of Welsh county histories, which began to appear in the 1580s following the appearance of William Lambarde's *Perambulation of Kent* in 1576: histories of Glamorgan by Rice Merrick and Rice Lewis (1578–84, 1596–1600 respectively), of Pembrokeshire by the great master of the genre George Owen (1584–1604), of Breconshire by the obscure and little-regarded Thomas ap John (1584–1604).[22] Even John Dee, who was a Welsh as well as an English and European humanist, dabbled for a while in this field during the 1570s before becoming wholly captivated by imperial visions and cabbalistic mysteries.[23] On a less ambitious level, Sir Edward Stradling of St Donat's in the 1560s, and Sir John Wynn of Gwydir early in the following century, wrote brief treatises designed to illuminate the history of their own families: Stradling's was dedicated to Cecil and achieved not only publication (by Powel in 1584) but also translation into Welsh.

Such works as the family and county histories depended heavily on detailed knowledge of the vast corpus of Welsh genealogical and heraldic lore preserved in the main by the professional poets.[24] In the sixteenth century, the new humanist gentry assiduously collected and compiled genealogical manuscripts, and indeed manuscripts of all kinds— inspired partly, no doubt, by the myth of the lost Welsh books and partly by the enthusiasm of humanists like Erasmus in the search for lost or neglected manuscripts. Nearly all Welsh humanists of note had extensive manuscript collections, again beginning with Sir John Price, who used to good effect his position as a Visitor of the Monasteries in order to rescue the contents of dispersed monastic libraries (I am aware that his activities could be described in less kindly terms). At the other end of the period stands Robert Vaughan of Hengwrt who, by the time of his death in 1667, had succeeded in assembling under his roof almost all the important medieval Welsh manuscripts and a high proportion of the Renaissance ones as well: this was to become the major manuscript foundation collection of the National Library of Wales in 1909. Vaughan was to be much aided by his friends, such as that talented profligate, John Jones of Gellilyfdy, nearly a hundred of whose manuscripts, many of them written in debtors' prisons, eventually found their way into the Hengwrt collection. Vaughan and Jones were in fact much more than mere transcribers and collectors, as recent studies—unfortunately unpublished—have clearly shown, but it is their activities in those fields that have justly gained them lasting fame.[25]

We now move on to consider briefly humanist scholarly endeavour in the field of the Welsh language. Here the humanists had a decisive advantage, because the guild of professional poets had over the centuries built up an unparalleled knowledge and mastery of the language, had evolved a largely standardized form of it which was used by them all over Wales, and even had in their possession so-called grammars (I say 'so-called' because they were heavily dependent on the standard textbooks of Priscianus and Donatus and so described Latin rather than Welsh), and quite extensive specialized vocabularies.[26] Late in 1545 William Salesbury of Llanrwst, possibly like Sir John Price with the support of William Herbert, Earl of Pembroke, obtained from the ailing King Henry VIII a seven-year patent allowing him and the stationer, John Waley, to publish an English–Welsh dictionary: this appeared early in 1547 as a Welsh–English dictionary and is interesting but elementary—it has been recently suggested in a highly illuminating survey of Welsh Renaissance dictionary-making that it had its origin in a vocabulary constructed by Salesbury for his own use when he himself was learning English.[27] There followed nearly a century of assiduous lexicography: indeed, a high proportion of the major Welsh humanists are known to have compiled dictionaries, although most of them are now lost. Their prince was undoubtedly 'Sir' Thomas Wiliems of Trefriw in the Conwy Valley, who began his career as an Oxford-trained Anglican priest but was reclaimed for Roman Catholicism and renounced his orders, becoming a somewhat inept country physician; between 1604 and 1608, after thirty years' preparation, he compiled a vast Latin–Welsh dictionary based on Thomas Thomas's *Dictionarium Linguae Latinae et Anglicanae*. This was, unhappily, never published, but a digest of it was included, with the consent of Wiliems's patron, Sir John Wynn of Gwydir, as the second part of Dr John Davies of Mallwyd's *Antiquae Linguae Britannicae ... Dictionarium Duplex* in 1632; the first part of the *Dictionarium Duplex* was a Welsh–Latin dictionary by John Davies himself, again the fruit of nearly thirty years' labour. Of that dictionary it may suffice to say that it is still useful today, especially for those parts which *Geiriadur Prifysgol Cymru* has not yet reached (if I may paraphrase a famous television advertisement). A few years after the *Dictionarium Duplex* appeared, Henry Salesbury of Henllan in the Vale of Clwyd, another Oxford-trained country physician, completed at an advanced age his *Geirfa Tafod Cymraeg*, a full (early eighteenth-century) transcript of which has only just come to light; it has not yet been thoroughly studied, but it is already clear that Salesbury is unlikely to dislodge John Davies from his position as the king of Renaissance lexicographers.

John Davies is also the king of Renaissance grammarians; but, as in the case of the *Dictionarium Duplex*, he was able to some extent to build on the achievement of his predecessors. The first Welsh humanist grammar, *Gramadeg Cymraeg*, began to appear in Milan in 1567; later parts were published in Milan or Paris, probably between 1584 and 1594.[28] Its author was Dr Gruffydd Robert, a Roman Catholic exile who became for a time a Canon Theologian of Milan Cathedral under St Charles Borromeo. The grammar is in Welsh and cast in dialogue form, presumably in imitation of such humanist models as Pietro Bembo and Castiglione, and the dedication (again, significantly, to William Herbert, Earl of Pembroke) and introduction, as well as some parts of the treatise proper, contain passages of exquisite Ciceronian prose.[29] The first two parts deal with orthography and morphology, respectively, and do so with remarkable discernment and relative (although not complete) freedom from Latin models: in this, Robert may have been helped by the work of earlier Italian grammarians such as Gian Francesco Fortunio (1516), Bembo (1525), and Nicolo Liburnio (1520), but his steady emphasis on the validity of spoken usage may reflect the views of the Sienese school of philologists headed by Claudio Tolomei ([1527–8], published 1555). Robert, in fact, aimed to provide the new Welsh scholar-gentleman with a manual of acceptable usage, both spoken and written; technical terms could, when necessary, be borrowed from Latin according to laws which Robert, following William Salesbury, both perceived and described; if Latin did not serve, other languages could be pillaged. The reception of Robert's grammar in Wales poses large problems, but the first part at least arrived here in some numbers and was well received. It was certainly seen by the second of the Welsh Renaissance grammarians, Dr John Davies of Brecon, 'Siôn Dafydd Rhys', who also spent some time in Italy as a Roman Catholic exile but returned to Wales in the early 1570s, becoming first a schoolmaster and then a country physician.[30] His grammar, *Cambrobrytannicae Cymraecaeve Linguae Institutiones*, was finished by 1590 and published in 1592, with the financial help of Sir Edward Stradling of St Donat's, to whom it is dedicated; the grammar itself is mostly in Latin but has a long introduction in Welsh, in which Davies displays truly remarkable powers of invective (it is in fact a splendid piece of writing). Like Gruffydd Robert's grammar, only the earlier portion deals with the language as such, and the most valuable section in it is that which treats of phonology, on which Davies was a considerable expert; the section on morphology, although not without merit, is in general too beholden to Latin and Greek grammarians to be of much use (Davies had in fact produced an Italian handbook on Latin grammar, and may also have produced a Latin handbook on Greek grammar, while he was in Italy). Some two years later, a much slighter work appeared, Henry Salesbury's *Grammatica Britannica*, dedicated to Henry Herbert, second Earl of Pembroke; this is again remarkable because of its respect, perhaps in deference to Gruffydd Robert, for the spoken language. Finally in 1621, John Davies of Mallwyd published his *Antiquae Linguae Britannicae . . . Rudimenta*, dedicated to Archdeacon Edmwnd Prys, sometime Fellow of St John's College, Cambridge, in a long epistle which is virtually a *Défense et illustration de la langue galloise*. Although certainly not flawless—for example, Davies firmly believed that Welsh and Hebrew were closely related—this relatively short book reveals a grammarian of genius at work, systematically analysing and describing the language used by the professional poets, some eighty of whom are referred to.[31] I cannot forbear from quoting once again Sir John Morris-Jones's remarks in the Preface to his own *Welsh Grammar, Historical and Comparative* of 1913 (although they admittedly say as much about Sir John as about John Davies):

> the author's analysis of the modern literary language is final; he has left to his successors only the corrections and amplification of detail.[32]

It may seem a far cry from what has been called 'the crowning glory of the Renaissance in Wales'[33] to a small practical handbook for Welsh learners published more than fifty years earlier, William Salesbury's *Brief and a plain introduction teaching how to pronounce the letters in the British tongue* (1550; a second edition bearing the title *A plain and a familiar introduction* appeared in 1567), and yet Salesbury displays in it not only a familiarity with some eight languages beside his own (including Latin and Greek pronounced as Erasmus wished)[34] but also an acute ear for speech-sounds: his work may, in fact, have inspired John Davies of Brecon's no less remarkable *De Italica Pronunciatione . . . Libellus*, published in Padua in 1569, which in turn laid the foundation for the excellence of the phonological section in his Welsh grammar of 1592.[35]

We now turn to the efforts of the humanists in the field of Welsh poetry. Their relationship with the professional poets was at best ambivalent. Theoretically, as we have seen, the humanists regarded the poets with the utmost respect as the heirs of the learned classes founded by the descendants of Samothes, or, alternatively, of the Greek sages brought over by Brutus and his successors. Certainly they thought of the earliest Welsh poets such as Taliesin and Myrddin, and a number of others more or less invented by John Leland and John Bale, as ancient savants replete with all kinds of knowledge. Moreover, they often speak of the poets of their own day, and of the two or three generations preceding them, in terms of the highest praise: this is true of William Salesbury, Gruffydd Robert, Edmwnd Prys, John Davies of Brecon, and John Davies of Mallwyd alike; the only totally discordant note was struck by Maurice Kyffin in his introduction to his translation of John Jewel's *Apologia Ecclesiae Anglicanae* in 1594, where he flatly denies—in response to an assertion by William Midleton—that the poets of his own day had inherited any of the learning and philosophy of the Druids of whom Caesar wrote, and this in spite of having once sat at the feet of the greatest of contemporary masters, Wiliam Llŷn. Edmwnd Prys and the two John Davieses all boldly claim that the Welsh poets were fully equal to those of ancient Greece and Rome; Gruffydd Robert, on the other hand, could not bring himself to go as far as that! However, the general attitude was undoubtedly favourable, which meant that in this respect Welsh humanists corresponded more closely to their Italian confrères, who revered the great Tuscan poets of the Trecento, than to their counterparts in France and England, who tended to be dismissive of medieval poetry in their own tongues—although there were, of course, exceptions to this rule. This generally favourable attitude, however, did not prevent the humanists from attacking the poets quite uninhibitedly on several specific counts; in short, for being what they perceived in their own day as a once-glorious profession in steep decline, a decline which they sought to arrest. The specific charges which they levelled against the poets were chiefly four—mendacity, lack of learning, lack of eloquence, and secretiveness— and I would like now briefly to consider these.

Mendacity took the form of undue flattery of patrons and also of false utterance of pedigrees. These were symptomatic of what the humanists perceived as a lack of respect for truth so profound that they sometimes derived, as Siôn Cent had done a century and a half earlier, the Welsh muse from the devil rather than the Holy Ghost—the great matter of Welsh literary criticism, as Professor R. M. Jones once remarked.[36] (It must be admitted, however, that the humanists' view of truth was excessively literal.) The fault was condemned by many humanists and also by one of the poets' own number, Siôn Tudur.[37] It was most powerfully addressed, however, by Archdeacon Edmwnd Prys in his renowned poetic debate with the hapless professional poet, Wiliam Cynwal, which extended over seven years in the 1580s and has recently been edited in a most exemplary manner.[38] It was also implicitly dealt with in the famous open letter, 'To the Poets and Learned Men of Wales', which Dr John Davies of Brecon wrote in 1597 as a riposte to Maurice Kyffin's attack on the poets in his translation of Jewel's *Apologia* three years previously; this letter, too, has been perceptively discussed recently.[39] The immediate remedy for mendacity was to desist from flattery and the forging of pedigrees and declare instead the unvarnished truth, even if this were to be unpalatable at times. The ultimate remedy was for the poet to devote himself to divine poetry, the praise of God based on the Bible.

Secondly, the poets were criticized for lack of learning. Gruffydd Robert, Edmwnd Prys, and Maurice Kyffin are the most specific of those who bring this charge against the poets, but they are clearly expressing a commonly held humanist view. By learning, of course, they meant book-learning, preferably in the ancient languages, of the kind disseminated in grammar schools and particularly in universities. They assuredly did not mean the kind of information with which the minds of the professional poets were stocked: the detritus of medieval oral story and medieval manuscript lore. Once again, it is Edmwnd Prys in his debate with Wiliam Cynwal, and John Davies of Brecon in his open letter, who address this question to best effect. Prys and Davies in fact present the poets with a list of disciplines on which they are to sing, with the help (as Davies in particular stresses) of the appropriate academic expert in each discipline. Neither list precludes praise—humanists, too, sought fame—but the emphasis, apart from divine poetry, is on historical and scientific verse: that is, their recommendations were in the humanist mainstream and they were thinking particularly, perhaps, of the Italian epic poets and the French scientific poets, especially Guillaume de Salluste du Bartas.

The third charge levelled by the humanists against the professional poets was lack of eloquence, by which they meant ignorance of the art of rhetoric as practised by humanists: rhetoric was, of course, the Renaissance art *par excellence*. Only William Salesbury and, possibly, Edmwnd Prys formulate this charge precisely, but it is probably implicit in general complaints about decline of poetic craftsmanship made by other humanists as well. It was not that the professional poets did not employ figurative language, as one of their number, Simwnt Fychan, gently pointed out, but rather that the figurative language they employed tended towards sameness and monotony. To help them, William Salesbury produced in 1552 an adaptation, with Welsh examples, of Petrus Mosellanus's *Tabulae de Schematibus et Tropis* with a dedication to his friend, the professional poet Gruffudd Hiraethog—the only professional poet ever to eulogize him, by the way. This may have had some effect—Simwnt Fychan made a copy, and Wiliam Cynwal and Robert ab Ifan, another professional, had kindred texts in their possession—but it was never printed. In 1595, however, Henry Perry, an Anglesey clergyman, took Salesbury's text as the basis of his own work, *Egluryn Ffraethineb*, adding material from the most recent edition of Henry Peacham's *Garden of Eloquence* and casting the whole into a Ramist mould; the work was carried out under the patronage of Sir John Salusbury of Llyweni and dedicated to him. Somewhat later, another Ramist rhetorical manual was constructed by the Denbighshire gentleman and poet, Tomos Prys of Plas Iolyn, and a translation of the old-fashioned pseudo-Aristotelian *Rhetorica ad Herennium* essayed by the Caernarfonshire gentleman, Siôn ap Hywel; but neither achieved print, and of the latter only a fragment remains. (There is a very useful survey of Welsh Renaissance rhetoricians which remains unpublished.)[40]

Finally, the humanists accused the poets of secretiveness about their art: William Salesbury, Gruffydd Robert, John Davies of Brecon, and Siôn ap Hywel wax eloquent about this. The poets were, in fact, enjoined to keep their art secret in the so-called Statute of Gruffudd ap Cynan promulgated at the First Caerwys Eisteddfod of 1523, but such an attitude was wholly at variance with the Renaissance ideal of the cultured courtier, who was encouraged to acquire and practise artistic skills that had hitherto been the preserve of professionals. Undaunted by the poets' lack of co-operation, several Welsh humanists published treatises dealing with the traditional poetic art, particularly the intricate system of alliteration and internal rhyme known as *cynghanedd* and the twenty-four 'strict' metres (that is, syllabic metres employing *cynghanedd*). They all had access to copies of the poet's 'grammar-book', first compiled by Einion Offeiriad *c.* 1330 and later revised, but in the absence of expert guidance they were not always able to interpret its injunctions correctly. The latter parts of both Gruffydd Robert's *Gramadeg Cymraeg* (1584) and John Davies of Brecon's *Institutiones* (1592) are given over to metrics, but differ somewhat in intention. Robert's Welsh treatise, which is unhappily full of errors, either because he had too few sources to hand in Milan or because he misinterpreted those that he had, was clearly meant to teach aspiring young humanists to write Welsh verse, and he is willing to cut corners and admit Italian metres (but not, surprisingly, the *ottava rima*), and the Welsh so-called 'free' or accentual metres, into the canon of acceptable modes. Davies, on the other hand, writes in Latin and attempts to present as much material as possible—some of it, admittedly, rather ill-digested—in order to display to the learned world what William Salesbury once called 'the unspeakable felicity and wondrous graces of the British metres'; that is, his intention was scientific as well as pedagogic. Hard on Davies's heels came his friend, Captain William Midleton, with his *Barddoniaeth, neu Brydyddiaeth* (1593/4); but Midleton's little manual was largely independent of that used by the professional poets and was designed, as he himself says, to teach his fellow-countrymen the quickest way to learn *cerdd dafod* ('tongue-craft' or 'verse-craft'): that is, he belongs more to the method of Robert than to that of Davies.[41] In the same category must be placed the short handbooks compiled by Midleton's neighbour, Roger Morris, and by his friend and fellow-buccaneer, Tomos Prys—Prys actually borrowed Midleton's title— but, accomplished as these are, neither of them achieved publication.

What effect did this concerted campaign of the humanists have on the professional poets? The short answer is, very little. The latter did not abandon praise as their staple; they did not take to composing lengthy theological, historical, or scientific poems; they took only cautious note of the new rhetoric; and they were naturally unhappy about the drive to flood the market with amateurs. Salesbury's friend, Gruffudd Hiraethog, was something of an exception: not only did he go out of his way, as it seems, to praise humanists, he also prepared a little book in which some easily accessible portions of the poets' traditional lore were set out for the pleasure and edification of Welsh gentry living in exile—of their own free will, of course—in England; but this, too, remained unpublished.[42] Some of Gruffudd Hiraethog's pupils, graduates of the Second Caerwys Eisteddfod of 1567, shared their teacher's inclinations to some extent: Siôn Tudur in particular, but also Simwnt Fychan and, perhaps, Wiliam Llŷn and Wiliam Cynwal as well. Of a somewhat later generation, Siôn Phylip and Huw Machno appear to have had some grammar schooling. All these from time to time display some innovatory tendencies, which may have been in response to humanist pressure. But the bulk of their work remains firmly traditional and—it must be admitted—of variable quality. Gradually, for a number of reasons, poet and patron drifted apart and the organization of professional poets was not able to survive the ravages of the Civil War and the political upheavals which followed, although a few individual professional poets continued to ply their trade for some years after the Restoration.[43]

Nor, unhappily, did the humanist campaign bring into being a flourishing new breed of amateur poets. It is true that there was a quickening of interest among some Welsh gentlemen and clergymen, most of them university-trained, in the composing of Welsh verse in the traditional strict metres during the late sixteenth and early seventeenth centuries: prolific examples are Huw Roberts, an Anglesey clergyman, and (again) Tomos Prys of Plas Iolyn.[44] It is true that in their work some broadening of thematic range may be discerned—it includes, for example, a number of satires on contemporary life—but in the main it remains overwhelmingly devoted to praise (except that these poets mercifully eschew the professional poets' malign practice of versifying pedigrees in their praise-poems). One exception to this rule was the importance attached to divine poetry, particularly (although not exclusively) the versifying of the psalms, which enjoyed a considerable vogue in Wales as in England. Gruffydd Robert managed to put into print a small collection of both divine and secular poetry, probably in Milan, very likely between 1584 and 1594. Around the latter year William

Midleton, too, printed, perhaps in Oxford, a collection of his own divine verse, of
which only a fragment survives. His complete collection of the Welsh psalms in the
strict metres was published in 1603, after his death at sea, by the stationer, Thomas
Salisbury, whose aspirations to become the scholar-printer of the Welsh Renaissance
were unhappily dashed by the Great Plague of 1603, in which he lost most of his
manuscripts. Of all the amateur poets, only Edmwnd Prys displays evidence of true
greatness and even he is overshadowed by his professional contemporary, Wiliam
Llŷn. A promising development was the adoption by the amateurs of the 'free' or
accentual metres, which had hitherto been the preserve of the lower grades of poets
and which were generally (although not invariably) shunned by the professionals. Much
interesting verse in this mode survives but it is again limited in range both metrically
and thematically.[45] Some enchanting love-lyrics were composed, especially by the
courtier-poet, Richard Hughes of Llŷn, in whose name a broadside pastoral ballad
of *c.* 1620 survives (balancing neatly Simwnt Fychan's rendering in the *cywydd* metre
of Martial's epigram on the happy life, which William Salesbury had had printed
as a broadside some fifty years earlier). Otherwise, the emphasis is again on religious
verses, particularly metrical psalms. A partial collection of psalms in the free metres
by Edward Kyffin, Maurice Kyffin's brother, was published by Thomas Salisbury
in 1603, shortly after their author had died in the Plague. But it was Edmwnd Prys,
at the age of 77 or 78, who finally published the complete metrical psalter in Welsh,
in every way a notable achievement. Prys has two or three other fine free-metre poems
apart from the psalms, and one of these is indeed a harbinger of things to come:
a poem constructed to fit a popular British or Continental air—in this case 'About
the Banks of Helicon'—and invested with full *cynghanedd* (as has recently been finely
shown; Richard Hughes has another such, but Prys's is probably much earlier).[46]
This was to become the dominant mode of Welsh poetry from the mid-seventeenth
century onwards, especially in north Wales, and someone less musically illiterate than
I could surely relate the development firmly to the spread of Renaissance music.

You will have noticed that few of the characteristic Renaissance poetic genres took
root in Welsh, in spite of the hopes of the humanists: there were no heroic epics,
no long philosophical and scientific poems, no sonnets, no lengthy pastorals, no true
epigrams (although the *englyn* was pressed into service to fill that particular gap). It
is all the more surprising, therefore, to find that there has survived a single example
of poetic drama in Welsh, *The Tragedy of Troilus and Cressida*. The sources are mostly
medieval—Chaucer and Henryson—and the metres mostly drab-age English, but the
play does have a certain grandeur in its apprehension and presentation of the role
of Fate in human affairs. It survives in a transcript made in the early seventeenth
century by John Jones of Gellilyfdy, but it has recently been cogently argued that
it was, in fact, written by Humphrey Lhuyd some fifty years earlier.[47] There is evidence
that dramatic presentations were made at Llweni and Chirk Castle as well as in
Ludlow Castle, the headquarters of the Council of Wales and the Marches (where
John Milton's *Comus* was presented), and there is no reason why the Welsh *Troilus*
should not have been performed in some gentleman's house somewhere in the rich

north-east, the 'Tuscany of Wales' as Peter Smith called it (see Chapter VI, p. 111).[48] That the play stands alone is, of course, symptomatic of a more general failure.

Before I deal with that, however, let me discuss briefly the impact of humanism on Welsh prose-writing. This was profound and almost entirely beneficial. I have mentioned the list of themes for poets, presented to them by Edmwnd Prys and John Davies of Brecon. A similar list for prose-writers may be found in the dedication of Gruffydd Robert's *Gramadeg Cymraeg* to William Herbert, Earl of Pembroke, and it included not only grammar, rhetoric, and dialectic—the medieval *Trivium*—but also moral philosophy (which we may assume embraced history as well), medicine, politics, natural philosophy, military science, and divinity. Of these themes it was divinity alone which achieved something approaching satisfactory treatment, and that only because the Welsh Protestant humanists accepted the challenge of translating the Bible into Welsh. The first Welsh printed book, Sir John Price's devotional manual of 1546, *Yn y Lhyvyr hwnn*, had as its stated objective 'to put into print part of holy Scripture', although the bulk of the material was taken from a medieval mystical treatise, which Price certainly thought of as a remnant of the lost theological learning of the Welsh.[49] The second Welsh printed book was William Salesbury's *Dictionary*, but the third was *Oll Synnwyr Pen Kembero Ygyd*, 'All the wisdom in a Welshman's head gathered together'—it is a very small book!—again by Salesbury, which is a collection of proverbs filched from Gruffudd Hiraethog but whose preface contains a ringing appeal to the Welsh to insist on having the Holy Scripture in their own tongue, for learning's sake as well as for religion's. Salesbury was not one to stand idly by, as the politicians say, when there was work to be done. In 1551 he himself produced a Welsh version of the Lectionary. In 1563—after the Marian interim—he appears to have organized the passage of a Bill through Parliament compelling the Welsh bishops and the Bishop of Hereford to have the Bible and Book of Common Prayer translated into Welsh by St David's Day 1567, on pain of being fined £40 each: a remarkable reversal, on Protestant principle, of the language clause of the Act of Union. By 1567 Salesbury himself had translated the whole of the Book of Common Prayer and the bulk of the New Testament: Bishop Richard Davies, the patron of the whole enterprise, and Dr Thomas Huet, Precentor (or head of the Chapter) of St David's, took care of the rest. After 1567, so Sir John Wynn of Gwydir says, Salesbury and Davies began to translate the Old Testament but quarrelled 'for the general sense and etymology of one word, which the Bishop would have to be one way and William Salesbury another'—which is far too good a story to discard, even if it is not likely to be wholly true! Salesbury was a kind of genius, immensely learned and painfully opinionated. His translations are brilliant, but obscured by an archaic and Latinized orthography and an unrelenting emphasis on variety—on copiousness—in both morphology and vocabulary. Plain country clergymen found them simply baffling, and even humanists like Maurice Kyffin found their artificiality intolerable. The situation was saved by Dr William Morgan, Vicar of Llanrhaeadr-ym-Mochnant and Edmwnd Prys's friend at Cambridge: by 1587 he had revised Salesbury's work and had himself translated the Old Testament and Apocrypha. The whole Bible appeared in 1588, to universal acclaim. Morgan regularized and modernized Salesbury's irregularities and archaisms and curbed his copiousness: he appears to have taken as his guide in matters orthographic and grammatical the practice of the professional poets, whose work he knew well (he may also have had Edmwnd Prys as a kind of linguistic consultant). Later, in 1599, when he was Bishop of Llandaff, Morgan revised Salesbury's Book of Common Prayer as well. Finally, in 1620, John Davies of Mallwyd and his brother-in-law, Bishop Richard Parry of St Asaph (Morgan's successor in that see, to which he had been translated from Llandaff) ironed out any remaining anomalies in the language and style of Morgan's translation and gave us what has ever since been regarded as the Welsh Authorized Version. When it is recalled that Davies's *Rudimenta*, which appeared the following year, was based almost exclusively on the work of the poets, it will be realized even more clearly what was the linguistic rock out of which the Bible was hewn. The Welsh Bible was a major triumph of humanism as well as Protestantism in Wales: at one stroke, it gave the country a substantial body of regular, copious, and eloquent prose, employing a variety of literary forms, which at the same time bore the intangible but efficacious seal of divine inspiration and approval. At one stroke, one might say, the status of Welsh as a learned language was henceforth assured. The heroic labours of the Revd Dr Isaac Thomas—and here I am deliberately breaking my rule of not naming present-day Welsh Renaissance scholars in the text of this lecture—have demonstrated clearly that the Welsh translators were splendid biblical scholars, able to handle the original languages in the best available texts with ease and assurance and able, too, to make discriminating use of the best contemporary versions in Latin and at least three modern languages, French, German and English.[50] Those researches have also shown how complete was the translators' command of Welsh in all its periods, with the single exception of Thomas Huet. If any complaint can be laid against their work it is that it was linguistically rather too formal: in particular, the omnipresent abnormal sentence construction, involving an initial subject (without emphasis) and concord between subject and verb, while agreeing happily with the rules of Latin grammar, may actually have forced Welsh into a slightly foreign mould.[51] But this is a matter on which far better linguistic scholars than I are far from agreed!

Building largely on the success of the biblical translators, a small school of Anglican prose-writers emerged in Wales, seeking to put into the hands of the Welsh reading public a judicious selection of books which, in one way or another, had been influential in English religious life. Somewhat surprisingly with regard to the modesty of the aim, but not unjustly considering their quality, a number of these have achieved the status of Welsh prose classics: Maurice Kyffin's translation of Jewel's *Apologia*; Edward James's version of 'The Book of Homilies'; Robert Lloyd of Chirk's vivid rendering of Arthur Dent's *Plain Man's Pathway to Heaven*; John Davies of Mallwyd's translation of Edmund Bunny's Protestant adaptation of the *First Book of the Christian Exercise, appertaining to Resolution*, by the Jesuit, Robert Persons—to name only four. But even in this favoured field of divinity, as you will have noticed, hardly any original works were produced by the Anglican humanist writers, although Bishop Richard Davies had set them an inspiring example in his long introduction to the Welsh New Testament of 1567, in which the myth of Joseph of Arimathea was first given authoritative expression in Welsh. The Roman Catholic authors did rather better in this respect, but they were somewhat outside the humanist mainstream and they also, for obvious reasons, found it difficult to get their books into print (there are, I should add, intriguing exceptions to both generalizations). The Puritans, too, did much better than the Anglicans in the matter of producing original religious works, but only after the high tide of Welsh humanism (if it may be so called) had already receded.[52]

However, *theologyddiaeth* (theology or divinity) was only one of nine fields of learning mentioned by Gruffydd Robert as clamouring for treatment in his dedication to the *Gramadeg Cymraeg*. The others, as you will recall, were grammar, rhetoric, dialectic, moral philosophy (including history), medicine, politics, natural philosophy, and military science. Of these, as we have seen, grammar and rhetoric were fairly adequately dealt with in print in Welsh but not (alas!) dialectic. Of the remainder, there was no attempt to deal with political thought or with military science, although William Thomas was among the first to introduce Machiavelli into England and Roger Williams was the foremost Elizabethan writer on military matters (just as Robert Recorde and John Dee were pioneers of mathematics, which Gruffydd Robert does not mention). In the remaining three fields mentioned by Robert, however—medicine, natural philosophy, and moral philosophy (which we may assume included history)—there was some movement. The normal mode of procedure in the major countries was firstly the translation into the vernacular of a flood of Latin and Greek texts in the various fields of learning, and then original works in the vernacular in those fields. This procedure is only faintly reflected in Welsh. Disappointingly, few translations from Latin authors were made and none from Greek, although the Welsh humanists were steeped in the classics and although some of them participated in the process in England: William Salesbury, for example, put into English Thomas Linacre's Latin translation of Proclus's *Sphere*, and Maurice Kyffin versified in English Terence's *Andria*. Part of Cicero's *De Senectute* was translated and put into print by Gruffydd Robert, and part of Seneca's *De Remediis Fortuitorum Liber* was excellently translated by an unknown scholar but remained in manuscript: as the editor of this fragment perceptively points out, the translator may have been attempting to provide for Welsh humanist prose-writers an alternative model to that presented by Cicero.[53] Sixteenth-century European humanist writers fared a little better: Juan Luis Vives's treatise on the education of women, *De Institutione Feminae Christianae*, was early translated into Welsh by an otherwise unknown writer, Richard Owen,[54] and one of Desiderius Erasmus's amazingly popular dialogues, the *Colloquium Adolescentis et Scorti*, was likewise put into Welsh by an unknown translator.[55] Erasmus's influence on the Welsh humanists was, in fact, pervasive, as was clearly demonstrated at this Congress four years ago, and it is surprising that so few of them attempted to translate or adapt him.[56] Neither of these translations was printed, but a happier fate awaited the Welsh version of the meditations of the obscure French (or, rather, Breton) humanist, Pierre Boaistuau, on the miseries and excellence of man, *Le Théâtre du Monde*, by the Roman Catholic exile, Dr Roger

Smyth: this was published, either in Paris or, surreptitiously, in London, in 1615. (The *Nouvelle Biographie Générale* [vi, 282] says rather damningly of Boaistuau that 'he did not lack a certain erudition', but this may be a somewhat harsh verdict on someone who is reputed to have influenced no less a thinker than Blaise Pascal.)

All these works may broadly be classified as belonging to the field of moral philosophy. Also subsumed under moral philosophy in Gruffydd Robert's list is history. We have already seen that substantial Welsh manuscript treatises in this field were produced by Roger Morris, Ifan Llwyd ap Dafydd, and John Davies of Brecon. I would like here to stress the importance of John Davies's work, now made much more accessible to us than before in a transcript prepared by Ffred Ffransis while he was serving terms of imprisonment when President of the Welsh Language Society.[57] The original text was written in 1597 in response to an attack in manuscript on Geoffrey of Monmouth by someone whom Davies calls 'the second, unprinted, gentleman' (the 'first, printed, gentleman' was Maurice Kyffin, to whose strictures on the poets in the preface to his translation of Jewel's *Apologia* Davies had already replied in the same year). This 'second, unprinted, gentleman' had attacked Geoffrey on four counts, some familiar, others relatively unfamiliar: the fact that Brutus was unknown to classical historians; the problem of the Oracle of Diana, which had foretold what Brutus's fate would be; the question of the giants, who had allegedly inhabited the island before Brutus; and the credibility (or rather, incredibility) of the prodigious feats of arms performed by some Galfridian heroes, notably Arthur. To all these charges Davies replies learnedly and at length, drawing not only upon his vast reading but also on folk memory—for example, of Welsh giants or of feats performed by Welsh and other heroes during the Wars of the Roses (his willingness to admit oral evidence may have had something to do with his stubborn, if covert, Roman Catholicism). But the manner of his argument is even more interesting than its substance. He argues like a humanist, making full and effective use of dialectic as well as rhetoric. The treatise is, in fact, 50,000 words of pure Welsh humanist prose, and its publication is an urgent desideratum. Other fields mentioned by Gruffydd Robert were medicine and natural philosophy; and here, William Salesbury again makes an appearance with a fine treatise on medicinal plants, based primarily on the work of the pioneer botanists, Leonhard Fuchs and William Turner, but incorporating also a significant element derived from Salesbury's own observations. This used to be regarded as a mere practical herbal, but its most recent editor has persuasively argued that it is, in fact, a work of humanist science in Welsh; it, too, remained unprinted.[58] A few fields of learning not mentioned by Gruffydd Robert also received some attention. John Davies of Brecon allegedly translated a compendium of Aristotelian metaphysics into Welsh, but this—if it ever existed—is now lost. Treatises on music by John Case and by Andreas Ornithoparcus (as Englished by John Dowland) were translated by the important Flintshire gentleman, John Conway, and the royal harper, Robert Peilin, respectively; but neither was published—happily in Conway's case, since his Welsh is pretty debased.[59]

The final conclusion must be that, although a sustained and partially successful effort was made during the period to treat of most of the main branches of learning in Welsh, the effort inevitably lacked depth and was also vitiated by the failure of many of the authors, for whatever reason, to see their work into print. It must be added that the remnants of the ancient native learning, on which the humanists set such great store, fared little better as regards achieving publication: John Price (as we have seen) printed some theology, John Davies of Brecon some material relating to metrics in his *Institutiones*, and William Salesbury and John Davies of Mallwyd various collections of proverbs and proverbial lore; proverbs were, of course, the distilled wisdom of the ancients *par excellence*, as well as being much in fashion in Renaissance Europe because of the influence of Erasmus. It is much to be regretted that the finest of all the Renaissance collections of Welsh proverbs, that of Thomas Wiliems of Trefriw, remained, and remains, unprinted.[60]

It is now time to sum up. What Wales saw, in the apt phrase of my colleague, Miss Morfydd Owen, was 'a limited Renaissance'.[61] In some fields it succeeded magnificently, in others it proved abortive. In the field of scholarship, the works of grammar and lexicography which it produced were truly remarkable, the works of historiography and chorography less so but still commendable; most important of all, perhaps, the medieval manuscripts inherited by the Renaissance were in the main safeguarded, and a plethora of others added to them. In the field of poetry, on the other hand, the standpoints of the humanists and the professional poets were too far apart from the beginning, so that they could not have been reconciled, and the humanists may, in fact, have hastened the decline of professional strict-metre poetry rather than arrested it as they sought to do; on the other hand, it is still not clear to what extent the flowering of free-metre poetry, of both the old and the new kinds, during the period may have been due to humanist influences. In the sphere of prose we have a triumph to surpass even that in the realm of scholarship, the resplendent Welsh Bible of 1588, but even in this field the triumph was not fully followed up: little original religious prose was written, and few contributions were made, with one or two notable exceptions, in other branches of learning. Symptomatic of the failure was the shortage of printed books in Welsh or about Wales, perhaps as few as 115 between 1546 and 1642, and of the 115 only some 67 at most may properly be described as humanist.[62]

Why then did the humanists achieve only a limited success in Wales? The basic reason was first clearly set out by the opening speaker of this Congress in a Welsh pamphlet published twenty-three years ago and recently reprinted.[63] It was that the state of Welsh society did not correspond to the humanistic literary ideal: that ideal belonged properly to a courtly and urban milieu, whereas Welsh society was still essentially agricultural and even largely pastoral. Therefore, it failed to generate patronage on a sufficient scale to make fulfilment of the humanists' dream possible. One might add that politically, too, circumstances were far from propitious. There was no Welsh Renaissance state to support Welsh humanism, as there most assuredly was a Scottish Renaissance state. The political centre of gravity lay outside Wales, so that the class which was politically aware—that is, the gentry—became drawn into the main currents of English politics, gradually losing much of its Welsh identity, including eventually the language itself. This process was never completed, but it had already gone quite far by the second half of the seventeenth century. Since most of the humanists, and virtually all their patrons, were gentry of one kind or another—indeed, the humanists have been called the organic intellectuals of the gentry class[64]—it is not surprising that the middle years of the seventeenth century saw the effective end of humanism, as well as of professional poetry, in Wales.

Yet there were lasting gains. No one who read John Davies's grammar and dictionary could doubt that Welsh was a learned language, able to hold its head high in the most exalted contemporary company: and Edward Lhuyd, after a good deal of making up for lost ground, was able to build upon John Davies's work when he embarked upon his own remarkable researches sixty years later. The claim of the language to learned status was clinched by the magnificence of the Welsh Bible and some of the lesser works that accompanied it, in spite of the fact that the range of learning available in Welsh was narrow. The Morgan Bible, as revised by Parry and Davies, became the fuel of the eighteenth-century Evangelical Awakening and the staple sustenance of the Protestant Nonconformist civilization (as it has been called) which evolved in the last century on the basis of that Awakening. Even the pronouncements of Edmwnd Prys were not forgotten—only last year there appeared in Welsh the first (very modern) Renaissance epic—and his metrical psalter became a popular as well as a learned classic and the basis for the evolution of a remarkable hymnology. But more than anything it is the image of a small but varied group of extraordinarily gifted men, all working together in the service of a high ideal, which still serves to awaken admiration and uplift the spirit.

Notes

1. I am very grateful to Emeritus Professor J. E. Caerwyn Williams for reading and commenting upon an early draft of this paper. I regret that its annotation has had to be so selective, particularly with regard to the historical background and the activities of the professional poets.
2. P .O. Kristeller, *Renaissance Thought* (New York, 1961), pp. 120–1.
3. See in particular G. M. Logan, 'Substance and form in Renaissance humanism', *Journal of Medieval and Renaissance Studies*, VII (1977), 1–34.
4. For an uniquely authoritative account of the period, see Glanmor Williams, *Recovery, Reorientation and Reformation: Wales c. 1415–1642* (Oxford and Cardiff, 1987); Professor Williams makes the point that the application of the Reformation to Wales was not dependent upon the Acts of Union.
5. J. I. Catto (ed.), *The History of the University of Oxford ... Volume I: The Early Oxford Schools* (Oxford, 1984), p. 186.
6. W. P. Griffith, 'Welsh students at Oxford, Cambridge and the Inns of Court during the sixteenth and early seventeenth centuries' (unpublished University of Wales (Bangor) Ph.D. thesis, 1982).
7. Gwyn Williams, 'Shakespeare's Phoenix', *The National Library of Wales Journal*, XXII (1981-2), 277–81, elucidates the relationships which lay behind the poem. See further John Rowlands, 'A critical edition and study of the Welsh poems written in praise of the Salusburies of Llyweni' (unpublished University of Oxford D.Phil. thesis, 1967/8).
8. Ceri Davies, *Rhagymadroddion a Chyflwyniadau Lladin 1551-1632* (Caerdydd, 1980); idem, *Latin Writers of the Renaissance* (Cardiff, 1981).
9. R. Brinley Jones, *The Old British Tongue: The Vernacular in Wales 1540-1640* (Cardiff, 1970); another seminal volume is the collection of essays by G. J. Williams, *Agweddau ar Hanes Dysg Gymraeg*, ed. A. Lewis (Caerdydd, 1969).

10. T. D. Kendrick, *British Antiquity* (London, 1950) has not been wholly superseded by F. J. Levy, *Tudor Historical Thought* (San Marino, 1967) and May McKisack, *Medieval History in the Tudor Age* (Oxford, 1971); on the European impact of 'Berosus' see C. G. Dubois, *Celtes et Gaulois au XVIe siècle* (Paris, 1972).

11. R. F. Treharne, *The Glastonbury Legends* (London, 1967); G. Williams, *Reformation Views of Church History* (London, 1970).

12. G. J. Williams, 'Leland a Bale a'r traddodiad derwyddol', *Llên Cymru* IV (1956-7), 15-25.

13. A. O. H. Jarman, 'Cerdd Ysgolan', *Ysgrifau Beirniadol X* (Dinbych, 1977), 51-78.

14. T. D. Kendrick, op.cit., p. 88; Kendrick has a lucid account of the debate, as does A. O. H. Jarman, 'Y Ddadl Ynghylch Sieffre o Fynwy', *Llên Cymru*, II (1952-3), 1-18.

15. On Vaughan and Maurice see T. Emrys Parry, 'Llythyrau Robert Vaughan Hengwrt (1592-1667) gyda rhagymadrodd a nodiadau' (unpublished University of Wales (Bangor) MA thesis, 1960).

16. E. D. Jones, 'Rowland Fychan o Gaer-fai a Brut Sieffre o Fynwy', *Llên Cymru*, IV (1956-7), 228.

17. E. B. Fryde, *Humanism and Renaissance Historiography* (London, 1983), p. 22.

18. J. E. Lloyd, 'The Welsh Chronicles', *Proceedings of the British Academy*, XIV (1928), 387.

19. R. Geraint Gruffydd, 'Humphrey Llwyd of Denbigh: some documents and a catalogue', *Denbighshire Historial Society Transactions*, XVII (1968), 53-107 (with corrigenda at ibid., XVIII, 178-9); idem, 'Humphrey Llwyd: dyneiddiwr', *Efrydiau Athronyddol*, XXXIII (1970), 57-74.

20. Ieuan M. Williams, 'Ysgolheictod hanesyddol yr unfed ganrif ar bymtheg', *Llên Cymru*, II (1952-3), 111-24, 209-23.

21. R. I. D. Jones, 'Astudiaeth feirniadol o Peniarth 168B (tt. 41a-126b)' (unpublished University of Wales (Aberystwyth) MA thesis, 1954); Nia Lewis, 'Astudiaeth destunol a beirniadol o "Ystorie Kymru neu Cronicl Kymraeg" (Ifan Llwyd ap Dafydd)' (unpublished University of Wales (Aberystwyth) MA thesis, 1957).

22. For a general survey see Q. E. Deakin, 'The early county historians of England and Wales *c*. 1570-1656' (unpublished University of Wales (Aberystwyth) Ph.D. thesis, 1982).

23 Gwyn A. Williams, *Welsh Wizard and British Empire: Dr John Dee and Welsh Identity* (Cardiff, 1980); in a paper delivered at the Congress, Mr R. J. K. Roberts, Deputy Librarian of the Bodleian Library, argued convincingly that Dee's interest in Welsh history went far beyond what can properly be described as 'dabbling'.

24. For a survey, see Peter C. Bartrum, 'Notes on the Welsh genealogical manuscripts', *Transactions of the Honourable Society of Cymmrodorion*, Session 1968, pp. 63-98; idem, 'Further notes on the Welsh genealogical manuscripts', ibid. 1976, pp. 102-18.

25. On Vaughan see the unpublished thesis cited at n.15 above; on Jones, see Nesta Jones, 'Bywyd John Jones, Gellilyfdy' (unpublished University of Wales (Bangor) MA thesis, 1964) and Nesta Lloyd (née Jones), 'A history of Welsh scholarship in the first half of the seventeenth century, with special reference to the writings of John Jones, Gellilyfdy' (unpublished University of Oxford D.Phil. thesis, 1970).

26. G. J. Williams and E. J. Jones (eds.), *Gramadegau'r Penceirddiaid* (Caerdydd, 1934) is important for the study of the Renaissance as well as the medieval period.

27. J. E. Caerwyn Williams, *Geiriadurwyr y Gymraeg yng Nghyfnod y Dadeni* (Caerdydd, 1983); on Salesbury see, most conveniently, the two chapters by W. Alun Mathias in Geraint Bowen (ed.), *Y Traddodiad Rhyddiaith (Darlithiau Rhydychen)* (Llandysul, 1970), pp. 27-78, which summarize his important unpublished University of Wales MA thesis of 1949, 'Astudiaeth o weithgarwch llenyddol William Salesbury'.

28. G.J. Williams (ed.), *Gramadeg Cymraeg gan Gruffydd Robert* (Caerdydd, 1939): a classic edition, which is basic to the study of the Renaissance in Wales.

29. T. Gwynfor Griffith, 'Italy and Wales', *Transactions of the Honourable Society of Cymmrodorion*, Session 1966, pp. 281-98; Heledd Hayes, *Cymru a'r Dadeni* (Bangor, 1987).

30. R. Geraint Gruffydd, 'The Life of Dr John Davies of Brecon (Siôn Dafydd Rhys)', *Transactions of the Honourable Society of Cymmrodorion*, Session 1971, pp. 175-90; the narrative requires some modification in the light of more recent discoveries.

31. Rhiannon Francis Roberts's University of Wales MA thesis of 1950, 'Bywyd a gwaith Dr John Davies, Mallwyd', remains, unhappily, largely unpublished.

32. J. Morris-Jones, *A Welsh Grammar, Historical and Comparative* (Oxford, 1913), p. v.
33. G. J. Williams, *Agweddau*, p. 72 (in Welsh).
34. Glyn E. Jones, 'William Salesbury a chynaniad Groeg a Lladin yn yr unfed ganrif ar bymtheg', *Y Traethodydd*, CXXXVIII (1983), 40-3.
35. J. Gwynfor Griffith, 'De Italica Pronunciatione', *Italian Studies*, VIII (1953), 71-82.
36. Bobi Jones, 'Pwnc mawr beirniadaeth lenyddol Gymraeg', *Ysgrifau Beirniadol III* (Dinbych, 1967), 253-88.
37. Enid Roberts (ed.), *Gwaith Siôn Tudur* (Caerdydd, 1980), pp. 606-11.
38. Gruffydd Aled Williams (ed.), *Ymryson Edmwnd Prys a Wiliam Cynwal* (Caerdydd, 1986): another classic edition of a basic Welsh Renaissance text.
39. Branwen Jarvis, 'Llythyr Siôn Dafydd Rhys at y Beirdd', *Llên Cymru*, XII (1972-3), 45-56.
40. Bedwyr Lewis Jones, 'Testunau rhethreg Cymraeg y Dadeni' (unpublished University of Wales (Bangor) MA thesis, 1961).
41. On Midleton, see Gruffydd Aled Williams, 'William Midleton, bonheddwr, anturiwr a bardd', *Denbighshire Historical Society Transactions*, XXIV (1975), 74-116.
42. D. J. Bowen, *Gruffudd Hiraethog a'i Oes* (Caerdydd, 1958); idem, 'Cywyddau Gruffudd Hiraethog i dri o awduron y Dadeni', *Transactions of the Honourable Society of Cymmrodorion*, Sessions 1974 and 1975, pp. 103-31.
43. Idem, 'Canrif olaf y Cywyddwyr', *Llên Cymru*, XIV (1981-4), 3-51; idem, 'Y Cywyddwyr a'r Dirywiad', *Bulletin of the Board of Celtic Studies*, XXIX (1980-2), 453-96. An ambitious research project, conceived and directed by Professor Bowen, tracing the rise and decline of patronage county by county, is now nearing completion.
44. William Rowlands, 'Barddoniaeth Tomos Prys o Blas Iolyn' (unpublished University of Wales (Bangor) MA thesis, 1912).
45. Brinley Rees, *Dulliau'r Canu Rhydd 1500-1650* (Caerdydd, 1952).
46. Idem, 'Tair cerdd a thair tôn', *Bulletin of the Board of Celtic Studies*, XXXI (1984), 60-73.
47. W. Beynon Davies (ed.), *Troelus a Chressyd o Lawysgrif Peniarth 106* (Caerdydd, 1976); R. I. Stephens Jones, 'The authorship of *Troelus a Chressyd*', *Bulletin of the Board of Celtic Studies*, XXVIII (1978-80), 223-8.
48. P. Smith and M. Bevan-Evans, 'A few reflections on Gellilyfdy and the Renaissance in north-eastern Wales', *Flintshire Historical Society Publications*, XXIV (1969-70), 19-43; other articles on this key region are G. J. Williams, 'Traddodiad llenyddol Dyffryn Clwyd a'r cyffiniau', *Denbighshire Historical Society Transactions*, I (1952), 20-32 and Enid Roberts, 'The Renaissance in the Vale of Clwyd', *Flintshire Historical Society Publications*, XV (1954-5), 52-63.
49. R. Geraint Gruffydd, '*Yny lhyvyr hwnn* (1546): the earliest Welsh printed book', *Bulletin of the Board of Celtic Studies*, XXIII (1968-70), 105-16.
50. Isaac Thomas, *Y Testament Newydd Cymraeg 1551-1620* (Caerdydd, 1976); articles on the Welsh Old Testament in the *National Library of Wales Journal* between Summer 1980 (Vol. XXI, No. 4) and Winter 1985 (Vol. XXIV, No. 2): these are soon to be gathered together and published as one volume.
51. See, for example, the opinion of that foremost authority on Welsh syntax, T. J. Morgan, 'Cymraeg naturiol gywir', *Ysgrifau Beirniadol V* (1970), 254-74.
52. R. Geraint Gruffydd, 'Religious prose in Welsh from the beginning of the reign of Elizabeth to the Restoration' (unpublished University of Oxford D.Phil. thesis, 1952-3); Geraint Bowen, 'Rhyddiaith reciwsantaidd Cymru' (unpublished University of Wales (Aberystwyth) Ph.D. thesis, 1978).
53. Nesta Lloyd, 'Cyfieithiad o ran o *De Remediis Fortuitorum Liber* Seneca i'r Gymraeg', *Bulletin of the Board of Celtic Studies*, XXIV (1970-2), 450-8.
54. Garfield H. Hughes, '"Dysgeidieth Cristnoges o Ferch"' in Thomas Jones (ed.), *Astudiaethau Amrywiol* (Caerdydd, 1968); Branwen Jarvis, '"Dysgeidieth Cristnoges o Ferch" a'i gefndir', *Ysgrifau Beirniadol XIII* (Dinbych, 1985), 219-26.
55. Nesta Lloyd, 'Cyfieithiad o ran o *Colloquium Adolescentis et Scorti* i'r Gymraeg', *Bulletin of the Board of Celtic Studies*, XXV (1972-4), 32-46.
56. Ceri Davies, 'Erasmus and Welsh Renaissance learning', *Transactions of the Honourable Society of*

Cymmrodorion, Session 1983, pp. 48–58; cf. Garfield H. Hughes, '"Ffasiynau'r" Dadeni', *Ysgrifau Beirniadol V* (Dinbych, 1970), 62–70.

57. The original text is at the National Library of Wales [= NLW] Peniarth MS 118, 731–864; copies of Mr Ffransis's transcript are available at the National Library of Wales.

58. Iwan Edgar, 'Llysieulyfr William Salesbury: testun o lawysgrif Ll.G.C. 4581, ynghyd â rhagymadrodd ac astudiaeth o'r enwau llysiau Cymraeg a geir ynddo' (unpublished University of Wales (Bangor) Ph.D. thesis, 1984).

59. D. Gwenallt Jones, 'Clod Cerdd Dafod', *Llên Cymru*, I (1950–1), 186–7; Gwendraeth Jones, 'Siôn Conwy III a'i waith', *Bulletin of the Board of Celtic Studies*, XXII (1966–8), 16–30: it should be noted, however, that it was the Latin treatise *Apologia Musices*, certainly by Case, that was translated by Conway, rather than the English *Praise of Musicke*, which is of uncertain authorship. Robert Peilin's treatise is at Cardiff Central Library Hafod MS 3: its antecedents have been established by Mrs Irwen Cockman, who is preparing an edition.

60. The collection is at NLW Mostyn MS 204: see J. E. Caerwyn Williams, 'Thomas Wiliems, y geiria-durwr', *Studia Celtica*, XVI/XVII (1981–2), 280–316.

61. Morfydd E. Owen, 'The prose of the *cywydd* period' in A. O. H. Jarman and Gwilym Rees Hughes (eds.), *A Guide to Welsh Literature*, II (Swansea, 1979), 338–75, esp. p. 373.

62. Eiluned Rees, *Libri Walliae* (Aberystwyth, 1987), *passim*.

63. Glanmor Williams, *Dadeni, Diwygiad a Diwylliant Cymru* (Caerdydd, 1964), reprinted in idem, *Grym Tafodau Tân* (Llandysul, 1984), pp. 63–86.

64. Gwyn A. Williams, op.cit., pp.20–1.

CHAPTER III

THE RENAISSANCE IN SCOTLAND
John MacQueen

THE Scottish Renaissance may be approached in a variety of ways. Still the most usual is to assume that it did not happen—that Scottish circumstances provided nothing equivalent to the revival and extension of classical culture which so potently influenced western Europe in the fifteenth and sixteenth centuries. However economic of time and effort such a viewpoint may be, it fails to take into account a number of achievements which, in different media and at different levels, fit the pattern set on the Continent: these include the portraiture on the coinage of the kings from James III (1460–88) onwards; Gavin Douglas's translation of the *Aeneid*, completed in 1513; the *Scottorum Historiae* of Hector Boece (1527); John Bellenden's translation of Boece (1531) and the first five books of Livy (1533); the anonymous Mar Lodge translation of Boece; the Latin works of George Buchanan (1506–82); the architecture of Linlithgow and Falkland Palaces; the defence of the vernacular, theoretically presented in the treatise of James VI, published in 1584, and directly exemplified in the Asloan, Bannatyne and Maitland manuscript collections of 1515, 1568, and 1570 respectively.[1]

This record, respectable in itself, might easily be augmented, and a number of scholars have written on individual items or aspects. Still almost totally neglected, however, is the Gaelic and Celtic dimension. Little thought has been given to the question of whether there was any purpose common to the Gaelic manuscript anthology, *The Book of the Dean of Lismore*,[2] written between 1512 and 1526, and the more or less contemporary anthologies of poetry in Scots. Although it is usually noted that George Buchanan was a native Gaelic speaker, his Gaelic is disregarded as a factor in his work as Renaissance humanist. The relationship between the distinctive Renaissance view of early Scottish history and the older tradition of the Irish synthetic historians and genealogists[3] is not often discussed. Yet all three are aspects of the Renaissance, and all three show ways in which tradition comes together with innovation to produce something new, and sometimes of considerable importance even for the present generation.

Others are better qualified than I to talk about the problems of the Dean's *Book*. Here I shall do no more than make a few tentative suggestions. The *Book* is mainly the compilation of Sir James MacGregor (*c*.1480–1551), and his brother Duncan, poet and genealogist. Sir James was Dean of Argyll, a diocese whose cathedral was on the island of Lismore, whence the name by which he is usually known; but he was a pluralist, vicar also of Fortingall in the diocese of Dunkeld, which was his usual residence and the place where he compiled the *Book*. The brothers were helped and encouraged in the work of collection by their father Dugall, by members of the local gentry, such as Finlay Macnab of Bovain, who died in 1525, and possibly by such national figures as Archibald Campbell, second Earl of Argyll, who died at Flodden in 1513. The intention was to be representative, and much effort went into the collection:

> Ná biodh annsan domhan-sa,
>   do shagart ná do thuathach
> 'gá bhfuil ni 'na gcomhghar-san
>   nach cuirthear é san Duanair.

('Let there not be in this world one single priest nor layman who has aught by him that is not put in the Song-book.') This was the exhortation given by Finlay Macnab to Dugall, father of the Dean.[4]

The Dean's intention, presumably, was not to reserve the MS for a limited circle, but to make it available for anyone, priest or layman, who wished to read or hear the contents. The Gaelic title would seem to have been *Duanaire na Sracaire* (*Song-book of the Pillagers*),[5] the last word possibly a reference to Clan Gregor. The word *duanaire* probably implies that the book was intended more as a basis for public performance than for private reading. Of the other Scottish MS compilers, George Bannatyne at least probably hoped to publish, although his plans came into effect only some centuries later; it is possible that the Dean and his brother also had print in mind. It should be remembered that the earliest specimens of Scottish printing, the Chepman and Myllar tracts dated in or about 1508,[6] contain for the most part vernacular verse texts, comparable to the contents of the Dean's *Book*.

The anthology is not in any sense defeatist; in reading it, one does not feel that it is an attempt on the part of a few survivors to preserve whatever they can of a literature that will soon be gone. In terms both of period and style, the range is wide, embracing as it does classical bardic poetry in syllabic metres (Irish as well as Scottish), Ossianic lays, and the satirical, often bawdy, compositions of poets who wrote primarily for local audiences. Duncan himself contributed five pieces, the most notable of which is an arrogant panegyric of Clan Gregor.[7] One purpose of the compilers was certainly to encourage the composition as well as the preservation of Gaelic verse under the new circumstances of the sixteenth century. In terms of their respective languages, much the same might be said of the Bannatyne and Maitland collections and their English equivalents, the Egerton and Devonshire MSS and *Tottel's Miscellany* (1557), which gave pre-eminence to the classical and Italianate style of poetry introduced by Sir Thomas Wyatt (1503–42).

It is thus particularly significant that the Dean's *Book* was written, not in the traditional Gaelic orthography which the poetry really demanded, and with which the compilers must have been familiar, but in an adaptation of the foreign spelling conventions which had become established in Lowland Scots. This can only mean that the brothers saw their primary readership as being not so much among Gaels literate in the native tradition, as among those who had received a Lowland education in grammar schools and the fifteenth-century Scottish universities, St Andrews, Glasgow, or King's, Aberdeen.

James IV's Education Act of 1496[8] may have exerted some influence. Possibly they hoped to rouse the interest of at least some Lowlanders. These might well, for instance, have felt a kinship with the good knight, Sir Duncan Campbell of Glenorchy, who was a more ribald Gaelic equivalent of William Dunbar, and who was killed, as Dunbar may have been, at Flodden. Nine of his poems appear in the Dean's *Book*, although W. J. Watson, in his *Scottish Verse from the Book of the Dean of Lismore*, prudently or prudishly included only one, a satirical funeral eulogy on a certain Lachlann Galbraith. This is comparable to Dunbar's *Tesment of Maister Andro Kennedy*; Lachlann, however, was a beggar rather than a toper:[9]

Tá 'na díleacht giodh olc linn
    an phléid ar n-éag do Lachlann;
is béad sin ar lár gach lis,
    an phléidar easbhaidh eólais . . .

I gan mháthair gan athair,
    an phléid bhocht ar anamhain;
ar n-éag Mheic an Bhreatnaigh bhinn,
    a cnead-se créad nach caoinfinn? . . .

Cia iarras iasacht dá bhróg?
    cia iarras sgiatha phéacóg?
cia iarras iadhadh dá chrios?
    cia do-ní leamh gach aoinlios?

Cia iarras seanada pill?
    cia iarras leabhair léighinn?
cia iarras díota go moch?
    cia ara mbí íota anmoch? . . .

Deacra linn ná éag an fhir
    gan a oighre dá éis-sin,
d'eagal na pléide dhul d'éag,
    's nach feadar cia ní a coimhéad . . .

Má theasta Lachlann lá Luain,
    is subhach bhitheas gach duain;
dá éag is buidhe gach bioth,
    is ní cuibhe giodh éinchioth.

('After Lachlan's death, begging, though sore we deem it, is an orphan; it is a sad thing in the midst of every court, that begging knows not where to go . . . Begging, poor thing, remains without mother or father; now that sweet-voiced Galbraith is dead, surely I should lament its moan . . . Who asks for the loan of two shoes? Who asks for peacocks' wings? Who asks for a clasp for his belt? Who disgusts each court? Who asks for old hats of shag? Who asks for reading books? Who asks for dinner in the morning and is late athirst? . . . Harder than the man's death we deem it that he leaves no heir behind him, for fear that begging may die out, since we know not who will preserve it ... If Lachlann had died on Monday, glad is every song; for his death, every being is thankful; not meet is a single tear.')

It is, of course, entirely probable that Lachlann was very much alive when this lament was composed. In his account of George Buchanan's comparable *Pro Lena Apologia* (*Apology for a Bawd*), Professor McFarlane notes that 'the poem is very much in keeping with the humanist spirit of the times: it is a mock-encomium, inspired in its style no doubt by Erasmus and more especially Lucian (*De Parasito*) and belonging to the same tradition as Panurge's famous praise of debts'.[10] It is at least remarkable that Sir Duncan's poem, while remaining firmly in the Gaelic tradition, should also fit so well into a distinctively Renaissance kind.

The fate of the MacDonald Lords of the Isles, commemorated in a number of poems,[11] and the activities of these sometimes uncomfortably close neighbours, the MacGregors, were other matters of some interest in the Lowlands, where there is also evidence that Ossianic material was familiar. Indeed, it is easy to forget the extent to which in the sixteenth century Gaelic remained a living language south and east of the High-land line; in Ayrshire and Galloway certainly, very possibly in pockets over much of the country, and certainly in major burghs such as Edinburgh, Glasgow, Dundee, Stirling, Perth, and Aberdeen. Under such circumstances, although the language would continue to be spoken, knowledge of the traditional orthography would inevitably disappear, to find an inadequate replacement in the conventions of Middle Scots. It is unlikely that the Dean and his brother invented the system which they used; legal documents contain many earlier instances of Scotticizations of Gaelic names, both Lowland and Highland. It may thus be significant that the Dean was a qualified notary public. The *Book*, it should also be remembered, was written in Fortingall, Perthshire, towards the eastern fringes of the full *Gaeltacht*. The Dean and his brother adapted the tradition to their own circumstances, which were relatively new, even revolutionary, but not by any means without hope for the Gaelic language. It seems to me very probable that all the vernacular anthologies, Gaelic, Scots, or English, were compiled with intentions similar to those of Dante when he wrote *De Vulgari Eloquentia*, or Du Bellay when he wrote his *Défense et illustration de la langue française* (1549). Dante's is the earliest example of this humanist activity, Du Bellay is much later and closer in time to the Scottish and English examples.

George Buchanan is an example of a Gael who took full advantage of Lowland and Continental education, and whose achievement must be assessed in terms of Renais-sance literary ideals. Thus the *Odes* and *Epodes* of Horace provide the vehicle for his Latin paraphrase and interpretation of the Psalms,[12] and he clothes the biblical Jephthah in all the trappings of classical tragedy.[13] He is aware of contemporary vernacular literature in Scots; he describes his anti-Franciscan poem, the *Somnium*, written in 1535, as a translation of an old Scots epigram into Latin verse: '*epigramma vetus nostrate lingua scriptum in Latinos versus transtuli.*'[14] The *epigramma vetus* is easily identifiable as the first six stanzas of William Dunbar's 'How Dunbar wes desyrd to be ane Freir',[15] composed some thirty years earlier. Interestingly, Buchanan's literary terminology shows that he linked Dunbar with such classical figures as Martial and the poets of the Greek anthology. I have indicated elsewhere a similar sense in which Dunbar may be regarded as a Renaissance poet.[16]

Buchanan's knowledge and use of Gaelic are most clearly seen in his *Rerum Scoticarum Historia*,[17] first published in 1582, although traces are also visible in *De Iure Regni apud Scottos*,[18] published in 1579, but written more than ten years previously. These historical and political works are based primarily on the *Scottorum Historiae* which Hector Boece, first Principal of King's, Aberdeen, had published at Paris in 1527.[19] Boece claimed, in turn, to have derived the earlier part of his work from the shadowy Veremundus, who has been tentatively identified with Richard Vairement,[20] a culdee of St Andrews in the 1250s, possibly author of the *Historia* which formed the eighteenth item in the lost *registrum* of the Augustinian priory attached to St Andrews Cathedral.[21] We shall return to Boece presently; here it is sufficient to point out that he was a credulous, perhaps an inventive, Renaissance historian, who wished to give an account of early Scottish history which would rival Livy's account of early Rome, and which consequently would contain more detail than was to be found in the *Scotichronicon*,[22] written during the 1440s by Walter Bower, Abbot of Inchcolm, the island monastery in the Firth of Forth. As himself pre-eminently a Renaissance scholar, Buchanan intended 'to free our ancient history from the uncertainty of fable, and rescue it from unmerited oblivion';[23] as a consequence, it was particularly necessary for him to tackle Boece's presentation of early Scots history.

His scholarly ire was particularly roused by the rival and mutually contradictory origin legends current in Britain and Ireland, the second of which could claim Boece's authority; the story, on the one hand, of the Trojan Brutus, on the other, of the Greek Gathelus and his Egyptian wife, Scota, daughter of Pharaoh. Buchanan devotes more space to the former, and enjoys some excellent philological fun when demolishing the claims of the supposed oracle of Diana to Brutus.[24] Clearly, however, the story of Gathelus gives him more trouble, not least because he is closer to it, and intellectually and emotionally more involved. He regards the story of Brutus as essentially the work of the Monk of Monmouth,[25] for whom, as a Renaissance and Protestant humanist, he has nothing but contempt. As opposed to this, he recognizes that the Gaelic poetic tradition is the source for the Graeco-Egyptian origin and the early kings of the Scots, and he has temperamental inclinations to accept as much of this as he can, short of betraying his scholarship. Twice in the course of Book II he refers to Bards, on the second occasion at least in terms that are unequivocally favourable:

> The same description of Poets, too, was held in the highest honour by the Gauls and the Britons, and by both were styled Bards, the name and function of whom are still preserved, among all nations who use the ancient language of the Britons; and in such respect are they held in many places, that their persons are esteemed sacred, and their houses sanctuaries; and during the fiercest wars, carried on between the most exasperated enemies, accustomed to use their victories in the most cruel manner, they and their attendants may pass and repass through the midst of the enraged opponents without injury. When they visit the nobles, they are received honourably, and dismissed magnificently; and they compose songs, far from being rude or inelegant, which the Minstrels (*Rhapsodi*)

either recite, or sing, accompanied by the harp, to the chiefs and their vassals, who listen to them with the keenest avidity and delight. Many of these ancient institutions still exist, nor are they in Ireland changed almost in anything, except in the religious rites and ceremonies.[26]

This should be set against the earlier and more dismissive passage, in which he emphasizes the illiteracy and consequent reliance on fallible memory of the 'shennachies' (*seneciones*),

who were retained by the chiefs of ancient families, and, likewise, often by other men of property, who recited from memory the genealogies of their patrons. But these, too, were wholly destitute of learning, and, besides, what reliance could be placed on men whose expectations and subsistence depended on adulation; and, even had their veracity been undoubted, all they told must have been but of little service to the historian.[27]

Even so, Buchanan does not find it impossible to attain a degree of historical probability; a more certain way to knowledge of ancient times, he suggests, is provided by onomastics, particularly the names of 'things which are eternal, as the heavens, the earth, and the sea, mountains, countries and rivers'.[28] Nor is it easy, he adds,

to give new names to cities or nations, or change the old ones, because these were not given rashly, but imposed at first, with the consent and advice of the people, by founders to whom antiquity has frequently prescribed divine honours, and as far as possible, clothed with immortality; these names are, therefore, deservedly stable, nor do they give way, except in consequence of some mighty revolution; even after a whole language is changed, these pertinaciously remain ... and in emigrations, those who were either driven from their ancient habitations, or, of their own accord, sought new ones, when they had lost their country, yet retained the name, delighting in a sound so grateful to their ears, and reposing under the shade of a similar appellation, they alleviated their regrets for an absence from their native land, and seemed to be no longer in exile, or wandering at a distance from home ... A more certain argument of affinity may, therefore, be drawn from such words.[29]

This evidence he links to the bardic tradition by the words, 'I do not think the opinion of any nation, respecting their ancestors, is to be rejected, if it rest upon likely conjectures, and is confirmed by ancient tradition'.[30]

On such grounds Buchanan builds his theory of the early history of the British Isles. His case turns largely on his knowledge of Gaelic and his familiarity with Renaissance principles of textual criticism. By a comparison of some elements common in settlement names, he demonstrates that much of western Europe, including Britain and Ireland, had been populated by people of Gaulish or Celtic descent. His concentration on single repeated elements and on settlement names is a particularly good indication of his critical powers; the elements chosen by him—*briga, dunum, dur-*, and *magus*—retain importance in modern scholarship; Rivet and Smith, for instance, comment that '*briga* means "hill"', often particularized as "hill-fort"'. It seems to belong to an early period of Celtic expansion, through Gaul into Iberia, and to represent an older stratum than *dunum*.'[31] *Dunum*, they say, is 'one of the most important elements in Celto-Latin toponymy'.[32] *Duro* is '"fort, walled town"', apparently usually on low ground (and named in contrast to **duno*- "hill-fort") . . . The element was very widely used.'[33] '*Magus* is a common element in British and Gaulish toponymy. It seems to belong to the later stages of Celtic settlement, when permanent habitation was possible in settled conditions and in undefended lowland sites . . . it represents a later stratum than *briga* and *dunum*, and it is significant that it is unknown in Iberia . . . The sense of original British **magos* was "field, plain", then "market".'[34] The scholarly instincts of Buchanan, in other words, did not fail to lead him to the most significant elements in the material open to him. It is now possible to say that he makes errors of detail, but the method adumbrated by him remains standard to the present day.

In the introduction to their book, Rivet and Smith comment on the astonishing, but characteristically Renaissance, grasp of historical fact, topography and cartography, and especially of linguistic matters, shown in the *Britannia* (1586) of William Camden.[35] None would question this, but it is a pity that they do not even mention Buchanan, whose remarkable investigations had appeared four years earlier and may have been written long before.

Buchanan was thus able to establish the likelihood that, at a remote period, settlers had taken their language from Gaul, not only to Britain and Ireland, but also to Germany, Spain, and other parts of Europe, and even to the Near East. On the early authority of Tacitus he accepts that the west coast of Britain had been occupied by immigrants of Spanish origin.[36] Such immigrants, he claimed, could have come only by way of Ireland, a conclusion which allows him to accept the tradition that Scotland had thrice been invaded by Irish Scots, who, in turn, were the descendants of the traditional Iber of Spain. The ancestors of Iber would have come to Spain, however, from Gaul rather than Egypt. Gathelus and Scota are rejected, but Buchanan was able to retain the forty traditional Scottish kings from Fergus I to Fergus II. The Picts he regarded as Celtic immigrants from the more easterly expansion of the Gauls into the Low Countries, Germany, and Scandinavia. The Britons were direct immigrants from Gaul. In terms of his theory, the linguistic kinship of Welsh with Irish and Scottish Gaelic was thus easily explicable. The mockery subsequently aimed at him, chiefly because he continued to accept the first forty kings, has obscured the most substantial part of his achievement as humanist and historian.

The first forty kings are, in detail, themselves a Renaissance contribution to Scottish history, although their origins belong to a tradition as old and distinctively Celtic as the Irish *Lebor Gabala* and the related genealogies. The kings are to be found in Books I to VII of Boece's *Scottorum Historiae*, occupying the period between Fergus I and Fergus II. The basic source for this and much of the later material was, it seems fair to say, the *Scotichronicon*,[37] compiled by Walter Bower, and including the earlier work of John of Fordun. Fergus I and II both appear there, the first establishing the monarchy in Scotland in 330 BC, while the second, a genuinely historical figure, is unhistorically crowned in AD 403, a century too early.[38] Boece puts the coronation in 422,[39] and so reduces the error to some eighty years. In *Scotichronicon* III.2, forty-five kings are said to have reigned during the period separating the namesakes, but names and details are given for only a few. Royal genealogies, however, parallel to extant early Irish genealogies, are found in V.60, in X.2, and in the Poppleton MS;[40] the names included in these have a more or less direct correspondence to those found in Boece, in whose work the two Ferguses are separated by a sequence of thirty-nine kings.

Boece, however, claims a different source, the notorious Veremund, now tentatively identified, as has been indicated, with the thirteenth-century Richard Vairement of St Andrews.[41] In VII.3, Boece tells the remarkable story of the alliance between the youthful Fergus II and Alaric the Goth in the sack of Rome in 410. (This date, incidentally, helps to explain why Boece, in comparison with Bower, delayed Fergus's coronation for almost twenty years; if he was a young freebooter in 410, he could scarcely have been crowned king seven years earlier. The fact that all the chroniclers of the fourteenth to sixteenth centuries give Fergus an unjustifiably early date is to make him precede the *adventus Saxonum* in 447/9 by a substantial margin.)

> It is haldin that, by vthir sacrate iowellis and mony precios arraymentis, Fergus, be cavill, gat ane schryne, full of bukis, to his parte, keping the samyn with incredibill diligence, incertane be quhat inspiracioun, and, aftir mony lauborios iournayis with the Gothis, brocht the samyn bukis vntwichit throw Germany to the Ilis, plaissing thame finalie in Colmkill, and, with diligent cure, gart big fare housis quhare perpetualie mycht be obseruit the honorabill memorie of antecessouris, as he belevit, togiddir with the vailyeand actis of his nacioun; and assignit tharto apprisit writaris in volwmys and bukis to collect thai historyis. Sum allegis, (as we have oft tymes herd), that Eneas Silueus, of singular erudicion, (quhilk eftirwart Pape was namyt Pius), directit fra Pape Eugenius the Ferde to King Iames the First in Scotland, was inflammyt be fame of thir bukis to pas to Colmkill and explore gif he mycht fynd ony volumys of the Decadis made be Titus Liuis, be weris and crudelite of inhumane pepill tynt, (for weris may do mare skaith than proces of tyme to distroye antiquiteis). Be suddane slauchter of the king, he desistit fra his purpois becaus without grete convoyance, (sen all the cuntre was on flocht), he mycht nocht pas throw the kinrik. Ferder, to vnderstand quhat bukis ar in Colmkill that are sa mekill namyt and of quhat mater thai trete, we tuke purpois to knaw, and at the religios men of the place, be ane messagere, thryis to thame send; finalie, be speciall diligence of Schir Iohnne Campbell, Knicht,[42] thesaurare to oure Souerane Lord, we optenit that five ald bukis, writtin with Romane lettres, be ane faithfull servand suld be send to ws to Aberdene. Quharefore in the yere of God j^m v^c v yeris we resauit of ald bukis certane rewyne quaris, of quham sum excedit nocht the palme of ane hand in breid, writtin in hard, inflexibill parchement, mervellus craftelie, as be the plesand forme of the lettir may be considerit. Bot thai war sa consumyt and worne be proces of yeris or erare be necligence of keparis, that with difficulte euery tent worde mycht be red. Nochttheles quhidder thir bukis, (of quhilkis thir ar the fragmentis and remanis), war writtin in Albion in Romane hand, of the Romane actis, or brocht to Albion fre vthir partis, we knaw nocht clerelie. Bot be iugement of euery man that on thame lukit, thai erare resembill the eloquence of Salust than the ditement of Liuius. Be the samyn berare to mee was brocht the historie of Veremwnd, archidene of Sanctandros, writtin of oure actis, quhilk, (how beit the

style be rude), comprehendis haboundantlie all thingis done fra begynnyng of the Scottis name to the tyme of King Malcolme Canmore. And becaus we fynd this Veremwnd without dissymulacion rehers oure actis, we haue in this oure werk, (as clerelie may be sene), writtin eftir him and the reuerend bischop, William Elphinstoun of Abirdene,[43] quhilk diligentlie in historijs of oure nacion follois Veremwnd, sen maist clerelie as apperis thai schaw the verite thereof.

The possible identity of Veremund is less important than the context in which Boece places him. The search for copies of classical MSS, especially those of 'lost' authors, was a characteristic occupation of certain Italian humanists in the fifteenth century. Boece uses the name of one, not usually regarded as a collector, Aeneas Sylvius, later Pope Pius II (1458–64), whose visit to Scotland in 1435[44] he sees as preluding the quest for MSS of the lost decades of Livy instituted by Pope Nicholas V (1447–55), a quest which in the case of Aeneas was directed towards the monastic library of Iona. Boece prides himself on following in the footsteps of these Renaissance pioneers; there is a palpable note of scholarly disappointment at the condition of the recovered MSS, and a touch of pedantic pleasure in the fact that, although it was possible to read only every tenth word, yet the style was recognizably more like Sallust than Livy. There is no necessary suggestion that the MS of Veremund came from the same place, but mere association gives it something of the glamour and authority of the classical discovery. One notes in passing that Boece sees Iona as a centre of religion and scholarship well before the time of Columba.

Long ago, Thomas Innes noted how Boece used Livy and other classical models to give flavour to the new anecdotes which he brought into his *History*. 'In effect', he says, '*Boece* was one of the first in these northern parts who, by assiduous reading, and imitation of the ancient *Latin* authors, began to restore the *Latin* tongue to its purity, instead of that barbarous style which, from the fall of the *Roman* empire, had overrun all till later ages'.[45] And in the course of his Section VI, 'Fourth Proof: Boece's History stuffed with Fables', he demonstrates the extent to which classical reading penetrated the very structure of the *History*. Innes refers to 'the fabulous stories in his history, copied from the *Roman* or other histories, such as the *Scottish* women married to the *Picts* interceding between their husbands and parents, like the *Sabine* in *Titus Livius*; King *Mainus*, like *Numa*, establishing the sacred rites; the table of the laws made by *Fergus* I, *Dornadilla*, and others. And all politic deliberations he puts in his *Scottish* grandees' mouths, from the same *Titus Livius* and others'.[46] The identification of Scotland with Rome under the kings and the early republic, subsequently made by John Bellenden in his translation of Livy (1533), was preceded and in a sense authorized by the tenor of events in Boece's *History*, which the Bellenden (1531) and Mar Lodge translations had made more widely available and influential.

There is a genuine as well as a spurious aspect to Boece's antiquarianism. He attempts to follow Livy's example by making a pretext of investigating the origins of ancient monuments and calendar customs, which fascinate and often puzzle him. Innes, in the passage quoted, refers to King Mainus establishing the sacred rites, but does it (II.4) scant justice. It is intended not only to draw a parallel between Mainus and

Numa Pompilius, but also to explain the existence and function of the megalithic stone circles found in Scotland, together with the religious origins of certain superstitions which survived into his own day and later. The passage runs as follows:

> And the king considering weill that without iustice, godlynes and divyne reuerence, the prosperite of men couth nocht incres, and that all kinrikis and erdlie curis ar vnder power of goddis, and gif the samyn be nocht propiciant, all attemptatis of men and counsale ar vane, and to realmes was na thing sa sikkir as the beneuolence of goddis; to the effect he mycht draw the pepill to godlynes to the ancient haly rytis, he ekit certane solempnit ceremonis of new to be done in reuerence to immortale goddis, that certane grete stanys in diuers partis of euery regioun, quhare was maist convenient, suld be invirone and in cirkill, and the gretest stane suld be erectit towart the south, to be vsit for ane altare. Apoun the samyn to immortall goddis suld hoistis be offerit and sacrifice be brynt. For verificacioun hereof yit in thir oure dayis ar sene thir roundis of stanys and ar callit the ald templis of goddis be the vulgarre pepill. Treulie quha sall behald thir roundis, sall mervell be quhat craft or corporall strenth stanys of so grete wecht mycht in ane hepe be placit. In this age the offerandis of the pepill, assignit to thare immortale goddis, conforme to the ritis of gentilite, was ane porcioun of corne or vther store quhilk was remanant of the sustentacion of thare preistis, of quham grete skantnes was for the tyme. Alsua he institute that euery moneth suld be had in reuerencee the cours and change of the mone, (othirwayis callit Dyane), quham the pepill anornit as protectrix of waist woddis and huntaris. Quharethrow how sone thai saw the mone eftir the coniunctioun with the son, be certane devot wourdis, with reuerence thai maid it salutacioun. Lang tyme amang the posterite was the prophane consuetude obseruit. Syne be the king to divine service war depute preistis, to quhais power war the iuris and all thingis concernyng divinite subiectit. And to thame of all offerandis made to the goddis was assignit ane liffing. By thir war diuers vtheris solempnit rytis and ceremonis be him institute, of the Gentile fassoun, like as in the ald bukis of Egipcianis war providit.

Diana is singled out because Boece has already (I.4) made the point that the economy of the early Scots, as opposed to that of the more urban Picts, was based on hunting. The Egyptians are mentioned because it was from Egypt that the Scots began their migration to Spain, Ireland, and Scotland. The priests are the Druids mentioned by Tacitus. The two philosophers who visited the later King Iosyne (II.10) 'affermyt that Scottis vndirstude nocht the verite of divyne ceremonis becaus, (following the ritis of Egipcianis), thai comparit ymagery of brutall beistis to the goddis immortall'; as a consequence, people temporarily gave up sacrificing to Isis and Apis. Diana, as mentioned in the passage, is perhaps to be identified with Isis. When Boece says that a ceremony 'was lang vsit', he probably implies that it was still followed in his own day.

The beginnings of modern archaeology are to be found in the collections made by Renaissance Italian humanists and their patrons of objects and works of art found on ancient sites, whether by chance or by deliberate excavation. Often these finds were a ready-made excuse for speculation. The *History* contains several notices of discoveries made in Scotland and the deductions made by Boece in consequence. In III.20 he gives as his opinion that the cremation of the body of the Roman general Plancius (by whom he seems to intend Aulus Plautius) in Britain in AD 43–7 affected Scottish and Pictish funeral customs:

> Hereof in thir our dayis mony signis yit are sene, for in the yere of our Redempcioun j^m v^c xxj, in the towne of Fyndour[47] in the Mernis, v mylis distant fra Abirdene, ane ald sepulture was fundin quharein was twa veschell, like laym piggis ['clay vessels'], of strange fassoun, replete with powder and as, and apoun thame baith war Romane lettrez gravin. How sone thai war producit to the aire, incontinent thai war dissoluit in powdir. Siklyke in ane towne in Mar callit Kenbatten,[48] ten mylis fra Aberdene, about the samyn tyme be pleuchmen twa sepulturis war fundin, of square assillare and hewin stane. In thame war foure vrnis half full of powder, wrocht of siclike craft, of the samyn quantite and siclike lettrez as of the tothir twa is remembrit. Diuers vtheris siclike antiquiteis to testify this consuetude has oftymes bene sene in diuers partis of Albion, like as antecessouris has left in remembrance.

In V.10 he traces the origin of the Scots coinage to the reign of Donald, first Christian king of Scotland, whose conversion was in AD 203: 'this nobill prince was the first Scottis king quhilk strake the cunye and prent of the goldin penny, siluer or vthir metall; gravin apoun the tane side, the image of the crucifix, with the figure of his awne visage on the tothir, signifying to the posterite the gude remembrance of him quhilk first of vthir Scottis princis resauit the Catholic faith.' The description fits the oldest Scots coinage, that of David I (1124–53), save that no gold coins were produced until much later; it is interesting that in the same passage Boece distinguishes clearly between the medieval Scots coinage, and the earlier Roman *as* found in hoards up and down the country:

> like as in the yere of God j^m v^c xix yeris. Nocht fer fra the mouth of Levyn in Fyffe was fundin be the hirdis grete nowmer of pennyis hid in ane veschell of bras: parte gold parte siluer. Of sum the prent was ane doubill port, representing the doubill yett in Rome, quhilk in tyme of weris wes patent and closit in tyme of pece. In vtheris was gravin the figure of Mars, Venus, Marcurius, or sum vthir idole. Euery cunye had on the ta side the figure of the emprioure, with scripture abone the samyn, or lettres gravin in this sorte, S P Q R, quhilk is to say, Senaturis and Pepill of Rome. Alsua in the yere of God j^m iiij^c lx, in Murray be the hirdis apoun the sey coist amang ald wallis of ane failyete castell, ane veschell of marbill was fundin quhareapoun ane ganer ['gander'] fechtand contrare twa edderis was gravin and replete of siclike money. And als oure authoure, Maister Hectoure affermys, he herd be trew famous men that the veschell was to the behalderis als mervellus as the cunye, ane clere argument that sum tyme amang oure forebearis the Romane cunye was in vse.

Fairly clearly, Boece at Aberdeen expected to pronounce on any discovery made in the neighbourhood, or even at some distance. Although he cannot be trusted in every detail, he shows some knowledge of Roman coinage. Few coins, however, were inscribed S.P.Q.R.; S.C. was by far the more common device. But it is certainly characteristic of the humanist to be interested in such matters.

The supposed ancestral link between Scots and Egyptians allows Boece to see the Pictish sculptured stones as hieroglyphic memorials of the ancient kings in days which preceded the use of the Roman alphabet. In I.7, for instance, he states that Fergus I 'causit this haly affirmacioun of the pepill, vncoactit, be thare aith roborate, be with letteris gravin in tabillis of marbill, be figuris of certane beistis, as to the pepill was custume for the tyme to write secretis, or sic vthir thingis as thai wald haue kepit mony yeris, and committit the cure hereof to kirkmen to sett the samyn in sanctuare and thare diligentlie to be kepit'. King Rewtha (II.8) erected monuments to keep alive the memory of valiant men, 'quhareapon war gravin the figuris of certane fowlis, serpentis or dragons, bred amang watteris, (sic figuris in place of lettres in secrate writingis vsit that age), that thareby suld the passingeris be informyt quhat men thai war and quhat actis thai did in thare tyme'. It is possible that he similarly regarded the 'tabillis' on which the laws of Dornadilla and Fergus were preserved (II.5) as sculptured stones with hieroglyphic inscriptions.

He also insists that connections with Egypt long remained open; thus, in II.9 he tells how King Ptolemy of Egypt despatched 'his oratouris' (again a Renaissance touch!) to investigate the geography of the world. King Rewtha extended every hospitality to them, and they recognized the kinship between their own religion and way of life and that of the Scots. The eventual but long-delayed result of their visit was the Cosmography and Tables of Ptolemy, only completed some four hundred years later in the time of the Roman emperor Hadrian. It is not so much that Boece has mistaken Ptolemy the geographer for one of the earlier royal Ptolemies as that he is determined to adduce his work as evidence for the antiquities of the Scots in the pre-Christian era. Thus the castle of Berigone in Lochaber, where Fergus I established his seat, has its origin in Ptolemy's *Rerigonion*, probably situated in the vicinity of Loch *Ryan* in the modern Wigtownshire.[49]

One purpose of all this may be to explain how information was preserved about the early stages of a non-literate society, a point much stressed by the later Buchanan, but Boece does not say so, nor, as we have seen, is he always consistent with himself. An interest in Egyptian antiquities, incidentally, is characteristic of many humanists in Italy and elsewhere. Names which come to mind include Ficino, Pico della Mirandola, and Bruno.

The most remarkable instance in Boece of antiquarian flair is his realization (IV.15) that Inchtuthil on the Tay had earlier been a place of some importance. He makes it a town destroyed and abandoned by the Picts as part of their scorched-earth policy against the Romans:

> Be sa nere approcheing of Romanis, affrayit war Pichtis, and brynt Tulyne, thare nobill and populos ciete, in aventure gif it war randerit to Romanis, it mycht be to thame refuge and to thare self richt skaithfull: disturssing it first baith of inhabitantis and gudis. Sum tyme this ciete was of large boundis apoun the bank of Tay, lyke as yit schawis the signys thareof. In thir oure dayis Inch Tuthil namyt.

Only in this century was it realized that Inchtuthil had been intended for a legionary fortress, evacuated by the Romans before its completion. The site is by no means an obvious one, and it is a tribute to Boece that he grasped something of its fate and original significance.

As a humanist, Boece was well aware that literary, philosophic, and scientific achievement was part of the historical record. Thus in II.5 and 6 he discusses the development of medicine as an art in Scotland, perhaps with the Beaton family tradition in mind;[50] in V.3 he places the period between the deaths of Dardanus and Mogall in a highly intellectual context:

> Betuix deceiss of Dardan king and this tyme mony famous men war liffand, in the quhilk tyme succedit to the crowne thre kingis liniale of the blude of Gald. For to Gald succedit his son Lugthak, and to Lugthak this Mogall, dochteris son to Gald. Thir famous cunnyng men war Quintiliane, oratoure and rhetoure maist preclare; Serapio, philosophoure apprisit abone all vtheris; Philo the Iow, philosophoure and oratoure, of quham falslie is vsurpit that owther Plato fenyeis him Philo, or ellis Philo schawis him Plato; Plinius the secund, quhilk wrate the Naturale Historyis no les trewlie than cunninglie, contenyng xxxvij volymys; Cornelius Tacitus, historiographoure, quham in this mater we haue oftymes with diligence followit; Cecilius Plenius the Secund, oratour; Suetonius Tranquillus; Ptholome the astrolog, famous in his tyme, quhilk as sum apprisit authoris writis ordorit with new addiciouns the discripcioun of the erde, compilit be Ptolome callit Phaladelph, king of Egipt; Lucius Apuleius, Affrican oratoure; Aulus Gelius; Plutharchus Chironeus, philosophoure. Sum writes Egesippus, historiographoure of the actis of Christianis and Iowis, liffit this tyme. By thir war mony famous poetis, as Iuuenale, Sillius Italiane, Marciale, and diuerss vtheris cunnyng men, excelling in doctryne and vertewe.

This is by no means a jejune list of 'curriculum' *auctores*, and notably gives prominence to Greek as well as Roman writers. Such passages are recurrent throughout the *History*.

The reference to the second-century Church historian, Hegesippus, is appropriately cautious as to date; it is interesting that copies of his five books of 'Memoirs against the Gnostics', now lost, appear to have been extant in some libraries as late as the sixteenth to seventeenth centuries.[51] A MS, since lost, may have been the source for the list of early martyrs which immediately follows the passage quoted.

One of Boece's ambitions (hinted at in the quotation) was to reconcile the sequence of events in first-century Britain, as indicated in *Scotichronicon* and the regnal lists, with the detailed account given by the recently rediscovered Tacitus.[52] The crudity of his method is not, perhaps, totally surprising when allowance is made for the early date of his work. He mistakes *Mona*, 'Anglesey', for *Mona*, 'the Isle of Man', and as a consequence sets up there an influential college of Druids. He identifies Conaire Mór, the Irish 'peace-king', who figures in the earlier stages of the Scots royal genealogy, in Irish historical tradition, and in the extended Irish tale, *The Destruction of Dá Derga's Hostel*, with Caratacus (*Caratake*), the redoubtable British opponent of the Emperor Claudius, who was eventually brought captive to Rome. Caratacus's seat of power he places in the Ayrshire Carrick, influenced, no doubt, by the distant similarity of name. Voada, sister of Caratacus, is made the neglected wife of Arvirag, King of the Britons; she and her younger daughter Voadicia form, as it were, a gemination of Boudicca or Boadicea, warrior-queen of the Iceni, now adorned with the benefit of Scots ancestry. Calgacus or Galgacus, defeated by Agricola at Mons Graupius, becomes Galdus, nephew of Caratacus, defeated in battle 'beside the fute of Granyebene the mont' (IV.16). The Scots royal line is thus brought into direct and violent contact with the Romans, and Boece demonstrates to his own satisfaction that the classical record enhances rather than contradicts the native tradition.

The inadequacy of his method merits no comment. Like many other humanist ventures of his time, Boece's work is rather an extended rhetorical exercise on a historical theme, depending for its effect on stylistic flair and the extensive citation of authorities which he had not necessarily studied in any depth, and who may, on occasion, even be fictitious. He represents a side of the Renaissance quite different from the critically inductive method of Buchanan and the patient drudgery of the Dean of Lismore.

The Scottish Gaelic contribution to the Renaissance is epitomized in the work of these three; the Dean, Buchanan, and Boece. Only one, the Dean, was concerned with Gaelic as a living implement of speech and thought, and his attempt to promote the language by introducing an orthography more consonant with Lowland habits was accepted neither by Highlanders nor by Lowlanders. His book became a neglected curiosity, to reappear only with the Ossianic controversy in the eighteenth century. Buchanan was more successful, partly because he wrote in Latin, partly because he treated Celtic more as a dead than a living group of languages, which therefore was susceptible to the same scholarly treatment as classical Latin and Greek. His failure here, like his failure in *De Sphaera* to conquer the problems presented by the new astronomy, resulted from his innate conservatism, his tendency to interfere only minimally with received authority if it had any surface appearance of truth; thus he discarded Gathelus and Scota, but could not bring himself to reconsider the nature of the tradition involving the first forty kings. Boece wholly lacked the critical mind; his innovations are the result of his enthusiasm for Scottish as for classical history, and his unscrupulous determination to meld the one with the other. Unscrupulous, I think, is the only word; even in the infancy of Tacitean studies, no one, it seems to me, can seriously have thought that Caratacus or Boadicea belonged to North rather than South Britain. He was saved, at least for a time, by his virtues as a Latin stylist, which even his bitterest foe, Thomas Innes, was forced to recognize. But the paucity of editions and translations in the seventeenth century and afterwards is the best possible indication that in humanism as elsewhere crime does not pay.

Notes

1. For the coinage, see I. H. Stewart, *The Scottish Coinage* (2nd edn., London, 1967). The Asloan, Bannatyne and Maitland collections have been published by the Scottish Text Society in 1923–5 (2 vols.), 1928–34 (4 vols.), 1919–27 (Maitland Folio, 2 vols.) and 1920 (Maitland Quarto) respectively. James VI's 'Ane Schort Treatise, Conteining some Revilis and cautelis to be obseruit and eschewit in Scottis *Poesie*' is to be found in J. Craigie (ed.), *The Poems of James VI of Scotland* (STS, 1955), pp.65–83. There is no modern edition of Boece's *Historiae*; there are two early translations, one by John Bellenden in R.W. Chambers, E. C. Batho and H. W. Husbands (eds.), *The Chronicles of Scotland, Compiled by Hector Boece, Translated into Scots by John Bellenden, 1531* (2 vols., STS, 1938–41), and the anonymous

Mar Lodge translation in George Watson (ed.), *The Mar Lodge Translation of the History of Scotland by Hector Boece*. Vol. I (STS, 1946). Vol. II has not as yet appeared. This is the text quoted and referred to as *Mar Lodge*. The latest edition of Buchanan's *Opera Omnia* is that of Ruddiman (2 vols., Edinburgh, 1715). James Aikman translated the *Historia* (2 vols., Glasgow, 1827). *George Buchanan Tragedies*, ed. P. Sharratt and P. G. Walsh, appeared in 1983. The last three will be referred to as 'Ruddiman', 'Aikman' and 'Sharratt/Walsh' respectively. See also W. Gatherer, *The Tyrannous Reign of Mary Stewart; George Buchanan's Account* (Edinburgh, 1958).

2. There is at present no complete edition. See W. J. Watson (ed.), *Scottish Verse from the Book of the Dean of Lismore* (Scottish Gaelic Texts Society, 1937) and Neil Ross (ed.), *Heroic Poetry from the Book of the Dean of Lismore* (SGTS, 1939). The first will be referred to as 'Watson'.

3. See especially 'The Irish synthetic historians' and 'The ancient genealogies', chapters III and IV in Eoin Mac Neill, *Celtic Ireland* (Dublin, 1921; revised edn. with new introduction and notes, Dublin, 1981).

4. Watson, pp. 4–5.

5. Watson, pp. 2–3.

6. See W. Beattie (ed.), *The Chepman and Myllar Prints* (Edinburgh Bibliographical Society, 1950).

7. Watson, pp. 212–17.

8. R. Nicholson, *Scotland. The Later Middle Ages* (Edinburgh, 1974), pp. 590–1.

9. Watson, pp. 14–21.

10. I. D. McFarlane, *Buchanan* (London, 1981), p. 113.

11. Watson, pp. 82–99 (poems X, XI, XII).

12. See my 'Aspects of humanism in sixteenth and seventeenth-century literature', forthcoming in *Humanism in Renaissance Scotland*, to be published by Edinburgh University Press.

13. Sharratt/Walsh, pp. 5–19; McFarlane, *Buchanan*, pp. 194–6.

14. McFarlane, *Buchanan* p. 52.

15. James Kinsley (ed.), *The Poems of William Dunbar* (Oxford, 1979), pp. 165–6.

16. J. and W. MacQueen (eds.), *A Choice of Scottish Verse 1470–1570* (London, 1972), pp. 11–17.

17. This occupies the greater part of the first volume of Ruddiman, in which individual works are separately paginated.

18. The text succeeds that of the *Historia* in Ruddiman's first volume. Translation by Duncan H. MacNeill, *The Art and Science of Government among the Scots* (Glasgow, 1964).

19. Above, footnote 1.

20. See W. F. Skene (ed.), *Johannis de Fordun Chronica Gentis Scotorum* (2 vols., Edinburgh, 1871-2), I, xxxviii, footnote 1; G. W. S. Barrow, *The Kingdom of the Scots* (London, 1973), pp. 218–20.

21. M. O. Anderson, *Kings and Kingship in Early Scotland* (Edinburgh and London, 1980), pp. 54–8.

22. Walter Goodall (ed.), *Joannis de Fordun Scotichronicon cum Supplementis et continuatione Walteri Boweri Insulae Sancti Columbae Abbatis* (2 vols., Edinburgh, 1759). This will be referred to as 'Goodall'. The first volume of a new edition in eight volumes has recently appeared, D. E. R. Watt (ed.), *Scotichronicon by Walter Bower*, Vol. 8, Books XV and XVI (Aberdeen, 1987).

23. Aikman, I, 1 (*res gestas majorum nostrorum a fabularum vanitate liberare, & ab oblivionis injuria vindicare*, Ruddiman, bk. I, p. 1A).

24. Aikman, I, 72-4 (Ruddiman, bk. II, p. 25B-E).

25. Geoffrey of Monmouth (*c.* 1100-54), author of *Historia Regum Britanniae*.

26. Aikman, I, 94-7 (Ruddiman, bk. II, p. 32B-C).

27. Aikman, I, 66 (Ruddiman, bk. II, p. 22E).

28. Aikman, I, 104 (Ruddiman, bk. II, p. 35B).

29. Aikman, I, 104-5 (Ruddiman, bk. II, p. 35B-C)

30. Aikman, I, 84 (Ruddiman, bk. II, p. 29C).

31. A. L. F. Rivet and C. Smith (eds.), *The Place-names of Roman Britain* (London, 1979), p. 278, *s.v.* 'Briga'. Hereafter 'Rivet/Smith'.

32. Rivet/Smith, p. 274, *s.v.* 'Branodunum'.

33. Rivet/Smith, p. 346, *s.v.* 'Durobrivae'.

34. Rivet/Smith, p. 287, *s.v.* 'Caesaromagus'.
35. Rivet/Smith, p. 5.
36. Aikman, I, 84 (Ruddiman, bk. II, p. 29C).
37. See above, footnote 22.
38. Goodall, I, 104 (bk. III, c. 1).
39. *Mar Lodge*, p. 384.
40. Anderson, *Kings and Kingship*, pp. 256–8.
41. See above, footnote 20.
42. John Campbell of Lundy, Lord High Treasurer, 1515–26, appointed one of the first Lords of Session in 1532. He died in 1563. For his career see *DNB*.
43. See the fine study by Dr L. J. Macfarlane, *William Elphinstone and the Kingdom of Scotland* (Aberdeen, 1985).
44. Nicholson, *Later Middle Ages*, p. 297; F. A. Cragg (trs.), L. C. Gabel (ed.), *Memoirs of a Renaissance Pope. The Commentaries of Pius II* (New York, 1962), pp. 32–4.
45. Thomas Innes, *A Critical Essay on the Ancient Inhabitants of the Northern Parts of Britain, or Scotland* (2 vols., London, 1729), p. 216.
46. Innes, *Critical Essay*, p. 250.
47. Findon or Finnan, fishing village in Banchory-Devenick parish, Kincardineshire.
48. Perhaps Kinbattoch, farm in Towie parish, Aberdeenshire.
49. See W. J. Watson, *History of the Celtic Place-names of Scotland* (Edinburgh and London, 1926), pp. 34–5; Rivet/Smith, p. 447, *s.vv.* 'Rerigonium', 'Rerigonius Sinus'.
50. J. Bannerman, *The Beatons* (Edinburgh, 1986), pp. 82, 91–3, 96.
51. *Oxford Dictionary of the Christian Church*, *s.v.* 'Hegesippus'.
52. See E. H. Warmington, 'Tacitus' minor works. The Hersfeld Manuscript', *Tacitus* I (Loeb Classical Library, 1970), ix–xiv. The unique MS of Tacitus's *Opera Minora* was brought from Hersfeld to Rome in 1455 (L. D. Reynolds and N. G. Wilson, *Scribes and Scholars* (2nd edn., Oxford, 1974), p. 123). Enoch of Ascoli, perhaps helped or encouraged by Aeneas Sylvius, was responsible. The *editio princeps* of Tacitus appeared in 1472, but did not contain the *Agricola*, first printed by F. Puteolanus at Milan, *c.* 1475–80, 2nd edn., Venice, 1497.

CHAPTER IV

GAELIC IRELAND AND THE RENAISSANCE

by Mícheál Mac Craith

For into the Ireland of 1500 were already entering the forces of the new, the Renaissance Europe. In the brief spell of 1450 to 1530, when Ireland was ruled by a native aristocracy, she progressed in art and literature, in the amenities and luxuries of life.[1]

The Irish preoccupation with antiquity may have been a fault in the Gaelic aristocracy, making them incapable of that compromise with the modern world of the Tudors which alone could have saved them. But in literature, as in all else, the native race of 1500 was taking the impress of a new, a Renaissance Europe.[2]

THESE two statements by Edmund Curtis are taken from his *History of Medieval Ireland*, a work that was not really concerned with the Renaissance as such. Curtis, unfortunately, never found the opportunity to develop his views on this subject, but judging from the above remarks, he believed that Gaelic Ireland, though definitely influenced by the Renaissance, was unable to come to terms with the new Tudor state.

The question was stated much more forcefully by David Mathew in his work, *The Celtic Peoples and Renaissance Europe*. Mathew's thesis can be best summed up in the following quotation from Christopher Dawson's introduction to his book:

Strictly speaking, Celtic culture outside Wales had no Middle Ages. It passed directly and without transition from the heroic atmosphere of the pre-classical Celtic warrior culture to the hard practical world of Renaissance statecraft—the world of Machiavelli and Granvelle and the Cecils . . . But there was no room for . . . compromises between the ancient Celtic society and the new Renaissance state. No sociological contact was possible between the Tudor courtier, with his mind attuned to all the subtleties of political intrigue and to all the refinements of Renaissance culture, and the Celtic chieftain, who still reckoned his wealth in cattle and his renown by the praise of his hereditary bards, while between the new national middle class, who provided the personnel of Tudor administration, and the long-haired swordsman and retainers the gulf was wider still.[3]

While Mathew, the historian, stressed the unbridgeable gulf between Gaelic society and the world of the Renaissance, Daniel Corkery, the littérateur, felt that the Gaelic world's virtual independence of the Renaissance was something to be celebrated. The great strength of Gaelic literature lay in the fact that it was firmly rooted in the Middle Ages and but barely contaminated by the new world view. This was one of the firmest tenets of Corkery's literary credo and was the guiding principle behind his famous work, *The Hidden Ireland*:

Whatever of the Renaissance came to Ireland met a culture so ancient, widely-based and

well-articulated, that it was received only on sufferance: it had to veil its crest and conform
to a new order; it did not become acclimatised, as had happened elsewhere; it was rather
assimilated, assimilated so thoroughly that its features can no longer be discerned, though
its effects are felt when the subsequent culture of the Gael is compared with the pre-Renais-
sance.[4]

And again:

In Aodhagán Ó Rathaille (1670–1729) one finds many touches that remind one of Villon—in
whom there is so little of the Renaissance spirit, so much of the Mediaeval; and if these
touches are found more frequently in Ó Rathaille than in any other poet of that century,
it is so simply because he was himself the best of those poets.[5]

For Corkery, the words 'Mediaeval' and 'Renaissance' are far from being value-free;
in fact, they are almost synonymous with good and bad in aesthetic terms and, as far
as he was concerned, the Renaissance implied artificiality, rootlessness, and a weaken-
ing of national art. When Pádraig de Brún lamented the fact that Gaelic culture
was barely touched by the Renaissance and was thus lacking in *Humanismus*,[6] Corkery
immediately went on the offensive:

Sé rud a deirim-se ná gurbé an buadh is mó atá againn féin ná dúthchas cruinn a bheith
againn sa Ghaedhilg, go bhfuilimíd, toisg é sin a bheith amhlaidh chun tosaigh ar gach
tír gur chuir cló an Renaissance, isteach uirthi; go bhfuilimíd, sa méid sin, níos comhgaraí
ná iad don tSean-Ghréig.[7]

(I affirm that our greatest asset is that we have a definite national culture in Gaelic, that
we are consequently superior to every country that the Renaissance interfered with, that
we are, in fact, much closer than they to ancient Greece.)

Corkery and Mathew, then, hold mutually exclusive views on the role of the Renaissance in Gaelic Ireland. For the former, a vibrant native culture assimilated the Renaissance so completely as to render it virtually unrecognizable, while the latter saw an
ancient, stagnant civilization inevitably being crushed by the new, dynamic, modern
world of Renaissance values. Curtis is less extreme than Mathew, but the end-result
of the meeting of the two cultures was the same. Over half a century has elapsed
since these scholars first formulated their ideas. In the mean time, much work has
been accomplished in the fields of Irish history and Gaelic literature, and a fresh examination of the whole topic of the Renaissance in Ireland is long overdue. The following
remarks are intended as a preliminary effort to remedy this defect.

In a recent study of the biography of Manus O'Donnell, lord of Donegal 1537–63,
Brendan Bradshaw suggests that his career conforms to different facets of the typical
Renaissance prince as portrayed in three key works of the period, Castiglione's *Book
of the Courtier*, Erasmus's *Education of a Christian Prince* and Machiavelli's *The Prince*.[8]
'Machiavelli's hard-headed political entrepreneur, Erasmus's scholarly Christian ruler,
Castiglione's prince-aesthete, all of these in varying degrees was Manus O'Donnell.'[9]
Given O'Donnell's well-documented taste for sartorial splendour, his renown as a
love-poet and composer of humorous epigrams, and the fame of the castle he built

at Lifford, he reflects the predilections of an aesthete—though not necessarily of a specifically Renaissance outlook.

In his political career Manus displayed a resourcefulness that would have obtained full marks from Machiavelli, especially in the light of his conduct *vis-à-vis* the Geraldine League. The level of diplomacy involved, both local and international, was relatively sophisticated. The origin of diplomacy of this scale and complexity has been traced back to Renaissance Italy, and the presence in Manus's entourage of a 'right sober and well learned young man' who had been brought up in France, may be of particular relevance in this regard.[10]

But it is when we consider his life of Colm Cille, a distinctively Renaissance product, as a work both of history and of literature, that O'Donnell's humanism really comes to the fore.[11] We must remember that Manus was neither a cleric nor a professional scholar, but a gifted layman. Yet he considered himself the author of this work and not just the originator of the project. As a work of history the *Betha Colaim Chille* shows its Renaissance stamp in the way its methodology displays the antiquarian enthusiasm for examining all the available sources so characteristic of this period:

'Et do thimsaig 7 do tinoil an cuid do bi spreite ar fedh shenlebor Erenn di.'[12]

(And he collected and assembled the part of it that was scattered throughout the ancient books of Ireland.)

Manus was very concerned to avoid the learned literary language of the *filí* and consequently employed simple language so as to be understood by all:

do furail an cuid do bi a Laidin don bethaid-si do cur a n-Gaidhilc, 7 do furail an chuid do bi go cruaid a n-Gaidilc di do cor a m-buga, innus go m-beith si solus sothuicsena do cach uile.[13]

(He ordered the Latin part of this life to be translated into Irish, and ordered the part that was in difficult Irish to be turned into easy Irish, so that all would find it clear and easy to understand.)

Here in typical Renaissance fashion the author is vindicating the claims of the vernacular as a literary language and it is worth noting that he seems to equate Latin with the literary dialect of the learned classes—both being scholarly languages for the élite but not for the general public.

It is noteworthy that the three features which characterize *Betha Colaim Chille* as a product of the Renaissance—its lay authorship, its antiquarian character, its stress on the vernacular—are precisely the very features that Manus himself emphasizes in the preface to his work. It appears that Manus was quite aware that he was being different, and this self-conscious attempt to break with traditional moulds is also typical of the Renaissance. The *Betha*, however, is not merely a humanistic work of literature. It was also inspired by pastoral concern and a desire for reform and renewal:

'a tarba dona poiplechaib leghfes 7 éstfes é, 7 a tarba anma 7 cuirp dom fén, 7 a n-esonoir 7 a ndigbail imarcach don diabhul.'[14]

(For the benefit of those who will read and listen to it, for my own benefit, both of soul and body, and to the devil's dishonour and great harm.)

It preaches a message of religious renewal in unmistakably humanist tones, and this concern for the renewal of religion is an aspect of the role of a Christian prince much stressed by Erasmus. A number of the episodes recounted in the *Betha* provide evidence for the humanist emphasis on the interiority of religion. For example, one particular story tells of a priest who languished in Purgatory for quite a long time until finally released through the intercession of Colm Cille. The particular sin was that the priest had spent too much time ornamenting his church, concerning himself with the external rather than the internal aspects of religion.[15]

Given that *Betha Colaim Chille* was such an innovatory work, one wonders if its author ever considered publishing it, thus providing the first printed book in Gaelic. The first book to be printed in Ireland was the *Book of Common Prayer* in 1551, nineteen years after the completion of the life of Colm Cille, and the first printed work in Gaelic came off the press in Dublin in 1571. In this regard Manus's reference in the preface to all those 'who will read and hear it' is also interesting. Such musings, however, are mere speculation and are of no real benefit to the task in hand. Suffice it to say that the evidence of history shows Manus O'Donnell to be very much in the Renaissance mould. 'For Manus was not just a political entrepreneur in the Machiavellian manner. He was also scholar, humanist, aesthete: something of the *uomo universale* that Castiglione and Erasmus in their varying ways idealized.'[16]

Lest one think that O'Donnell was an exception rather than the rule it is interesting to note that R. D. Edwards observed that the career of Shane O'Neill, a younger contemporary of O'Donnell, displays features characteristic of the Renaissance despot: the single-minded pursuit of power and the ruthless use of force to attain one's end; a high notion of territorial sovereignty; an independent attitude to ancient traditions and a willingness to adapt and innovate in the light of new conditions.[17] His efforts to secure support from Philip II and Charles IX to maintain his independence of Elizabeth led him to express himself very much as a man of the new age.[18] The conflict between the Crown and Ireland's dynastic lords has traditionally been presented as a conflict between a progressive modern civilization and a stagnant archaic one, the latter being inevitably destroyed, a victim not of colonial aggression, but of the march of progress. The pattern of national monarchy is not the only design for the consolidated Renaissance state. Such was the model developed in England, France, and Spain. In Italy and Germany another model evolved, that of the regional principality. James Lydon has recently shown some striking parallels between the dynastic lordships of Ireland and the regional principalities of Italy.[19] Far from being a conflict between a modern and an archaic civilization, it would now seem more correct to represent the struggle in sixteenth-century Ireland as one between two new political systems, between a centralizing monarchy and consolidating regional lordships. While Gaelic Ireland may have been characterized by certain aspects that appeared archaic to the Elizabethans, it was, none the less, a society coming to terms with the Renaissance.[20]

It is one thing to single out the career of one or two individuals as evidence of Renaissance influence; it is quite another matter to prove that this influence permeated society as a whole. And even if the developing political systems of Gaelic Ireland exhibited Renaissance characteristics, it does not follow that the literature of that society was similarly marked. When one turns to consider the corpus of Gaelic literature in the sixteenth century or of any other century, one immediately thinks of bardic poetry. The student of bardic poetry is apt to be disappointed, however, if he hopes to find evidence of a new world view readily present in the lines of eulogistic verse. Tadhg Dall Ó hUiginn (1550–91) is usually taken as the paradigm of the professional poet, and the impression conveyed by his work is aptly summarized by Eleanor Knott:

> He shows in most of his poems a calm acceptation of contemporary strife as though it were the natural order. Poetry flourished in it, and for him, like most Bardic poets, the profession was the thing ... We may take him as a typical figure, thoroughly adapted in mind and custom to the existing order, utterly unaware of the imminent dawn of a new world.[21]

It is usually overlooked that Ms Knott also penned the following lines in the same introduction:

> Towards the end of the sixteenth century we find Eóghan Rua Mac an Bhaird attempting to express a more intellectual outlook in verses which reflect a faint gleam of the humanizing influence, which was beginning—too late—to rise over the schools. Another poet of the same period whose work shows signs of intellectual advance is Eochaidh Ó hEódhusa, one of the first prominent writers to use freer forms. He was a master of the strict metres, and his originality is not completely obscured even by the conventional eulogy which formed the main ware of the bardic poetry.[22]

Even in the lines above, however, it is clear that Eleanor Knott regarded Mac an Bhaird and Ó hEódhusa as exceptions and departures from the norm. But given the role of the bardic poet in Gaelic society and the function of eulogizing verse in legitimizing and sustaining the power of the local prince—and this entailed assimilating change into the traditional world view—one may properly question the value of seeking evidence of a new outlook in the professional work of the poet. Did not the ritualistic, semi-religious, and even liturgical nature of official encomiastic verse, by very definition, preclude openness to change? Evidence of an altered outlook, if it is to be found at all, is much more likely to be present in the personal poetry of the period than in the conventional, professional verse of the *fili* as preserved in the family *duanairí*. Such of this unofficial verse as has come down to us, has been preserved by chance rather than by design, but we are fortunate that quite a substantial body of light poems, all connected with love, has been assembled by T. F. O'Rahilly in his famous anthology, *Dánta Grádha*.[23] This collection of 106 poems is usually taken as displaying many characteristics of *amour courtois*, and, given that the earliest recorded practitioner, Gearóid Iarla (d. 1398), is the first known author of Norman stock to compose in Gaelic, it has more or less been taken for granted that these poems are ultimately of French origin. Most of the evidence supporting this hypothesis is based on thematic similarities. This approach is notoriously fallible—in love poetry even more than in other fields—given the universality of the topic. Thematic similarities between two literatures are in no way conclusive evidence of direct influence, and the whole question of the provenance of the *Dánta Grádha* needs to be looked at anew.

In his introduction to the earlier and smaller edition of O'Rahilly's anthology, Robin Flower took two poems by Thomas Wyatt from *Tottel's Miscellany* (1557), translated them into Gaelic using Rannaíocht Mhór metre, and then more or less asked the reader if he could decide for himself which was the original:

> Illustrating in this way one may be accused of manufacturing the evidence. But let anyone read the poems in this volume carefully and compare them with Tottel's collection, and he will not be able to escape the conclusion that this is the same matter, the same witty and well-favoured verse speaking with different tongues. These are collaterals descended from a common ancestor, but by a different way. Surrey and Wyatt got their inspiration out of Italy; it is a probable conjecture that our Irishmen derived the matter of their art from French sources, though in the later stages an English influence is certainly to be reckoned with.[24]

Even allowing for the fact that Flower's argument is based mainly on thematic similarities, there is a certain *non sequitur* in his displaying similarities between Wyatt and Gaelic verse and then going on to postulate French provenance. It is as if Flower could not accept the value of his own evidence, manufactured or otherwise. Even more to the point is the fact that the translations from Wyatt were omitted from the 1926 edition. It is hard to resist the impression that Flower wanted to find French influence and French influence alone. English provenance, if allowed at all, is late and vague. One feels tempted to ask whether or not the growing nationalism of Conradh na Gaeilge, heightened after the 1916 rising and maintained into the heady days of the new Free State, had had an undue effect on the aesthetic views of Gaelic literary critics—even if the one in question was an Englishman?[25]

Flower's views on the provenance of these poems has prevailed until recently. One notable exception to the dominant view was Frank O'Connor. The *Dánta Grádha* are treated in his book, *The Backward Look*, under the significant title, *The Renaissance in Ireland*, and are, in fact, the only material covered in this chapter:[26]

> They have not been studied with any great critical attention, and vague suggestions of influence from Provençal strike me as far-fetched. There is no hint of French influence in the poems of the Earl of Desmond, and if French influence had not made itself felt by the end of the fourteenth century, when it was strongest in Wales, it is most unlikely that it had made itself felt at all ... So far as I can date the poems, they are Tudor, Jacobean, and one, at least, Restoration. In searching for origins I doubt if we need to go much further than English. By the sixteenth century it was beginning to play the same part as Latin had in the literature of the early Middle Ages; it was expanding the whole conception of literature and bringing the practice of it back where it belonged, to the amateurs, though the amateurs were now noblemen rather than churchmen ... and the professional poets joined in the game and made the rules a bit harder.[27]

O'Connor had a disconcerting habit of often hitting the nail on the head, though his conclusion tended to be based more on an instinctive hunch than on irrefutable evidence. Nevertheless, it is remarkable that the keywords in his argument are Renaissance and English. It is well worth the trouble to try to give substance to his hypothesis.

Cearbhall Ó Dálaigh's 'A Mhacalla Dheas'[28] is an echo poem, a genre that was itself a product of the Renaissance world. More importantly, it can be shown that Ó Dálaigh had used a poem from William Percy's *Sonnets to Coelia*, published in 1594.[29] Ó Dálaigh's poem is not a translation. In fact, his use of the echo technique is much more sophisticated than Percy's and he seems to have been highly conscious of the possibilities inherent in this device. It is only when he fails to exploit the full range of possibilities that Percy's influence comes through. Ó Dálaigh's poem is a prime example of Renaissance style being mediated into the Gaelic world through an English source. An even more interesting example is Riocard do Búrc's 'Fir na Fódla ar ndul d'éag?'[30] Seán Ó Tuama once said to me that in content and tone this poem is remarkably similar to John Donne's 'The Indifferent', but one can go much further and affirm that it is actually a translation of the poem that inspired Donne—Ovid's *Amores*, Book II, Number IV: 'Non ego mendosus ausim defendere mores'. The Gaelic literati have always been inclined to adopt a rather cavalier approach to the matter of translation. Their policy could best be described as select, adapt and revamp. This refusal to conform to the strictures demanded by faithful adherence to the original text often obscures the fact that we are actually dealing with a translation, and do Búrc's poem is a case in point. We know next to nothing about the translator. The question arises whether he was working from the original Latin or from an existing translation in another language. In either case, his interest in the classics is an indication of Renaissance values, but it is worth noting that the only translation of the *Amores* into another language before 1600 is that by Christopher Marlowe published in 1597, four years after his death. This work came under ecclesiastical censure, and copies of it were burned publicly in London in 1599. John Harington was the next English writer to undertake a translation of the *Amores*. His *Epigrams* were published posthumously in 1615 and 1618, the latter edition containing his translation of *Amores* II, IV. Harington visited Ireland on two occasions, met Hugh O'Neill on his second visit, and presented him with a copy of his famous translation of Ariosto's *Orlando Furioso*. Though the evidence is not conclusive, I feel that do Búrc used Harington's translation, since the Englishman's reasonably free approach to the original and his adaptation of the Latin metre into four-line verses could readily accommodate itself to Gaelic prosody. Even if we cannot advance precise evidence for do Búrc's source, his interest in translating from the classics is ample demonstration of a mind influenced by Renaissance values.[31]

The problems entailed in interpreting the *Dánta Grádha* are accentuated by the fact that most of them, 75 out of 106, are anonymous, and that of the 21 authors whose names we know, in a number of cases that is all we know about them. The anonymous poem, 'Fuar dó féin an croidhe tinn',[32] is worthy of comment for two reasons. In the first place it contains a very interesting acrostic. The first letters of lines a) and c) in each verse are the same, while the last letters of lines b) and d) are the same.

This pattern is maintained right through the poem, giving a man's name twice on the left, Fearflatha, and a lady's name twice on the right, Caitiríona. The poem has survived in only one manuscript, and a misspelling indicates that the copyist was quite unaware of the acrostic's existence, despite, or maybe because of, the enigmatic clue in the penultimate verse. The use of the acrostic device is telling in that it indicates a poem made for private reading rather than public recitation. Despite the flimsy nature of the evidence, this would appear to suggest a concept of poetry totally foreign to the Gaelic poetic tradition and may derive from the importance laid by the Renaissance on education and on the dignity of the human person.[33]

As regards content, the poem at first sight seems to be a Gaelic version of the medieval debate between the heart and the eyes as to which bore the greater responsibility in causing love. But a closer analysis of the poem shows that such is not the case:

> ... we are apt to mistake for mere conceits statements which in the sixteenth century were accepted as physiologically and psychologically true. The sonnets are full of references to murdering mistresses, whose eyes slay and whose eye-beams penetrate like arrows to the very heart; and it is necessary to recognize that these had a basis in what was taken to be fact. When Prospero says of Ferdinand and Miranda, 'At first thou art infected', he is speaking literally. The curious lore behind such statements can be found in Ficino's *Commentary on the Symposium*, much of which is reproduced in Castiglione's *Courtier*. It was believed that the soul controlled all bodily functions by means of the animal spirits which bridged the gap between material and spiritual and were concocted out of the purest of the blood. These spirits, collecting in the heart, were thought to flow out through the eyes in the form of a fine stream of particles which, hitting the eye of the other person, went down into the heart, and set up a disturbance among the animal spirits already there. This disturbance is love, an actual physical infection passing from one person to another.[34]

The process is described in Book III of Castiglione's *Book of the Courtier*, which was first published in April 1528. Sir Thomas Hoby translated it into English in 1561, and this work was influential in providing a proper code of conduct for young English noblemen. I would suggest that 'Fuar dó féin an croidhe tinn' provides us with a Renaissance dissertation on the origins of love, mediated into the Gaelic tradition via Sir Thomas Hoby's translation of the *Book of the Courtier*.[35]

Another interesting love poem is 'Féach orm, a inghean Eóghain'.[36] Unfortunately, all we know about the author is his surname, Ó Géaráin. Critics of Gaelic classical poetry have drawn attention to one glaring weakness in the poetic craft, a seeming inability to consider the totality of the poem as a cohesive artistic unit. Gaelic poets tended to concentrate their talent and art on the individual verse, while neglecting the poem as a whole. A certain formlessness pervades much of their work, leaving the modern reader with the impression that their poems would not be unduly affected by either the addition or omission of a number of verses. 'Féach orm, a inghean Eóghain' is a striking exception to this pattern. It contains thirty verses, neatly divided into two halves of fifteen verses each. Not only is the argument in the first half paralleled in the second, but so also is the sequence of thought in the deployment of the argument. This parallelism is achieved through the skilful use of rhetorical, linguistic, and stylistic devices, those in the second half of the poem containing a negative and contrary version of those used in the first. The poet is dying because of the refusal of his lover, a female Narcissus, to gaze affectionately at him. If she persists in this stance she will have no one to look at except herself, thus running the risk of incurring the same fate as her mythological precursor. To avoid such dire consequences she should abandon her coldness and turn in love towards her admirer.

Such a bald outline in no way conveys an adequate impression of the complexities of the argument and the means used to achieve it. Given the almost geometric pattern of the poem, one cannot help feeling that it was composed for private reading rather than public recitation, another example of a radical new concept of the role and function of poetry in Gaelic society. To appreciate the poem completely, one would almost need to have the two halves laid out in parallel columns. The precision and minuteness of the various degrees in the development of the argument, the sustained use of extended metaphor in depicting the lady as a female Narcissus, and the false logic entailed in the deployment of this metaphor, are all features that remind one of the Metaphysicals. Given its complex sense of unity and structure, its metaphysical mode, its composition for private reading instead of public recitation, 'Féach orm, a inghean Eóghain' bears all the hallmarks of Renaissance influence and is the work of a poet with a very clear concept of form as an aesthetic value.[37]

Seathrún Céitinn's 'A Bhean Lán de Stuaim'[38] is rightly acclaimed as the most famous of the *Dánta Grádha*. Early critics of this poem had difficulty in reconciling the sentiments expressed with the celibate, priestly vocation of the author, thereby confusing biographical detail with literary criticism. This confusion has led to the mistranslation of the word '*stuaim*' as 'wile', an interpretation that is without any linguistic justification, but an error that has persisted in nearly all the major translations of this poem. The equation of '*stuaim*' with 'wile' seems to derive from an a priori condemnation of the lady addressed in the poem as the sort of woman who would dare to seduce a priest. If, however, one abandons the interpretation of this poem as a priest warding off temptations to his celibacy, it becomes much less a poem of renunciation than one of regret. It can easily be fitted into the framework of 'The Aged Lover Renounceth Love'—a pattern apparently initiated by Lord Vaugh in *Tottel's Miscellany*, and imitated by such famous poets as Ralegh, Campion, Sidney, Shakespeare, and Donne. Céitinn's reluctant renunciation is based on the waning of his physical powers and one could almost construe John Wilmot's 'Song of a Young Lady to her Ancient Lover' as a reassuring reply to Céitinn's fears.[39]

It is ironic, indeed, that Corkery should have singled out this particular poem as an example of all that is best in the Gaelic literary tradition; best for Corkery, of course, since it implies no contamination by the Renaissance:

> Indeed, it seems to me that nearly all modern poets in English are trying, never, however, with the same triumphant success, to write lyrics in the manner of Keating's 'A Bhean

Lán de Stuaim'. When they succeed in doing so the Old Man of the Renaissance will have been flung from the shoulders of our civilisation.[40]

With all due respect to Corkery, it is precisely as an old man of the Renaissance that the persona of this poem stakes his claim to fame.

It has been pointed out that the *Dánta Grádha*, in common with most formal, courtly type of verse, contain quite an amount of trite, conventional posturing with no specific lady in view. In fact, only one of the poems mentions a real lady of flesh and blood, Eisibéal Stevin, and even that is not a serious poem.[41] Female personal names occur from time to time, but even if these actually refer to a specific lady, the emphasis is less on her personal qualities than on the cleverness of the poet in composing an anagram or an acrostic. Many of the anagrams could be detached from the poems to which they belong without in any way detracting from their artistic unity. A striking example of this is contained in Piaras Feiritéar's 'Léig díot t'airm, a mhacaoimh mná'.[42] The final verse of this poem contains an acrostic that reveals the name of the lady as Ursula Hussey,[43] but as this verse occurs after the *dúnadh* (closure), it probably did not belong to the original poem. One can thus easily imagine a poet hawking the same poem from court to court and, relying on his linguistic cleverness and metrical acrobatics, tacking on an extra verse for whatever lady managed to catch his fancy.

The reference to the lady is thus easily detachable from the poem as a whole. Of greater significance is the fact that Feiritéar also composed a poem for a historical lady, one Meg Russel; a poem not in fact contained in O'Rahilly's anthology. In this poem, the sentiments of the author and the factual reference to the lady are fused in such a way that any attempt to separate them would prove impossible without totally destroying the poem. Instead of the impersonal approach to love normally favoured by the *Dánta Grádha*, this piece is based on a real human relationship and, as such, bears witness to the dignity of the human person so much emphasized by the Renaissance.[44] It is also worth noting that Feritéar's contemporary, Pádraigín Haicéad, also composed love poems to a real, historical woman, Máire Tóibín. Indeed, one of Haicéad's poems contains unmistakable proof of English influence, in that he attempts to translate a pun from English into Gaelic that fails to come off because of the innate differences between the two languages.[45] In trying to Gaelicize the pun 'Marigold/golden Marie', he can do no better than 'nóinín/óigín óirnidhe . . . Máire Tóibín'. Haicéad's poem also contains a version of a story told by Ovid in *Metamorphoses IV* about a nymph called Clytie, who turned into a marigold after being spurned by the sun, except that in Haicéad's version he inverts Ovid's order, leaving Máire Tóibín as the sun and the poet as the marigold. A poem by Charles Best, 'A Sonnet of the Sun', was published in the famous anthology, *A Poetical Rhapsody*, in 1602.[46] Best's poem contains both an inverted version of Ovid's story and a pun on 'marigold' and 'goulden Marie'. Given the highly unusual combination of these two elements and the fact that Haicéad was working from English, it seems quite reasonable to suggest that 'Dála an nóinín' was inspired by Charles Best's sonnet. The earliest deliberate inversion of Ovid's story known to me is Thomas Watson's 'The Marigold so likes the lovely Sunne', published in 1582.[47] What is most relevant to the discussion here is that Watson gives a heading to the poem actually citing his sources and then proceeds to invert. Watson's citation of his sources is not in any way due to a sense of honesty and humility but a deliberate demonstration of the Renaissance principle of *imitatio*. He has strong claims to be recognized as a good poet precisely because he is imitating Ovid, universally acknowledged as one of the great models.[48]

Feiritéar and Haicéad are also unique in that they both wrote poems to their male friends; poems that are not merely verses composed for friends but are deliberate, self-conscious celebrations of friendship. It could even be said that these works reflect a greater depth of sincere, heartfelt emotion than most of the *Dánta Grádha*. In a poem marking the recuperation of a doctor friend from illness, Feiritéar wrote a line of deep significance: 'Is fearr duine ná daoine' ('An individual is better than a group').[49] Irish bardic verse was based on the *pobal* and praised the individual chieftain, not in his own right as an individual, but as representative of his *pobal* or community. Here, we find these values being set aside by Feiritéar as he lauds the individual in his own right over and against the community. The most recent editors of this poem have rightly drawn attention to the author's stressing of the dignity of the human person just like any contemporary of Shakespeare.[50] Another interesting feature of the poem lies in the manner in which Feiritéar praises his friend's knowledge of medicine:

> Fairsing t'eolas, a ghairt mhic,
> ó Arctic go hAntairctic.[51]

This is a most unusual phrase in Gaelic; and it does not seem to be mere coincidence that the words 'from th'Artique to th'Antartique famosed' are to be found in the long poem, 'Sir Francis Drake', published by Charles Fitzgeffrey in 1596, constituting the earliest example of this usage noted by the *Oxford English Dictionary*.[52] The *Commentarius Rinnucinianus* refers to Feiritéar's skill as a poet in both Gaelic and English: 'singularem linguae Anglicae atque Ibernicae facundiam, . . . et poetam utraque lingua praesertim Ibernica insignem.' ('singularly eloquent in the English and Irish language, and an eminent poet, especially in the Irish language.')[53] Though none of his English verse has survived, the evidence of his Gaelic poetry suggests that it was through the English world of letters that Feiritéar made his contact with the ideas of the Renaissance. A bilingual member of the Old English aristocracy, he was ideally suited to introduce modern concepts of man into Gaelic society.

The same holds true for Pádraigín Haicéad. He was also praised for his linguistic skills in the *Commentarius Rinnucinianus*: 'Author Ibernicam, Anglicam, Latinam et (credo) alias linguas eleganter callebat.'[54] Haicéad had the added advantage of spending a long period on the Continent, in France and the Spanish Netherlands. Much of his poetry bristles with difficulty, but when we read his poems of friendship there can be no doubt that we are in the same world as that of Thomas Carew and Robert Herrick.

One very important conclusion may be deduced from this all-too-brief survey of the surviving love poetry in classical Gaelic. These poems are important not for any special insight they convey concerning the Gaelic approach to matters of the heart, but for the evidence they produce of the growing influence of English culture on Gaelic literature in the period 1550–1650, and of the all-important role played by the Old English as a bridge between the two cultures. Most of these poems are anonymous, but the authors of the rest, men like do Búrc, Feiritéar, Haicéad, and Céitinn, were all of Old English stock, and it is mainly on the strength of their poetry that we have deduced evidence for Renaissance influence mediated through English channels. When one considers that what has come down to us of the love poetry has survived by mere chance, and is, therefore, probably but a fraction of the literary output composed in this genre, it is really remarkable that the evidence for Renaissance values and English influence is so clear. Many other members of Old English stock must have played a similar role to that played by the poets already noted. A brief look at the well-documented career of another member of this class could prove instructive.

When Richard Nugent, Baron Devlin, died in 1559, his two sons, Christopher and William, were placed under the protection of Sir Thomas Radcliffe, Earl of Sussex, and sent to England. Christopher went to Cambridge and, while there, wrote a Gaelic primer for Queen Elizabeth. William went to Oxford but returned to Ireland in 1573 without taking a degree. Richard Stanihurst refers to him as follows:

> William Nugent a proper gentleman and of a singular good wit, he wrote in the English toong diverse sonnets.[55]

These poems have not survived but his cousin, Richard, published a book of verse in 1604:

> Richard Nugent's Cynthia containing direful sonnets, Madrigalls and passionate intercourses describing his repudiate affections expressed in love's own language.[56]

William wrote a number of poems in Gaelic. His family were patrons to the bardic family of Ó Cobhthaigh; and MS G993 of the National Library of Ireland is William's *duanaire* or poem-book, containing poems by the Ó Cobhthaighs.[57] William was friendly with Cú Chonnacht Óg Mag Uidhir and composed two poems on his death in Genoa in 1608.[58] He was also friendly with Giolla Brighde Ó hEoghusa. Giolla Brighde composed a poem of solace for William's wife on the death of their eldest son,[59] and he composed a poem for William, when he took the name of Bonabhentura Ó hEoghusa, having joined the Franciscans at Louvain in 1607.[60] William himself was one of the first to compose poems of exile in Gaelic in the seventeenth century.[61] Exile was a topic which became quite prominent at this period, and, while naturally stimulated by physical absence from the poet's native land, may also owe something to the recovery of the classical concept of the *patria*, a theme much associated with the Renaissance.[62]

William Nugent was a very cosmopolitan member of the Old English aristocracy. He lived in England for fourteen years and also spent time in Scotland, Rome, Paris, and Madrid.[63] He composed verse in both Gaelic and English and was familiar with literati of both languages. Given his upbringing, training, and experience, he was ideally positioned to mediate new ideas via English channels into the Gaelic world.

The network of relationships involving Old English and Old Irish families at this period was very complex. William was a cousin of Henry, twelfth Earl of Kildare, who died in 1597 fighting against Hugh O'Neill. Gerald Nugent, a nephew of William, married Mary O'Donnell, a sister of Rory O'Donnell, first Earl of Tyrconnell, while his niece, Elizabeth, married Gerald Fitzgerald, fourteenth Earl of Kildare. Bridget Fitzgerald, daughter of Henry, married Rory O'Donnell in 1603 at the age of thirteen years. Sometime between 1603 and 1607 Cú Chonnacht Óg Mág Uidhir commissioned Eochaidh Ó hEoghusa to compose a love-poem for Bridget, but conveying the impression that it was Cú Chonnacht's own work, 'Ní mé bhur n-aithne, a aos gráidh'.[64] Bridget, whose knowledge of Irish would have been somewhat limited, was at least sufficiently *au fait* not to be taken in by the game. She in her turn hired a poet to compose a witty reply in which it was clearly manifested that she was in no way taken in by Cú Chonnacht's protestations of love or his claims to authorship, and that she had a pretty strong suspicion that Eochaidh Ó hEoghusa was the poet. All the protagonists in this harmless piece of fun were acquaintances of William Nugent. It is also remarkable that a professional poet such as Eochaidh Ó hEoghusa was prepared to join in the sport.[65]

We have previously remarked that the work of the professional poets, by its very nature, shows very little openness to new ideas. Eochaidh himself was very much in the traditional mould. He considered his relationship to his patron Aodh Mág Uidhir as a marriage, an idea that was part of the poetic order's pre-Christian inheritance, but an idea to which Eochaidh himself was extremely attached. 'He seems to have lived his whole life according to it, and he constitutes its most extreme expression.'[66]

Yet despite his traditional conservatism Eochaidh, possibly because of his contacts, was quite open to new influences. In 1593 he composed a poem for Aodh Mág Uidhir counselling caution in his thirst for war.[67] To bolster his advice Eochaidh makes use of the exemplary tale concerning the fate of the thirty philosophers and the rain of madness. This exemplum was quite well known throughout Europe, but Eochaidh's version corresponds so closely, not only in its general thrust but also in minute details, to a version recounted in the correspondence of St Thomas More that one feels bound to suggest an English intermediary for his rendering.[68] Eochaidh was prepared to doff his professional official *gravitas* on occasion and compose love-poems for his patron in a certain *jeu d'esprit*. The love-poem discussed above has been described by Frank O'Connor as 'all great fun, and very beautiful, but is as queer as a coot, and anyhow has more Donne than Wyatt in it'.[69] Two other love-poems are attributed to Ó hEoghusa, 'A bhean chridhe chompánta' and 'A fhir chroide charaimse'.[70] Given Eochaidh's involvement in the sally between Cú Chonnacht Óg Mág Uidhir and Bridget Fitzgerald, it is tempting to see these two latter poems as a further comment by the poet on the whole affair. Eochaidh, having taken up one role in the original skirmish, now shows himself at being equally adept in playing the roles of both male and female protagonists. It has not been previously pointed out that these two poems with their stress on verbal and mental jugglery correspond to the answer-poem, one of the most characteristic poetic productions in England in the first forty years of the seventeenth century. The answer-poem flourished in the social conditions of the Jacobean and the Caroline courts when the recently invented Italian art of solo recitative was being introduced to England. One is tempted to ask if Eochaidh was aware of the possibilities not only for witty repartee afforded by this new genre, but also for marrying the traditional *reacaireacht* technique of official bardic verse with the new technique involved in solo recitative.[71]

Eochaidh Ó hEoghusa may have been a traditional poet, every bit as traditional as Tadhg Dall Ó hUiginn, yet his work contains many indications of his being open to outside influences and to contemporary English literature. This may be partly due to personal disposition, but it must have been facilitated in no small way by his involvement in circles frequented by both Old English and Old Irish. This involvement may have been one of the reasons why he found it so easy to welcome the accession of James I to the throne in 1603,[72] a welcome that received its due reward when Eochaidh received a grant of land during the Ulster Plantation.[73] Eleanor Knott once aptly remarked that but for the Gaelic political collapse at this time Ó hEoghusa would have been the beginning of a new tradition rather than the end of the old.[74]

One of the striking features of the *Dánta Grádha* is that some of them seem to have been composed for private reading rather than for public recitation—thus challenging the whole concept of the role and function of poetry in Gaelic society. It is to be presumed that the authors of these poems envisaged this reading would be done from manuscripts. One wonders if they were in any way aware of the possibilities offered by the invention of printing. Printing was both one of the great discoveries of the Renaissance and one of its indispensable allies.[75] It is only with the Reformation that printing came to Ireland and it is to this turbulent period that we now turn our attention.

That the Church in Ireland was in need of reform at the beginning of the sixteenth century is not in question, irregularities being more prevalent in Gaelic Ireland than in the Pale. That the failure of the Reformation was inevitable is a view no longer held by serious historians.[76] There is evidence of sincere support for reform, inspired by humanistic principles among certain quarters in the Pale. It was not until about 1580 that it could safely be said that the Protestant Reformation had failed, but even then it was not clear to what extent Gaelic Ireland would become Catholic. To a certain extent, the upholders of the old faith were equally impervious to both the Protestant Reformation and the Catholic Counter-Reformation alike. The very English-ness of the Reformation militated against its success in Gaelic Ireland. Spiritual renewal went hand in hand with anglicization and military conquest, the guiding principles of the former being relegated by what were seen to be the exigencies of the latter. The use and cultivation of the Gaelic tongue were seen as disloyalty to the Crown, and the existing laws in Gaelic were reinforced in 1537 by an 'Act for the English order, habite and language'. When the Irish Parliament passed the Act of Supremacy in 1560, it added a rider permitting church functionaries who did not know English to conduct services in Latin:

that in every church or place, where the common minister or priest hath not the vse or knowledge of the English tongue, it shall be lawfull for the same minister or priest to say and vse the mattens, evensong, celebration of the Lord's supper, and administration of each of the Sacraments, and all their common and open prayer in the Latine tongue in such order and forme as they be mentioned and set forth in the said booke established by this act . . .[77]

One of the clarion calls of evangelical humanism was for a restoration of the original text of the Scriptures, coupled with the provision of accurate translations into the vernacular for the edification of the common people, a programme neatly encapsulated in a famous quotation from Erasmus:

I wish that every woman would read the Gospel and the Epistles of Paul . . . I wish these were translated into each and every language . . . read and understood not only by Scots and Irishmen, but also by Turks and Saracens . . . I hope the farmer may sing snatches of Scripture at his plough, that the weaver may hum bits . . . to the tune of his shuttle, that the traveller may lighten . . . his journey with stories from Scripture . . .[78]

The use of the vernacular for Scripture and public worship became one of the most significant features of the Protestant Reformation, yet this principle was easily discarded by the royal officials when faced with the problem of subduing Gaelic Ireland.

When the 1541–3 Parliament in Dublin granted Henry VIII the title of King of Ireland, this implied that all the inhabitants of the country, not merely those of the Pale, were subjects of the Crown. The Palesmen advocated a conciliatory policy towards the Gaelic world in the belief that their assistance would be indispensable in bringing the Gaelic lords to civility. Some of the Pale nobility were prepared to bring up young Gaelic noblemen in their own homes and there were repeated calls to erect grammar schools throughout the land, 'whereby the youghts of that wilde contrie by learning shalbe brought to know God and their Prince'.[79] This conciliatory policy was felt to be in accordance with the humanistic principles then in vogue in England, which proclaimed that the condition of primitive man could be improved by education. By the mid-sixties, however, these humanistic ideas were considerably modified in English circles. Social change was now held to be a very gradual affair. Civility could not be introduced overnight to a barbaric people such as the Gaelic Irish. The dominant element would first of all have to be overthrown and English settlers then introduced as a ruling élite. The Palesmen's philosophy had not taken account of the changing ethos in England. Those that attended university at Oxford and Cambridge found the intellectual atmosphere becoming more and more uncongenial and gradually withdrew to Continental centres of education such as Douai, Salamanca, and Louvain, thereby coming under the influence of post-Tridentine Catholicism.

Nicholas Canny has explained this development in England as a contrast between an older, Aristotelian school of thought and an aggressive new approach dominated by French political theorists such as Ramus, whose views were very much in vogue in Cambridge.[80] Canny's explanation has been strongly contested by Brendan Bradshaw.[81] Bradshaw holds that the notion of social progress as a gradual affair goes back to the 1530s. It was readily accepted that the natives could be introduced to civility only by degrees. It was only a question of which technique should be employed to achieve this end: persuasion or coercion. The persuasive technique, firmly rooted in Erasmian humanism, was based on an optimistic view of human nature that held man to be inherently reformable. The coercive technique, deriving from Protestantism, was based on a very pessimistic view of human nature as totally corrupt. This outlook made a very positive contribution to the Protestant doctrine of justification, but the results were far from positive in the political realm, as both Luther and Calvin stressed the coercive authority of government symbolized by the sword. Though humanism and Protestantism overlapped in many areas, the fundamental anthropologies of the two movements were diametrically opposed. It was this pessimistic view of human nature that provided the intellectual background to the Elizabethan conquest. Without civility there could be no Christianity; the natives must be subdued first, and this was the attitude that could induce even a person as refined as Spenser to call for a moratorium on evangelization in Ireland until the conquest was complete.[82]

It was only when John Carswell published a Gaelic translation of the Book of Common Order in Edinburgh in 1567[83] that the authorities in Dublin were finally galvanized into action to provide spiritual material for the native Irish. Carswell addressed his work to Gaelic speakers in Ireland as well as Scotland and, as this Presbyterian book[84] could have posed a threat to the Elizabethan ecclesiastical settlement, the authorities had to take pre-emptive measures. Elizabeth herself was not unfavourably disposed towards the Gaelic tongue. In the 1560s she sent the not inconsiderable sum of £66.13s.4d. to Adam Loftus, Archbishop of Armagh, and Hugh Brady, Bishop of Meath, 'for the making of character to print the New Testament in Irish'.[85] When nothing had been achieved by the end of 1567, she threatened to demand that the money be returned 'unless they do presently put the same in print'.[86] The same year, 'she provided characters and other instruments for the Presse, in hope that God in mercy would raise up some to translate the New Testament into their mother tongue'.[87] A poem by Pilib Bocht Ó hUiginn (d. 1487), 'Tuar ferge foighide Dé', was the first work to be printed in Gaelic in Ireland, but this broadsheet was just a test-piece.[88] The same year, 1571, Seán Ó Cearnaigh, treasurer of St Patrick's Cathedral, published *Aibidil Gaoidheilge, Caiticiosma*. The most interesting feature of this work was Ó Cearnaigh's willingness to cull some theologically neutral prayers from Carswell's book, prayers that would in no way cause offence to loyal Anglicans.[89]

Work on the New Testament proceeded apace under the direction of William Daniel (Uilliam Ó Domhnaill), one of the first three scholars to enter Trinity College, Ireland's first university, when it was founded in 1592.[90] The fact that Ireland had no university until this late date must have been a major obstacle to the spread of the Renaissance there. Given that Trinity College was founded specifically to advance Protestantism that had already failed to make significant progress on the Irish scene, the prospects for a belated flowering of humanism in Ireland cannot have been greatly enhanced by this foundation. The translation of the New Testament was not completed until 1602; only five hundred copies were printed, and were bound the following year.

In his dedicatory epistle to James I, Daniel explained that his translation was based on the Greek version of the New Testament:

> Vnder which burden how carefully and conscionably I have groned, they onely can judge that can confer this translation with the original Greeke, unto which I tyed my selfe as of dutie I ought.[91]

The 'original Greeke' was in fact the *Textus Receptus* published by Erasmus in 1516. This was a major breakthrough in biblical scholarship, though it must be conceded that some of the 'original Greeke' was, in fact, composed by the doughty Erasmus himself. Daniel also made use of the Latin Vulgate and the *English Geneva Bible* (1557). The team of translators were all university men trained in the classics, and Daniel's willingness to work from the best Greek text available at the time marks this Gaelic New Testament as a product of evangelical humanism. Daniel also undertook a translation of the *Book of Common Prayer* under the inspiration of Sir Arthur Chichester, who became Lord Deputy in 1605. This work, appearing in 1608, is remarkable for its faithful transposition of Cranmer's dignified prose into a natural, fluent, Gaelic style and for Daniel's use of Puritan rather than Anglican terminology.[92]

By the 1590s the Catholic Counter-Reformation was well under way, deriving its strength from the foundation of Irish colleges on the Continent.[93] But one must not forget the preparatory education given by a number of grammar schools in Ireland. The school run by Peter White at Kilkenny deserves special prominence. White, one-time fellow of Oriel College, Oxford, introduced his pupils to the writings of Erasmus in a work of his own composition, *Epitomae Copiae Erasmi*, and was also the author of four other small Latin works. His school attracted scholars from Dublin and from all over the south and received a glowing tribute from Richard Stanihurst:

> In our own time the school was run by Peter White whose great merits are recognised throughout the colony. From this school, educated men have sprung as if from a Trojan horse. I could commemorate here the learned and intelligent scholars—the Whites, Comerfords, Walshes, Waddings, Dormers, Shees, Garveys, Butlers, Archers, Strongs, and Lombards—all of whom committed themselves to that teacher's tutelage at an early age. My own boyhood was given to him. Indeed, I am so indebted to this school-master's attention and compassion that I am at a loss in paying tribute to him since I cannot reckon the full extent of his infinite merits in me.[94]

It is highly significant that so many of those mentioned by Stanihurst went on to the Continent and played a leading role in bringing the Counter-Reformation back to Ireland. One should not omit the school run by John Flahy in Waterford and the one conducted by the Lynch family in Galway.

The first Irish college to be founded on the Continent was that of Alcalà in Spain in 1590. Irish colleges at Alcalà, Salamanca, Lisbon, Santiago de Compostella, Seville, and Madrid trained their students in an atmosphere in which classical studies, biblical scholarship, and scholastic education flourished in harmony. And in the Low Countries many Irishmen flocked to the universities of Douai and Louvain. The Renaissance of the Low Countries was centred in Louvain, while Douai, newly founded in 1562, was like another Oxford, combining the traditions of English humanism with the spirit of the Netherlands Renaissance. Irish colleges were soon established in these regions at Douai, Antwerp, Lille, Charleville, Tournai, and Louvain. Other foundations in Rome and Paris should not be forgotten.

In 1600 an informer made a detailed report to Cecil on the Irish college at Douai:

> ... there are in the house sixty young gentlemen, eldest sons of the principal gentlemen of the Pale, ... besides many merchants' sons of Dublin and Drogheda ... the rebel rout in Ireland whom they call the Catholic army, and Tyrone, by name, is daily prayed for there; they all speak Irish, and it is to be feared that these young gentlemen, the offspring of the colonies of the English conquest, may become, in language and disposition, fermented with the ancient hatred of Irish to English which is so great that I know of no disputing among brutes greater.[95]

The Irish colleges catered for lay as well as clerical students. The fact that Gaelic was taught to the Old English testifies to the missionary nature of these centres of education, but they soon suffered from internal conflicts, the Old Irish forming a 'Spanish party' as against the Old English, who tended to seek accommodation with the English Crown, offering loyalty in return for freedom of religion. In 1602 O'Neill, O'Donnell, and the Franciscan, Florence Conroy, made allegations of partiality against Thomas White SJ, rector of the Irish college in Salamanca. He was accused of being biased in favour of Munster and showing no affection for Ulstermen and Connaught-men, who were for many years the true defenders of the faith in Ireland.[96] Within four years Conroy, with the support of Philip III of Spain, had founded the Irish Franciscan college of Louvain, a college that was to play a major role in the field of Gaelic literature and learning in the first half of the seventeenth century.[97] If the Old English in the towns took the lead in the Counter-Reformation, their dominance was being strongly challenged by the Gaelic Irish at the beginning of the seventeenth century. The friars at Louvain felt that something had to be done to counteract the production of spiritual books in Gaelic from the Protestant point of view and so procured their own printing press. Bonabhentura Ó hEoghusa, the former Giolla Brighde, pub-lished *An Teagasg Críosdaidhe*[98] in Antwerp in 1611 and republished it in Louvain in 1614/15. Other works soon followed: *Desiderius* by Florence Conroy (1616),[99] *Scáthán Shacramuinte na hAithridhe* by Aodh Mac Aingil (1618),[100] *Riail an Teas Oird* by Brian Mac Giolla Choinne (1641),[101] and *Parthas an Anama* by Antaine Gearnon (1645).[102] It was this literary output more than anything else that caused F. X. Martin to state that the Counter-Reformation in Ireland telescoped Renaissance, Reform, and Counter-Reformation all into one.[103] All these works are strongly imbued with a militant Counter-Reformation approach, Mac Aingil specifically stating in his introduction that it was the necessity of combating Protestant material in Gaelic that prompted him to take up his pen. Apart from refuting doctrinal error, clarifying the Catholic position, sometimes stooping to abuse and vilification of their adversaries—particularly in the sexual sphere—the authors are quite influenced by pietism, a result no doubt of their spiritual training in Spain or the Spanish Netherlands.[104]

Theology apart, however, the chief characteristic of these books is their deliberate rejection of the studied, artificial, literary language of the *filí* in favour of a direct, simple style. Ó hEoghusa, Conroy, and Mac Aingil are very aware of this innovatory aspect and, as if anticipating censure, take great pains to defend themselves in their prefaces to the reader. Their prime reason in writing is to teach the faith. Teaching clearly implies being understood. Simplicity and clarity take precedence over elegance of style; the message, and not the medium, matters. 'If I were to worry about gilding words I would make many of them obscure', declared O'Hussey.[105]

Conroy, in support of his contention that his main aim was to be understood by simple people not skilled in the subtleties of the literary tongue, has recourse to a quotation from his favourite author, St Augustine:

> Of what profit is the golden key unless it opens that which we need to open, when that is the only use we have for it; and why should we reject a wooden key if it opens that thing for us.[106]

Mac Aingil defends his choice as follows:

> If it is said that it is impertinent for us to write anything in Gaelic because we have not cultivated that language in the traditional way: our answer is this, that it is not to teach Irish that we write but to inculcate repentance and we deem it sufficient to be understood even though our Irish is not quite correct.[107]

It might not be out of place here to recall Manus O'Donnell's preface to his life of Colm Cille some eighty years earlier. Having assembled his sources, he translated the Latin into Gaelic and the difficult Gaelic into easy Gaelic so as to facilitate being understood by all. In this he was vindicating the use of the vernacular as a literary language, and at the same time putting 'difficult Gaelic' and Latin on the same scale.

In other countries, the growth of humanism and the invention of printing encouraged the cultivation of the vernacular for literary purposes, Du Bellay's *Defense et illustration de la langue françoyse* being a very good example of this development. But whereas in other countries it was simply a matter of comparing and contrasting the vernacular with Latin, in Gaelic Ireland the vernacular had to contend with two languages, Latin and *bérla na bhfileadh*, the language of the poets. The printing revolution, however, meant that knowledge was no longer the preserve of the élite; learning became democratized, as it were. As soon as the Gaelic literati came to terms with the printed word, their whole concept of literacy and learning had to change, and this change was further accelerated by Counter-Reformation necessity and strategy. The prefaces to the Louvain works are dominated by a mixture of humanistic values and Counter-Reformation technique. The self-conscious apologia of the authors is all the more acute, given that Conroy and Ó hEoghusa themselves belonged to the traditional learned caste, and even Aodh Mac Aingil may have received some training in a bardic school.[108] These scholars felt the same need to justify themselves to their peers as did many a Continental author abandoning Latin for the vernacular. As regards Conroy's apology for his lack of skill and fluency, even allowing for the fact that he spent most of his life out of Ireland, one wonders whether his admission is to be taken literally, or whether it was merely in accordance with the standard, stylized profession of humility common in literary introductions of the time, and ultimately of classical origin.

It is remarkable, too, that the three authors mentioned are very muted in their criticism of the learned classes and their medium. The most severe strictures on the arcane literary dialect are to be found in the preface of Theobald Stapleton's Irish and Latin catechism published in Brussels in 1639.[109] The author was of English extraction, and thus, his knowledge of Gaelic would have been confined to the vernacular, the common language of everyday speech. He would have been equally ignorant of the merits of the literary language and acutely aware of its disadvantages in the new world dominated by printing and the needs of the faith. Interestingly enough, Stapleton is equally hard on Latin and he vividly describes the ordinary people trying to recite the Our Father and the Creed in Latin, chattering like a parrot or jackdaw trying to talk, 'acht à gogalluig amhail Pioraide, no caoga do chuirfeadh chum cain te'.[110] As for 'an Tuata bocht simplidh Erenach',[111] the poor simple Irish peasant, both Latin and literary Gaelic were equally unintelligible to him, and therefore useless in the Counter-Reformation campaign.[112] Despite the advantage of vernacular Gaelic, however, the problem of literacy still remains. In the final analysis these religious works of the Counter-Reformation must have been aimed at a very restricted group, the literate members of the upper classes, both Old Irish and Old English.

The invention of printing and the consequent development of the vernacular froze the vernacular tongues into standard forms, and thus introduced the necessity for grammars and dictionaries.[113] Interest in philology and the classics entailed similar works for Latin and Greek. There was a corresponding spin-off in Louvain. Of the grammars, the most famous and most influential was Bonabhentura Ó hEoghusa's *Rudimenta grammaticae hiberniae*.[114] Despite its great influence on subsequent grammarians this was all achieved through the manuscript tradition, and it was only in 1968 that this grammar was finally published. Ó hEoghusa was the central figure of the Louvain scheme for producing work in Gaelic. Fully trained in the bardic schools, a poet of note, the author of the first published catechism in Gaelic and the first grammar in the language, he apparently had intended to accomplish much more, because he died, according to Mac Aingil,

> a ttosach a shaothair so chor a ccló, sul ráinig leis sinni do theagasg a tteangaidh ar máthar, iondas go ttiocfadh dhínn ní éigin do rachadh a leas na n-anmann do sgríobhadh, ó nách léigthear dhúinn tré bhurba an pherseacuision foircheadal do dhénamh ó bheól ... As mór do bhí faoi do sgríobhadh do rachadh a leas anama, a n-onóir shaoghalta don náision dá maireadh.[115]

> (... when he was beginning to put his work into print and before he managed to instruct us in our mother tongue, so that we could succeed in writing something that would benefit souls, since the severity of the persecution prevents us from teaching by word of mouth ... He had intended to write much that would have brought spiritual profit and worldly renown to the nation had he lived.)

The first Gaelic dictionary to be published was Mícheál Ó Cléirigh's *Sanasán Nua* (Louvain, 1643).[116] The title of this work, *Foclóir nó Sanasán Nua ina mínighthear cáil éigin dfoclaibh cruaidhe na gaoidheilge, arna sgriobhadh ar urd aibghitre* . . ., indicates that he was mainly dealing with archaic and difficult words. But it has recently been pointed out that the first English dictionary, that of Robert Cawdrey of 1604, contained a similar title:

> A Table Alphabeticall, conteyning and teaching the true writing, and understanding of hard usuall English wordes . . . Whereby they may the more easilie and better understand many hard English wordes.[117]

Other Franciscan lexicographers were Muiris Ó Maolchonaire, Baolach Mac Aogáin, Seán O Cuirnín, and Seosamh Pluincéad, all of whose work still remains in manuscript form,[118] though contemporary writers expressed hope of seeing at least some of these works in print:

> The labours of the Reverend Fathers of the order of St Francis in the college of Louvain will we hope once more revive the Irish language . . . We have already seen many works printed in the Irish type at the press at this college, and we are expecting soon from the same source, a copious Irish dictionary which some of the same friars are said to be compiling.[119]

Conroy and Mac Aingil were major European theologians as well as Gaelic scholars of repute, the former a student of Augustine, the latter a Scotist. Ó hEoghusa wrote from Douai that, though invited to pursue his studies at Salamanca and Valladolid, he would prefer Louvain as the best centre of learning.[120] Coming under the influence of contemporary theology, the aims of the Counter-Reformation, and the challenge and possibilities offered by the printing press, the Louvain friars seem to have deliberately adapted the resources of the Gaelic language to the needs of a new world. The other great prose writer of this period, Seathrún Céitinn, some of whose work was considerably influenced by English recusant literature, does not seem to have been of a like mind, perhaps because he was not working in conjunction with a printing-press.[121] Nevertheless, one feels that his poem, 'Milis an teanga an Ghaedhealg', owes much to the general European contemporary spirit of lauding the vernacular.[122]

The other great contribution of Louvain lay in the fields of history and hagiography. Some scholars have tended to treat the work of the Irish friars in isolation, but it is much more profitable to place it in the contemporary international context.[123] The growth of evangelical humanism and the Reformation gave a fresh boost to the study of hagiography. Fantastic, not to say unedifying, miracles were to be eliminated as unauthentic, the products of fertile and bizarre imaginations. The *vitae* would no longer be accepted credulously but would be subjected to stringent tests for verification. Such a scientific, critical approach had in fact begun in Brussels under the direction of the Jesuit scholars known as the Bollandists, some of whom were in close contact with the Irish Franciscans at Louvain.

Somewhat closer to the bone were the activities of the learned but erratic Scotsman,

Thomas Dempster. Basing his proof on a misinterpretation of the Latin word *Scotus*, Dempster claimed for Scotland many an Irish saint. The results of his labours can be gauged from his *Historia ecclesiastica gentis Scotorum*, published posthumously in 1627. Of the 4,300 famous Scotsmen recorded by Dempster, there are 5 popes, 14 cardinals, 679 saints, and 257 founders of Continental monasteries. Dempster's extravagant claims sufficed to goad a number of Irish to undertake the research necessary to vindicate their countrymen.[124] The first work of this kind to be published was Henry FitzSimon's *Catalogue of the Principal Saints of Ireland* in 1611. David Rothe and Stephen White were others to have engaged in hagiographical writing, but it was a meeting in Paris in 1623 between Thomas Messingham, rector of the Irish college there, and two Irish Franciscans, Hugh Ward and Patrick Fleming, that really got the Irish friars at Louvain interested in this area. They originally intended to help Messingham in compiling his *Florilegium Insulae Sanctorum* (1624), but the arrangement fell through and the friars undertook their own project.[125]

A renewed interest in history was part of the cultural inheritance of the Renaissance and, with the advent of the Reformation and other ensuing divisions of Christendom, this interest assumed a polemical colouring. The first salvo fired in the conflict was the appearance of the *Magdeburg Centuries* in 1559, a history of the Church undertaken by Protestant scholars, a work that was not completed till 1624. Its contentious nature is best indicated by its threefold division; the *Hidden Antichrist*, the *Public Antichrist*, the *Unveiled Antichrist*. A Catholic reply was not long in forthcoming, and the *Annales Ecclesiastici*, written by Cesare Baronio, librarian at the Vatican Library, appeared in 1597. It is interesting to note that all the contemporary libraries in the Irish colleges abroad included the early folio volumes of Baronio, and from the early seventeenth century onwards, works on the history and antiquities of Ireland appear on their shelves.[126]

A new interest in Scotism occurred in the seventeenth century, mainly among Franciscans, and, since John Duns Scotus was erroneously believed at the time to have been an Irishman, it was a matter of national pride as well as of religious *pietas* to conduct research into his life and work. It was only natural that Irish Franciscans should be among the foremost Scotists of the time, and Aodh Mac Aingil's work on Scotist philosophy and theology was not superseded until 1950.[127]

Luke Wadding of Waterford was engaged in writing the history of the Franciscan order at the time. His *Annales Minorum* were published in eight volumes between 1625 and 1654, and he was encouraged by David Rothe to do for the history of his own country what he had done for his order. Various works on the history of Ireland were appearing from the middle of the sixteenth century onwards. Many of these were unreliable, to the extent that they were written by men like Campion—Campion's *A History of Ireland* (1571), Stanihurst's *A Plain and Perfect Description of Ireland* (1577), *De Rebus in Hibernia Gestis Libri Quattuor* (1584)—men who, though Catholics, would not have known Gaelic and therefore would not have had access to source documents. Learned Protestant scholars like William Camden, James Ussher, and Sir James Ware, were also publishing works on Irish history. Camden had, in fact, republished the infamous Giraldus Cambrensis's two works, *Topographica Hiberniae* and *Expugnatio Hibernica*, in 1602. All these works provided the necessary background and stimulus for a Catholic, native Irish reaction. The Irish Franciscans hoped to produce works superior to those that had already appeared, works which would show the world that they were citizens of no mean country.[128]

Peter Burke has defined the sense of history as including three factors: the sense of anachronism, the awareness of evidence, and the interest in causation; three factors that were absent in the Middle Ages and only began to develop during the Renaissance.[129] These three areas seem to provide the ideal yardstick to judge the hagiographical and historical work of the Louvain friars. Fr. Canice Mooney adopted a somewhat parallel approach in assessing John Colgan's work, *Acta Sanctorum Hiberniae* (1645) and *Triadis Thaumaturgae* (1647). Mooney's scheme included heuristics, criticism, interpretation, synthesis, and exposition.[130] Colgan's greatest contribution would have been in the area of heuristics. Faithful to the Renaissance rallying cry, *ad fontes*, he was most diligent in searching out manuscripts not only in Ireland but all over Europe. On the other hand, his critical faculty was somewhat disarmed by the fact that he was dealing with the lives of holy men. Religious credulity tended to blunt the healthy scepticism needed to analyse documents objectively. His editorial method consisted of editing the best text rather than producing a critical text. In this he was faithful to the humanist tradition.

The historian, Mícheál Ó Cléirigh, was equally aware of the importance of primary sources and, during the ten years he spent in Ireland searching out and transcribing manuscripts, he was always careful to cite his source, the place and date of transcription, and actual owner of the document. As regards his critical faculty, he alludes on occasion to certain aspects of the saints' lives that he finds absurd (*'go neimhchiall'*).[131] But owing to his vow of obedience he faithfully transcribes all that occurred in the manuscripts:

óir do haithnitheadh díom lorg na seinleabhar do leanmhain.[132]

('since I was commanded to follow the pattern of the old books'.)

Given Ó Cléirigh's brief, it is difficult to comment on his critical faculty and it may have been intended to subject his work to more critical analysis back at Louvain prior to publication.[133]

Compared with Ó Cléirigh's *Annála Ríochta Éireann*, Céitinn's *Foras Feasa ar Éirinn* stands out, first of all, in its use of continuous narrative as against the annalistic style.[134] Céitinn seems to have been writing more consciously within the scheme advocated by Burke than Ó Cléirigh. His awareness of the value of primary sources is clearly seen in his virulent attack on previous historians who could neither speak nor read Gaelic.[135] Céitinn has often been condemned for excessive credulity, as seen in the following extract from Bishop John Roche's letter to Luke Wadding in 1631:

One Doctor Keating laboureth much in compiling notes towards a history in Irish. The man is very studious, and yet I fear that if his work come ever to light it will need an amendment of ill-warranted narrations; he could help you to many curiosities of which you can make better use than himself. I have no interest in the man, for I never saw him, for he dwelleth in Munster.[136]

On the other hand, an Irish antiquarian scholar called Thomas O'Sullevane, writing in 1722, adds new light to Céitinn's allegedly uncritical spirit:

> But when . . . the Doctor had an opportunity to confer with more judicious Men, concerning his Work, he found it would not stand the test of an History; not only for that—the first part of it which preceded the Milesian Conquest, was without any Probability or Appearance of Truth; as having even been exploded by all Cricks, . . . but because in the second which reaches down from the said Conquest; through the Series, and Succession of the Kings, with many of their Actions, might be depended on in the main, for Reality; yet these also were so blended and interwoven with Fables, that they would carry no greater weight than the first. Since therefore he could not help what was done, by getting in the copies already taken, which was not in his power to accomplish; he desir'd it should never be translated into any other Language, nor otherwise regarded, than as a Miscellany of indigested things, wherein judicious and discerning Natives might find something worth their perusal at leisure Hours.[137]

The above quotation, attributing a greater historical sense to Céitinn than the work itself warrants, is unfortunately not open to verification. If a copy in Céitinn's own hand was actually sent to Louvain, it would seem that he wished to be associated with the Louvain scheme and envisaged publication.[138] It also seems that one of the early copies of the *Foras Feasa* is in Mícheál Ó Cléirigh's hand.[139] All this seems to indicate that the two scholars were not working in isolation and independently of each other.

Céitinn composed an objective history of Ireland and finished with the Norman invasion mainly because of his expressed aim in refuting Giraldus Cambrensis, but recent scholarship has shown that he had an ulterior motive in mind. He extended the invasion myth of the Lebor Gabála to accommodate and include the Old English element and recounted the reform of the Irish Church in the twelfth century to vindicate the claims and aims of the Counter-Reformation conducted by the secular clergy of his own time:

> Keating's successful integration of the Old English community into the national myth, by viewing the Norman invasion in the same light as the Tuatha Dé Danann and the Sons of Míl demonstrated the relationship of the Old English to the natives while maintaining their distinctiveness. This and his vindication of the reform methods and objectives of the Counter-Reformation secular clergy, particularly the restructured diocesan system, are the essence, if not quite the stated objective, of the *Foras Feasa ar Éirinn*.[140]

All this goes to indicate that Céitinn was well aware of the moral value of history, of using the past to interpret the present. It further shows that it is totally incorrect to interpret the *Foras Feasa* as a 'monument to a doomed civilization'.[141] Both Céitinn and Ó Cléirigh were well aware of the imminent danger to priceless manuscripts owing to the troubled nature of the times, and a corresponding sense of urgency thus dominated their work. But their primary aim was to write for the present, for their contemporaries, to provide a history of the new Catholic nation that had come into being, *ríocht Éireann*, a nation composed both of *SeanGhael* and *SeanGhall* under the common title of *Éireannach*.[142] It is interesting to note that the most recent research on Richard Stanihurst, one of the prime targets singled out by Céitinn, shows a gradual process towards a vision of a unified Catholic community in Ireland composed of both Old English and Gaelic Irish.[143]

All that has been said above should be sufficient to dispel the myth that Céitinn wrote the *Foras Feasa* in a cave in the glen of Aherlow while on the run. He was a scholar with access to sources in Latin, English, and Gaelic, with the comfort necessary to peruse these works at length and leisure, and to select from them in accordance with the general aim of his history a vindication of the Old English and of the Counter-Reformation.[144] The same is true of Mícheál Ó Cléirigh. Though a contemporary remarked in a letter that it was little short of a miracle that Ó Cléirigh was not hanged in Ireland since everyone knew of his travels, this should not be interpreted to mean that he was working under extremely difficult conditions.[145] For one thing, apart from the year 1628/29, the period was one of comparative toleration, but of greater importance is the fact that Ó Cléirigh could not have achieved what he accomplished unless he was working under conditions conducive to scholarship, study, research and writing. Very relevant in this regard are the distinguished patrons who supported him. Toirdhealbhach Mag Cochláin gave his patronage to *Seanchas Ríogh Éireann* and *Geinealuighi na Naomh* in 1630. Mag Cochláin was both a Member of Parliament and a wealthy landowner.[146] Brian Mag Uidhir, lord of Enniskillen, was Ó Cléirigh's patron when he re-edited *Lebor Gábala Éireann* in 1631. Brian Rua and his cousin were the only two Old Irish chosen as King's Commissioners in Co. Fermanagh, an office that entailed collecting the royal taxes.[147] Sir Fergal O'Gara, a Member of Parliament for Co. Sligo, gave his patronage to Ó Cléirigh when he was engaged on his major work, *Annála Ríoghachta Éireann*.[148] O'Gara may even have instigated the project, as there is no indication that the writing of a civil history of Ireland was part of Ó Cléirigh's original brief when he was dispatched from Louvain to Ireland in 1626.[149] O'Gara, too, being an alumnus of Trinity College, may have been the link between Ó Cléirigh and Archbishop Ussher.[150] Ussher was on particularly friendly terms with Thomas Strange, guardian of the Franciscan convent in Dublin from 1626 to 1629.[151] In his correspondence with Luke Wadding, Fr. Strange indicates Ussher's willingness to make his library available to Irish scholarly friars. Given the difficulty of the times, Strange does not mention Ussher by name but uses the ironic pseudonym Jacobus de Turrecremata (Torquemada),[152] adding that this man 'could harm us more than any in the kingdom'.[153]

It seems, therefore, wrong to hold that the Annals were written in stealth and under duress. On the contrary, they were written under the patronage of men of substantial means, men of considerable standing in the land, men who had come to terms with the new political settlement. It even seems that love of learning and scholarship were able to break down the barriers of religious intolerance. The evidence is clearly available for Ó Cléirigh; further research should indicate similar patronage for Céitinn. Neither historian should be seen as making a last stand for Gaelic culture. They were working within the system, recognizing the King of England as legitimate ruler of the Kingdom of Ireland. In the final analysis, the Old English Céitinn and the Old Irish Ó Cléirigh were both using the best resources of learning available at the time, native documents and Renaissance techniques, to provide an authoritative history for the new Catholic nation that had come into being under the '*síoth coitcheann*' established by James I and continued by Charles.

In 1642 Rory O'Moore, one of the leaders of the 1641 rising, wrote to Hugh Burke:

> If we may afore Flan Mac Egan dies, we will see an Irish school oppened, and therefore could wish heartily that those learned and religious fathers in Louvayn did come over in hast with their monuments and with an Irish and Latin print.[154]

These fond hopes were unfortunately not realized. Lack of funds and the diversion of promised funds to the military campaign of 1642–9 saw the literary work of Louvain dwindle to an end. Much of what was accomplished remained in manuscript form; how many of these manuscripts perished through neglect, and even confiscation, no one knows. One copy of the Annals of the Four Masters was presented to Fergal O'Gara, the other sent to Louvain for printing. In 1755 Fr. Peter McCormack, guardian at Louvain, came across the Louvain copy and wondered what it was—such was the break in the tradition.[155] The Annals remained in oblivion until printed by O'Donovan in the last century.[156] Céitinn's work, too, was not put into print until the last century;[157] but at least his history entered and enriched the manuscript tradition. On the Continent, the printing-press played a major role in disseminating humanism and the new learning. Despite the initial impact, however, the printed word failed to gain a permanent foothold in the world of Gaelic letters, and the manuscript tradition of the Middle Ages continued right up to the end of the nineteenth century. This is by no means to affirm that the Gaelic world was a stagnant one, closed to change. On the contrary, a major work recently published demonstrates that much of the devotional and political poetry of the seventeenth century was strongly influenced by the Baroque movement; a product of post-Tridentine Catholicism, pious in scope, reacting against the optimism and paganism of the Renaissance.[158] Many Irishmen studying abroad came under the influence of this movement, and the rigours of the Cromwellian campaign at home served only to accentuate the pessimism of the age. Indeed, one could say that the Baroque caught up with the Renaissance in Ireland before the latter had time to come to fruition. In the final analysis, the initial flowering of the Renaissance in Ireland, late though it was, might have held out hopes for an Indian summer, but the fortunes of history decreed that instead of this Indian summer, we were left with the Wild Geese; instead of *Fómhar na nGéanna, na Géanna Fiáine*.

Notes

The most comprehensive overview of Gaelic literature for the period covered by this chapter is Brian Ó Cuív, 'The Irish language in the early modern period', in *A New History of Ireland, Vol. III, Early Modern Ireland, 1534-1691* (Oxford, 1976), Chapter XX, pp. 509-45. Bernadette Cunningham's 'Native culture and political change in Ireland, 1580-1640', in Ciarán Brady and Raymond Gillespie, *Natives and Newcomers* (Irish Academic Press, 1986), pp. 148-231, is also an important contribution.

An interesting, if somewhat controversial, analysis is Nicholas Canny's 'The formation of the Irish mind: religion, politics and Gaelic Irish literature 1580-1750', in *Past and Present*, No. 95 (May, 1982), 91-116.

Breandán Ó Buachalla's 'Na Stíobhartaigh agus an t-aos léinn: Cing Séamas', in *Proceedings Royal Irish Academy*, LXXXIII (1983), section C, 81-134, is also essential reading. Not many studies have dealt with the Renaissance as such. The main contributions have come from F. X. Martin OSA, 'Ireland, the Renaissance and the Counter-Reformation', *Topic: 13* (1967), pp. 23-33; John Silke, 'Irish scholarship and the Renaissance, 1580-1675', *Studies in the Renaissance*, Vol. XXI (1973), 169-205; Benignus Millett, 'Irish literature in Latin, 1550-1700', in *A New History of Ireland, Vol. III*, pp. 561-86.

1 Edmund Curtis, *A History of Medieval Ireland from 1086 to 1513* (London, 1938), p.366.
2 Ibid., p. 373.
3 David Mathew, *The Celtic Peoples and Renaissance Europe* (London, 1933), p. xix.
4 Daniel Corkery, *The Hidden Ireland* (Dublin, 1924; 2nd edition, 1967) p. 149.
5 Ibid., p. 151.
6 An tAth. Pádraig de Brún, 'Ars Scribendi', *Humanitas*, I (Márta, 1930), 4.
7 Domhnall Ó Corcora, 'Na hEorpaigh Seo Againne', *Humanitas*, I (Meitheamh, 1930), 1. There is a good summary of the controversy between O'Corkery and de Brún to be found in Frank O'Brien, *Filíocht Ghaeilge na Linne Seo* (Baile Átha Cliath, 1966), pp. 55-81. Corkery's clearest statements on the characteristics of Gaelic poetry are to be found in 'Filidheacht na Gaedhilge—a cineál', an introductory essay to R. Ó. Foghludha, *Éigse na Máighe* (Baile Átha Cliath, 1954), pp. 7-29. For a recent assessment of Corkery's literary views, cf. Seán Ó Tuama, 'Dónal Ó Corcora agus Filíocht na Gaeilge', *Studia Hibernica* No. 5 (1965), 29-41; Breandan Ó Buachalla, 'Ó Corcora agus an Hidden Ireland', *Scríobh*, 4 (1979), 109-37.
8 Brendan Bradshaw, 'Manus "the Magnificent": O'Donnell as Renaissance prince', in *Studies in Irish History presented to R. Dudley Edwards*, edited by Art Cosgrave and Donal McCartney (Naas, 1979), pp. 15-36.
9 Ibid., p. 23.
10 Ibid., p. 21.
11 A. O. Kelleher and G. Schoepperle (eds.), *Betha Colaim Chille* (Illinois, 1918).
12 Ibid., p. 6.
13 Ibid., p. 6.
14 Ibid., p. 9.
15 Ibid., pp. 337-8.
16 Bradshaw, op. cit., p. 35.
17 R. Dudley Edwards, 'Ireland, Elizabeth I and the Counter-Reformation', in S. T. Bindoff *et al.* (ed.), *Elizabethan Government and Society* (London, 1961), pp. 321-3. Cf. Bradshaw, op. cit., pp. 16-17. Cf. also Brendan Bradshaw, 'The Elizabethans and the Irish: a muddled model', *Studies*, LXX (1981), 237-8.
18 Edwards, op. cit., p. 322.
19 James Lydon, *Ireland in the Later Middle Ages* (Dublin, 1973), pp. 140-5.
20 Bradshaw, 'The Elizabethans and the Irish: a muddled model', 236-40.
21 Eleanor Knott, 'The bardic poems of Tadhg Dall Ó hUiginn', *Irish Texts Society*, Vol. XXII (London, 1922); Vol. 1, xlv.
22 Ibid., xxxiv-xxxv.

23 T. F. O'Rahilly, *Dánta Grádha: An Anthology of Irish Love Poetry (AD 1350–1750)* (Dublin and Cork, 1926).
24 Robin Flower, Introduction to T. F. O'Rahilly, *Dánta Grádha: An Anthology of Irish Love Poetry* (Baile Átha Cliath, 1916), p. xix.
25 Daniel Corkery's emphasis on 'national art' may also derive more from political rather than aesthetic considerations.
26 Frank O'Connor, *The Backward Look* (London, 1967), Chapter 8, 'The Renaissance in Ireland', pp. 97–108.
27 Ibid., pp. 97–8.
28 *Dánta Grádha* (1926) 19, pp. 26–8. All future references to this work are to the 1926 edition.
29 Mícheál Mac Craith, 'Ovid, an Macalla agus Cearbhall Ó Dálaigh', *Éigse*, XIX (1982), 103–20.
30 *Dánta Grádha*, 5, pp. 5–7.
31 The argument is set out at greater length in my unpublished Ph.D. thesis (NUI, 1986), *Lorg na hIasachta ar na Dánta Grá*, pp. 155–74.
32 *Dánta Grádha*, 20, pp. 28–9.
33 Mícheál Mac Craith, 'Deismireacht Fhileata', *Macalla* (1983), 59–71.
34 Maurice Evans, *English Poetry in the Sixteenth Century* (London, 1969), p. 97.
35 Mac Craith, *Lorg na hIasachta ar na Dánta Grádha*, pp. 191–202.
36 *Dánta Grádha*, 16, pp. 20–4.
37 Mac Craith, 'Féach orm, a inghean Eóghain', *Studia Hibernica*, XXI (1981), 75–94; *Lorg na hIasachta ar na Dánta Grádha*, pp. 230–65.
38 *Dánta Grádha*, 100, pp. 133–4.
39 Mac Craith, 'A Bhean Lán de Stuaim', *Reiviú Mhá Nuad*, VII (1984), 27–51, *Lorg na hIasachta ar na Dánta Grádha*, pp. 123–54.
40 Corkery, *The Hidden Ireland*, pp. 15–16.
41 *Dánta Grádha*, 60, pp. 80–1.
42 Ibid., 26, pp. 34–5.
43 Pádraig de Brún, Breandán Ó Buachalla, Tomás Ó Concheanainn, *Nua-Dhuanaire Cuid I* (Baile Átha Cliath, 1975), p. 26. The edition of the poem printed here has two extra verses not found in *Dánta Grádha*.
44 Pádraig Ua Duinnín (ed.), *Dánta Phiarais Feiritéir* (Baile Átha Cliath, 1934), pp. 103–5.
45 Máire Ní Cheallacháin (ed.), *Filíocht Phádraigín Haicéad* (Baile Átha Cliath, 1962), pp. 3–4.
46 H. E. Rollins (ed.), *A Poetical Rhapsody 1602–1621*, (2 vols., Cambridge, Massachusetts, 1932), pp. 285–6.
47 Thomas Watson, *The 'Εκατομπαθία' or Passionate Centurie of Love* 1582, English Reprints carefully edited by Edward Arber (London, 1870), p. 45.
48 Mac Craith, *Lorg na hIasachta ar na Dánta Grádha*, pp. 111–22.
49 Ua Duinnín, op. cit., p. 100.
50 Seán Ó Tuama and Thomas Kinsella, *An Duanaire 1600–1900: Poems of the Dispossessed* (Port Laoise, 1981), p. 96.
51 *Dánta Phiarais Feiritéir*, p. 100. This edition of the poem contains thirteen verses, the *Nua-Dhuanaire* version has ten, while *An Duanaire* has only six. The lines quoted are found only in the first edition.
52 *Oxford English Dictionary*, Vol. I (1961), p. 436.
53 Barnabus O'Ferrall and Daniel O'Connell, *Commentarius Rinnucinianas*, Vol. V (Dublin, 1944), p. 165.
54 Ibid., p. 76.
55 Liam Miller and Eileen Power (ed.), *Holinshed's Irish Chronicle* (Dublin, 1979), p. 105.
56 *Dictionary of National Biography*, Vol. XIV (Oxford, 1968), p. 709.
57 Tomás Ua Brádaigh, 'Clann Cobhthaigh', *Ríocht na Mídhe*, IV (1967), 26–32. Fr. Thomas Brady, MA; 'The O'Coffey Poets', appendix to Basil Iske, *The Green Cockatrice* (Dublin, 1978), pp. 179–82.
58 Éamonn Ó Tuathail, 'Nugentiana', *Éigse*, II (1940), 4–14.
59 Cuthbert Mhág Craith, OFM, *Dán na mBráthar Mionúr Cuid I* (Baile Átha Cliath, 1967), 'Deacair suan ar chneidh gcarad', pp. 31–4.

60 Ibid., pp. 35-8.

61 Gerard Murphy, 'Poems of Exile by William Nuinseann Mac Barún Dealbhna', *Éigse*, VI (1949), 8-15.

62 Bradshaw, 'The Elizabethans and the Irish: a muddled model', 241.

63 A good account of Nugent's career is to be found in Basil Iske's work, *The Green Cockatrice*, already cited, n.57.

64 *Dánta Grádha*, 47, pp. 66-9.

65 Cathal Ó Háinle, 'Flattery rejected: two seventeenth century Irish poems', *Hermathena*, CXXXVIII (Summer 1985), 5-26.

66 James Carney, *The Irish Bardic Poet* (Dublin, 1967), p. 13. Carney's views on the 'marriage relationship' between poet and patron have been somewhat refined, but not basically changed, by Pádraig Breathnach's article, 'The Chief's Poet', PRIA, LXXXIII (1983), Section C, pp. 37-79.

67 L. Mac Cionnaith, SJ, (ed.), *Dioghluim Dána* (Baile Átha Cliath, 1938), 'Bíodh aire ag Ultaibh ar Aodh', pp. 236-40.

68 Mac Craith, 'Cioth na Baoise', *Béaloideas*, 51 (1983), pp. 31-54; *Lorg na hIasachta ar na Dánta Grádha*, pp. 203-28. This exemplum also gave rise to a proverb that is found pretty frequently in seventeenth-century literature, 'dul fá uisce an cheatha'.

69 O'Connor, *The Backward Look*, p. 99.

70 *Dánta Grádha*, 96, pp. 128-9. O'Rahilly registers the two poems under one number in the body of his text, but records them as two distinct poems in the index of first lines. It is as two separate poems pertaining to the answer-poem genre that they are best understood.

71 E. F. Hart, 'The Answer-Poem of the early seventeenth century', *Review of English Studies, New Series*, Vol. VII, No. 25 (1956), 19-29.

72 Pádraig Breathnach, 'Metamorphoses 1603: Dán le hEochaidh Ó hEoghusa', *Éigse*, XVII (1977/78), 169-80. In this poem Ó hEoghusa contrasts the changes for the worse catalogued by Ovid in *Metamorphoses* with the changes for the better that the new reign will bring about. In verse 17 the poet says that we are all like the daisy: when light comes to it, then it opens its doors. If daisy/*nóinín* is translated as sunflower or marigold, a translation that is quite justified, it means that Ovid was adapting the tale of Clytie and the Sun from *Metamorphoses*, Book III, to his own ends. An examination of Ó hEoghusa's knowledge of the classics could prove most fruitful. For the literati's acceptance of James I, see Breandán Ó Buachalla, 'Na Stíobhartaigh agus an tAos Léinn: Cing Séamas', PRIA, LXXXIII (1983), 81-134.

73 *Calendar of State Papers, Ireland, 1611*, p. 210.

74 James Carney, 'Society and the bardic poet', *Studies*, LXII (1973), 249. Carney notes that one of the latest bardic poets to write in a classical manner, Diarmaid Mac an Bhaird, modelled one of his poems very closely on Ó hEoghusa's 'Fuar liom an adhaighsi dh'Aodh'. This is one of the few cases where we can see one bardic poem clearly deriving from another. Carney concludes that Eochaidh Ó hEoghusa was a 'self-conscious poet who intended his work to be read, and who, ... with this end in view, had copies multiplied and circulated' (ibid., p. 249).

75 Elizabeth Eisenstein, *The Printing Press as an Agent of Change* (2 vols., CUP, 1979).

76 For recent work on the Reformation in Ireland, see G. A. Ford, *The Protestant Reformation in Ireland, 1590-1641* (Frankfurt, 1985); Patrick Corish, 'King or Pope', Chapter III of his *The Irish Catholic Experience: a Historical Survey* (Dublin, 1985) pp. 63-95; Alan Ford, 'The Protestant Reformation in Ireland', in Ciaran Brady, Raymond Gillespie (eds.) *Natives and Newcomers: the Makings of Irish Colonial Society, 1534-1641* (Irish Academic Press, 1986), pp. 50-74. Two important articles are Nicholas Canny, 'Why the Reformation failed in Ireland: *une question mal posée*', *Journal of Ecclesiastical History*, XXX (1979), 423-50, and Karl Bottigheimer, 'The failure of the Reformation in Ireland: *une question bien posée*', *Journal of Ecclesiastical History*, XXXVI (1985), 196-207.

77 Richard Bolton (ed.), *The Statutes of Ireland . . . neatly perused and examined* (Dublin, 1975), p. 273.

78 Erasmus, *The Paraclesis*, quoted in Eisenstein, op. cit., Vol. 1, p. 342.

79 Quoted by Nicholas Canny, *The Formation of the Old English Élite in Ireland* (Dublin, 1975), p. 13.

80 Ibid., pp. 20–9. Canny further elaborated his views in *The Elizabethan Conquest of Ireland: A Pattern Established, 1565–1576* (Sussex: Harvester Press, 1976).

81 Bradshaw, 'The Elizabethans and the Irish', *Studies*, LXVI (Spring, 1977), 38–49; 'Sword, word and strategy in the Reformation in Ireland', *Historical Journal*, XXI (1978), 475–502.

82 Bradshaw, 'The Elizabethans and the Irish', p. 48. For the differences between humanism and Protestantism see A. H. T. Levi's introduction to the Penguin edition of *Erasmus: Praise of Folly* (1986), pp. 16–32.

83 R. L. Thomson (ed.), *Foirm na n-Urnuidheadh* (Edinburgh, 1972).

84 It may occasion some surprise to find Bishop Carswell, 'Easbug Inndseadh Gall', writing a book of Presbyterian thought and theology. Carswell was never actually consecrated bishop, but he was prepared to accept the title in order to procure the wealth of the diocese for his patron, the Earl of Argyll. Carswell's action earned him the rebuke of the General Assembly of the Church of Scotland.

85 Breandán Ó Madagáin, 'Bíobla: an Bíobla i nGaeilge', *Diagacht don Phobal*, I (Maigh Nuad, 1986), 43.

86 Ibid., p. 43.

87 Ibid., p. 43.

88 Bruce Dickins, 'The Irish Broadside of 1571 and Queen Elizabeth's types', *Transactions of the Cambridge Bibliographical Society*, I (1949), 48–60. A modern edition of the poem is found in L. McKenna, *Philip Bocht Ó Huiginn* (Dublin, 1931), pp. 114–18.

89 Nicholas Williams, *I bPrionta i Leabhar Na Protastúin agus Prós na Gaeilge 1567–1724* (Baile Átha Cliath, 1986), Caib. II, 'Seán Ó Cearnaigh', pp. 21–6.

90 Ibid., Caib. III, 'Uilliam Ó Domhnaill agus a Chúntóirí', pp. 27–42.

91 Ibid., p. 32.

92 Ibid., p. 38.

93 For the Counter-Reformation see Frederick M. Jones, *The Counter-Reformation, A History of Irish Catholicism*, Vol. 3, iii (Dublin, 1967); John Bossy, 'The Counter-Reformation and the people of Catholic Ireland', *Historical Studies*, VIII (1971), 155–70; Patrick J. Corish, *The Catholic Community in the Seventeenth and Eighteenth Centuries* (Dublin, 1981) and 'Not a mission but a Church', Chapter 4, *The Irish Catholic Experience*, pp. 96–122; Colm Lennon, 'The Counter-Reformation in Ireland, 1542–1641', in *Natives and Newcomers*, pp. 75–92.

94 Colm Lennon, *Richard Stanihurst the Dubliner, 1547–1618* (Irish Academic Press, 1981), p. 142.

95 John Brady, 'Father Christopher Cusack and the Irish College of Douai 1594–1624', in Sylvester O'Brien OFM (ed.), *Measgra i gcuimhne Mhíchíl Uí Chléirigh* (Dublin, 1944), p. 101.

96 Helga Hammerstein, 'Aspects of the Continental education of Irish students in the reign of Queen Elizabeth I', *Historical Studies*, VIII (1971), 149–50.

97 Tomás Ó Cléirigh, *Aodh Mac Aingil agus an Scoil-Nua Ghaedhilge i Lobháin* (Baile Átha Cliath, 1935), eagrán úr ag Tomás de Bhaldraithe (Baile Átha Cliath, 1986); Canice Mooney OFM, 'St Anthony's College, Louvain', *Donegal Annual* (1969), 18–48.

98 Fearghal Mac Raghnaill, OFM (eag.), *An Teagasg Críosdaidhe* (Baile Átha Cliath, 1976).

99 Thomas F. O'Rahilly, (ed.), *Desiderius* (Dublin, 1941). Conroy had previously translated a catechism from Spanish into Gaelic and sent it to Ireland in 1598. It remained in manuscript form until Brian Ó Cuív edited it some years ago; 'Flaithrí Ó Maolchonaire's Catechism of Christian doctrine', *Celtica*, I: Part II (1950), 161–206.

100 Cainneach Ó Maonaigh, OFM (eag.), *Scáthán Shacramuinte na hAithridhe* (Baile Átha Cliath, 1952).

101 P. Ó. Súilleabháin, OFM (eag.), *Rialachas San Froinsias* (Baile Átha Cliath, 1953).

102 Anselm Ó Fachtna, OFM (eag.), *Parrthas an Anma* (Baile Átha Cliath, 1953).

103 F. X. Martin OSA, 'Ireland, the Renaissance and the Counter-Reformation', *Topic*, 13 (1967), 24.

104 Nicholas Canny, 'The formation of the Irish mind: religion, politics and Gaelic Irish literature 1580–1750', *Past and Present*, No. 95 (May 1982), 97–8.

105 'Lé hóradh briathar dá mbeinn,/mór dhíobh fá chiaigh dho chuirfinn' (*An Teagasg Criosdaidhe*, lines 26–7).

106 'Créd an tarbha atá san eochair órdha muna osgailtear lé an ní iarrmaoid d'osgladh, an tan nách

fuil d'fheidhm againn ría acht sin; nó créd fá budh ionbhéime eochair mhaide dá n-osgla an ní sin dúinn.' (*Desiderius*, lines 44–8).

107 'Dá n-abarthaoi gur dána dúinn ní sgríobhadh a nGaoidhoilg, 's nár shaothruigheamar innti, as í ar bhfreagra ar sin, nách do mhúnadh Gaoidhilgi sgríobhmaoid achd do mhúnadh na haithrídhe, as lór linn go ttuigfidhear sin gé nách bíadh ceart na Gaoidhilgi againn.' (*Scáthán Shacramuinte na hAithridhe*, lines 74–8).

108 Anraí Mac Giolla Chomhaill, *Bráithrín Bocht Ó Dhún: Aodh Mac Aingil* (Baile Átha Cliath, 1985), p. 19.

109 T. Stapleton, *Catechismus, seu doctrina Christiana Latino-Hibernica* (Brussels, 1639, reflex facsimile printed by Irish Manuscripts' Commission, Dublin, 1945).

110 Ibid., introduction, paragraph 28.

111 Ibid., introduction, paragraph 27.

112 My colleague, Tadhg Ó Dúshláine, informs me that the stress on simplicity is found in early English recusant literature and he cites an example from a pamphlet published by Dr Thomas Harding in Antwerp in 1565: 'First the book being good, and conteyning true, holsome, and Catholike doctrine, the more it is made common, the more good thereby is done. Againe whereas many be desyrous of the same, as well in Scotland, Ireland as in England.' (*An Answer to Maister Ivelles chalenge*). I am indebted to Dr Ó Dúshláine for this reference.

113 Lucien Febvre et Henri-Jean Martin, *L'apparition du livre* (Paris, 1971), 'L'imprimerie et les langues', pp. 439–55.

114 Parthalán Mac Aogáin, OFM (eag.), *Graiméir Ghaeilge na mBráthar Mionúr* (Baile Átha Cliath, 1968), pp. 3–106.

115 *Scáthán Shacramuinte na hAithridhe*, lines 3080–7.

116 Mícheál Ó Cléirigh, *Foclóir no Sanasan Nua* (Louvain, 1643).

117 Alan Harrison, 'Graiméir agus Foclóirí Scuitbhéarla', *Féilscríbhinn Thomáis de Bhaldraithe*, in eagar ag Seosamh Watson (Dundalgan Press, 1986), pp. 51–2.

118 Cainneach Ó Maonaigh OFM, 'Scríbhneoirí Gaeilge an Seachtú hAois Déag', *Studia Hibernica*, I (1961), 193.

119 John Lynch, *Cambrensis Eversus* (? St Malo, 1662), translated by Matthew Kelly (3 vols., Dublin, 1848–52), quoted in Alice Stopford Green, *The Making of Ireland and its Undoing, 1200–1600* (London, 1909), p. 453.

120 Colm Ó Lochlainn, *Tobar fíorghlan Gaedhilge* (Baile Átha Cliath, 1939), pp. 67–8. For a clarification of the point at issue in the letter, see *Dán na mBrathar Mionúr*, II, pp. 111–12.

121 Tadhg Ó Dúshláine, 'Seathrún Céitinn agus an stíl Bharocach a thug sé go hEirinn', *Dúchas 1983–1984–1985* (Baile Átha Cliath, 1986), pp. 45–7.

122 Eoin Mac Giolla Eain, *Dánta, amhráin is caointe Sheathrún Céitinn* (Dublin, 1900), p. 17.

123 Fr Canice Mooney OFM, 'Father John Colgan, OFM, his work and times and literary milieu', in Terence O'Donnell (ed.), *Father John Colgan OFM* (Dublin, 1959), pp. 13–20; 'St Anthony's College, Louvain', already cited, pp. 29–32.

124 Mooney, 'Father John Colgan, OFM, his work and times and literary milieu', p. 18.

125 Ibid., pp. 15–16.

126 Ibid., pp. 13–14; Donal F. Cregan, 'The social and cultural background of a Counter-Reformation episcopate, 1618–1680', in *Studies in Irish History Presented to R. Dudley Edwards*, pp. 115–16.

127 Mooney, 'Father John Colgan', p. 18; Cathaldus Giblin OFM, 'Hugh McCaghwell, OFM, Archbishop of Armagh (+ 1626)—aspects of his life', *Seanchas Ardmhacha: Journal of the Armagh Diocesan Historical Society*, Vol. II, No. 2 (1985), 286–8.

128 Mooney, 'Father John Colgan', p. 17; 'St Anthony's College, Louvain', p. 31.

129 Peter Burke, *The Renaissance Sense of the Past* (London, 1970), p. 1.

130 Mooney, 'Father John Colgan', p. 29.

131 MS Bibliothèque Royale, Bruxelles, 2324–40, f.273b.

132 Ibid., f.273b.

133 In BR 2324–40, 226a, Ó Cléirígh mentions that his work is tedious but that the blame is to be put

on those who ordered him to follow the path of the old books, 'go ham a sgagtha' ('till the time of their sifting'). Is the sifting to be construed as Ó Cléirigh's own work? Or could this mean that Ó Cléirigh was to make no change at all until the transcribed materials were brought back to Louvain? His tendency to sidestep misconduct by those of O'Donnell stock in the Annals shows that Ó Cléirigh was not always a mere transcriber.

134 Breandán Ó Buachalla, '*Annála Ríoghachta Éireann is Foras Feasa ar Éirinn*: An Comhthéacs Comhaimseartha', *Studia Hibernica*, XXII - XXIII (1982-3) 59-105. This is a work of major importance, developing the views of Mooney, and placing Céitinn and Ó Cléirigh within the same international cultural context.

135 Cf. the following statements Céitinn makes about Stanihurst:

It is no marvel that Stanihurst should be without 'knowledge in this matter, since he had never seen the records of Ireland, from which he might have known her previous condition' (*An Díonbhrollach*, V, pp. 32-3, lines 16-18). 'Stanihurst also finds faults with the lawgivers of the country and with its physicians: although I wonder how he ventured to find fault with them, seeing that he understood neither of them, nor the languages in which the skill of either class found expression, he himself being ignorant and uninformed as regards the Gaelic, which was their language, and in which the legal decisions of the country and the (books of) medicine were written. For he was not capable of reading either the law of the land or the medicine in their own language, and if they had been read to him he had no comprehension of them ... it was not possible for him to form a judgement between the two aforesaid faculties, inasmuch as he never understood the books in which they were written, and did not even understand the doctors whose arts they were, because the Gaelic alone was their proper language, and he was out and out ignorant of it.' (*An Díonbhrollach*, V, pp. 38-9, lines 1-21).

'Understand, reader, that Stanihurst was under three deficiencies for writing the history of Ireland, on account of which he was not fit to regard himself as an historian ... The second defect, he was blindly ignorant in the language in which were the ancient records and transactions of the territory, and of every people who had inhabited it; and, therefore, he could not know these things.' (*An Díonbhrollach* V, pp. 40-3, lines 55-63). The above quotations are taken from David Comyn (ed.), *The History of Ireland by Geoffrey Keating*, ITS, Vol. IV (London, 1902).

136 Brendan Jennings (ed.), *Wadding Papers 1614-38* (Irish Manuscript Commission, Dublin, 1953), p. 544. For a modern assessment of Céitinn's credulity, cf. Donnchadh Ó Corráin, 'Seathrún Céitinn (*c*. 1580 - *c*. 1644): An cúlra Stairiúil', *Dúchas* (1983-84-85), pp. 63-4.

137 Brian Ó Cuív, 'An eighteenth-century account of Keating and his *Foras Feasa ar Éirinn*', *Éigse*, IX: Part IV (1960-1), 269.

138 *Historical Manuscripts Commission*, Rep 4, 1874, p. 603. Reference is made to a MS in 'Louvain: History of Ireland', in Irish, by Keating, with a date of 1636.

139 Myles Dillon, Canice Mooney OFM, Pádraig de Brún, *Catalogue of Irish Manuscripts in the Franciscan Library, Killiney* (Dublin, 1969), p. 27.

140 Bernadette Cunningham, 'Native culture and political change in Ireland, 1580-1640', *Natives and New-comers*, p. 167. Ms Cunningham has elaborated her argument in 'Seventeenth-century interpretations of the past: the case of Geoffrey Keating', *Irish Historical Studies*, XXV, 98 (1986), 116-28.

141 T. J. Dunne, 'The Gaelic response to conquest and colonisation: the evidence of the poetry', *Studia Hibernica*, XX (1980), 19.

142 Ó Buachalla, '*Annála Ríoghachta Éireann is Foras Feasa ar Éirinn*: an Comthéacs Comhaimseartha', pp. 79-80.

143 Colm Lennon, *Richard Stanihurst The Dubliner, 1547-1618*, pp. 117-28.

144 For Céitinn's secondary sources, see Anne Cronin, 'Sources of Keating's *Foras Feasa ar Éirinn*', *Éigse*, IV: Part IV, 235-79.

145 Cainneach Ó Maonaigh OFM, 'Franciscan Library MS A30.4', *The Irish Book Lover* (May 1940), p. 203.

146 Ó Buachalla, '*Annála Ríoghachta Éireann is Foras Feasa ar Éirinn*: an Comhthéacs Comhaimseartha', p. 94.

147 Ibid., p. 94.

148 Ibid., p. 94.

149 Alexander Boyle, 'Fearghal Ó Gadhra and the Four Masters', *Irish Ecclesiastical Record* (August 1963), pp. 112–13.

150 Ibid., pp. 109–10.

151 Fr. Aubrey Gwynn SJ, 'Archbishop Ussher and Father Brendan O'Connor', *Father Luke Wadding Commemorative Volume* (Dublin and London, 1957), pp. 270–2.

152 Ibid., p. 270. For recent research on Ussher's attitude to Gaelic culture, see J. Th. Leerson, 'Archbishop Ussher and Gaelic Culture', *Studia Hibernica*, XXII – XXIII (1982–3), 50–8.

153 Gwynn, 'Archbishop Ussher and Father Brendan O'Connor', p. 272.

154 Ó Cléirigh, *Aodh Mac Aingil agus an Scoil Nua-Ghaedhilge i Lobháin*, p. 27.

155 *Catalogue of Irish Manuscripts in the Franciscan Library, Killiney*, p. 26.

156 John O'Donovan (ed.), *Annála rioghachta Eireann: Annals of the Kingdom of Ireland by the Four Masters from the earliest period to the year 1616* (VII volumes, Dublin, 1851).

157 John O'Mahony (ed.), 'Foras Feasa ar Éirinn de réir an Athar Seathrun Ceiting, ollamh ré diadachta', *The History of Ireland, from the earliest period to the English invasion* (New York, 1866).

158 Tadhg Ó Dushláine, *An Eoraip agus Litríocht na Gaeilge 1600–1650* (Baile Átha Cliath, 1987). I am indebted to the author for his kindness in permitting me to read the proofs of this work.

CHAPTER V

TRADITION AND INNOVATION IN BRETON ORAL LITERATURE

by Donatien Laurent

THE accuracy of the term 'oral literature' has recently been questioned among French anthropologists. Some find it more appropriate to use a new term—ethnotext—which is, in fact, a wider one, since it refers to any text of ethnic interest, oral or written.[1] Rather than this new term which presupposes that the word 'literature' is strictly reserved to written material—and having regard to the privileged position in France of the Breton oral heritage—I prefer to keep to the expression 'oral literature' to deal with this body of orally transmitted texts, which will be the subject of this paper.

This term—*littérature orale* (oral literature)—was, as far as we know, concocted in the 1850s by one of the finest French writers of the time, George Sand, who knew what literature meant, and it is most likely that Breton folk poetry and tales were what she had in mind when she used this expression, as she was an enthusiastic admirer of La Villemarqué. I think it is, in fact, well suited to a traditional literature when we understand the word, as Marcel Mauss did when he wrote: 'Il y a littérature dès qu'il y a effort pour bien dire.' (Literature exists as soon as there is a quest for fine speech.) So I will use it in this sense.

Now, this quest for fine speaking presupposes a will to transmit, to pass on to younger generations; and this brings us back to the idea of tradition, the relation of which to oral literature we mean to define. Tradition in itself cannot stand, cannot exist, unless permanently renewed, readapted to fit in with the new interests of the people: tradition implies innovation, or at least renewal.

This being granted, before approaching the question of this twofold impulse in the field of Breton oral literature, one has to wonder whether one has grounds for trying to measure tradition and innovation in a matter about which nobody felt concerned until the beginning of the last century, which therefore was not committed to writing until a group of young, enthusiastic Breton aristocrats and gentlemen-farmers fell in love with it and, in the 1830s, decided to promote it out of its fostering milieu. In other words, are we entitled to judge tradition from a little more than one hundred years' observation? Are we not in danger of substituting hypothesis and extrapolation for lack of extant material?

An Ancient Literary Tradition

To this well-founded fear, one might answer first, that some of the roots of Breton oral literature stretch far back into the past. Professor Léon Fleuriot—who unfortunately will not attend our congresses any more and to whose memory I would like to dedicate this paper—has devoted much excellent and convincing work to this question of the sources of ancient Breton literary history, a theme which his assistant, Dr Y. B. Piriou, recapitulated some five years ago in his thesis on lost Breton literature.[2] They both collected, from every extant source of history and literature, elements which tend to restore the image of ancient Brittany as a land of rich literary tradition, a tradition which, we can presume, was for the greater part orally transmitted. To their works must be added all the concordant and conclusive arguments which have been provided by B. Merdrignac and B. Tanguy from their scrutiny of the 'Latin Lives' of Breton saints and of the ancient collections of charters, as well as from such valuable sources as toponymy and onomastics in general.[3]

In addition to these data one must keep in mind those parallel materials which can be found in other early texts coming from outside Brittany. Among them is the Irish tale, *Tromdam Guaire*, which tells how there came a time when none of the poets of Ireland could recite a complete version of the *Táin Bó Cuailnge*, and so they had to go abroad to Armorica (Letha) to find it, because it was the only place where the whole tale had been preserved. It is uncertain how far we can credit this text, but I think it is not unprofitable to refer to it in this context.

In addition, new research on ancient Brittany, carried out on both sides of the Channel, has brought to light a considerable amount of new material and knowledge in the last fifty years. It gives us a better idea of those Breton schools of learning, from which we still possess some 150 Latin MSS prior to the eleventh century, of which a hundred were written before the ninth century.

All these elements then concur to draw up an image of Celtic Brittany and of its society as a dynamic country, open to the rest of the world, having commercial relations with many partners in Europe.

Although it is, as yet, a debatable question for lack of conclusive evidence, it becomes more and more certain that Brittany played a central role in the composition and diffusion of the *Matière de Bretagne* and Arthurian tradition on the Continent. But why did no medieval Breton manuscript come down to us when we have, as we have seen, 150 Latin MSS prior to the eleventh century? This is an intricate question which is beyond the scope of this paper. It is enough for the moment to be able to assert that there has been a continuum in Breton literary tradition, which helps us to understand why we find in Breton oral tradition today literary themes and narratives which are still easily recognizable from the similarity of their roots to insular Celtic material. This will become clearer as we examine some of these oral texts.

Breton oral tradition falls into two main categories: narrative prose (tales, legends, memorates), and sung poetry (ballads, songs). In this short survey, I shall pass from one genre to another, since it is the content which matters. And I shall give more attention to sung poetry as it is easier to draw from it in order to observe the combined action of tradition and innovation in the transmission of the various texts.

1. Gwerz Skolan

I shall mention *Gwerz Skolan* (*The Ballad of Skolan*) only briefly, although it is one of the finest specimens we have of a poem obviously deep-rooted in ancient Brittonic poetry and still present today in the living tradition of Brittany. (I know of more than 30 original independent versions coming from various parts of Brittany.)[4] There is one version of this poem in the Black Book of Carmarthen:

> Du dy varch du dy capan,
> Du dy pen du du hunan,
> I adu ae ti yScolan?

to which the Breton verses seem to echo back:

> Du da varc'h ha du out-te
> Ken du hag an diaoul eo e voue,
> A blec'h e teues ha da blec'h hes-te?

I will not expatiate on this, though I wish to mention that a thorough study of these Breton versions gives a good illustration of the way these two opposite powers—tradition and innovation—exert influence on the poem, giving new strength to it and allowing it to remain alive after so many centuries. When analysed, Breton Skolan tradition falls into two different branches: one has stuck to the very archaic *englyn milwr* metre (three seven- (or eight-) syllable lines with one rhyme) and is also closer in tone and in colour to the Welsh poem in the Black Book of Carmarthen. The other branch had its metre displaced and transferred into a quatrain by adding a new line to the triplet, or rather singing the third line twice, so as to have a new melody with four lines—a type which had come to be more in favour than the old-fashioned three-lined melody. It is interesting to note the possible existence of a medieval French Skolan poem. There is, in Shrewsbury Library, a thirteenth-century list of Breton lays, in which can be found the item '*Luelan ly chler*'. I wonder whether it might not be a misreading by some copyist for '*Scolan ly cler*'—'Scolan the cleric'—in the transcription of the title?[5]

2. Gwerz Santez Enori

Another telling example is *Gwerz Santez Enori* (*The Ballad of Saint Enori*).[6] This, too, has evident parallels throughout pan-Celtic literary tradition: it tells about a king of Brest, *Roue Brest* (one version has *Roue Breiz*: the King of Brittany), who is slowly consumed by a big snake coiled up around him. And the only cure would be the virgin breast of a king's daughter (*bron werc'h merc'h eur roue*). Now he has three daughters, and he asks each of them in turn to deliver him. Only the last one, whom he had dismissed and disinherited, agrees. She has not uncovered her breast, when the snake leaves her father and fastens itself on to her breast which is cut off. A gold one is substituted for it by an angel. Then she marries a king of Goelo and the story goes on with the tale of the calumniated wife and the wicked mother-in-law. She is driven away over the sea and lands on the Irish shore, where she finds shelter in a monastery with her new-born child Beuzek (i.e. 'drowned'). Her husband, who had been searching for her for seven years, at last lands in Ireland and hears of her from fishermen who often come to visit her.

This story had already appeared in a Latin prose text of the fifteenth century, *Chronique de Saint-Brieuc*, but with only one daughter to the King of Brest, and it is a cruel stepmother who calumniates her and not a mother-in-law.[7] It is obviously related to the thirteenth-century French romance, *Livre de Carados*, an interpolation in the First Continuation of Chrétien de Troyes' *Conte del Graal*, where the heroine, named Guinor, sacrifices herself for her lover, the Breton king, Caradoc of Vannes, by relieving him of a serpent. Two other short thirteenth-century French romances about Caradoc's wife, who is portrayed as a model of chastity and fidelity, complete the story. Although the tale as a whole has not been preserved in a Welsh form, several references to Tegau Eurvron (Tegau Gold Breast), wife of Caradawc Vreich Vras (Caradawc Big Arm), in the *Trioedd Ynys Prydein*, as well as allusions in the works of fourteenth-century Welsh poets, bear witness to the existence of the tale in medieval Wales; while a thirteenth-century English lyric, *Annot and Johon*, attests a still more widespread extension, which is corroborated by two English ballads, 'The Boy and the Mantle' and 'The Queen of Scotland' (Child, nos. 29 and 301). To complete the survey, one should mention two versions of a Gaelic tale, the latter having been collected as late as 1974 by D. A. MacDonald and A. Bruford and published in 1978 in the journal *Tocher*, under the title 'The Weatherwise Mariner'. It is a long tale, obviously belonging to the same narrative set, where the snake coiling up round the hero's neck was, initially, a shirt given to him by his cruel stepmother, a detail which seems to point to the Greek legend of Nessus' shirt draining away Heracles' life.

Here again, Breton oral tradition under its double form—the fifteenth-century Latin prose version and the modern religious ballad of Saint Enori—is connected with old narratives, which apparently never extended beyond Celtic borders. (I could not find traces of anything of the kind in any catalogue of international folk-tales, and the Stith Thomson Motive Index of folk literature points only to these Celtic items I have mentioned.) The lesser role played in it by innovation is to be explained by the fact that it is a religious legend, which never lost touch with written ecclesiastical tracts or teaching. It is all the more interesting to compare the ten or twelve oral versions that have been collected, as they show noticeable variants.

3. Merlin

As a transition between sung folk poetry and prose, the Merlin legend in Breton oral literature requires a mention. The material here again appears in a twofold form, both poetry and prose, the former being better preserved than the latter. We only have one extant version of it, collected by La Villemarqué in 1837—a long Breton poem of 300 lines, which I presented in our Penzance Congress in 1975, as it appears in the original manuscript—whereas the prose tale, still surviving in scattered versions on both sides of the linguistic border line, in Breton and in French, reveals a sturdy capacity to survive.[8] With reference to the recent restatement of the Merlin Celtic material by Count Nikolay Tolstoy (*Studia Celtica*, 1983, pp. 11–29 : 'Merlinus redivivus'), the Breton material offers interesting elements which, unfortunately, I have no time to discuss here.

4. Ar boudenn wi (The Egg-shell)

Now I should like to come to a short prose narrative with rhymed formulas, which this time shows a widespread diffusion throughout northern Europe. We are here more in the field of beliefs than that of literature, properly speaking; but it is worth having a look at it in this context of tradition and innovation with which we are dealing at present.

It tells the story of the changeling which a woman finds in place of her seven-month child, which she had left alone for a while in a cradle. At first, she did not discover the trick, but after some time had passed by, the child did not grow at all. She questioned the parish priest, who told her to go back home and take an egg-shell (*boudenn wi, pluskenn wi*) and ten acorn-cups, and to fill them with soup, as if she meant to prepare dinner for ten reapers, and then listen to what the child would say. If he began to speak, she would have to seize a whip and spank him. So she did all this and, when she had the soup prepared in the egg-shell, she heard the changeling exclaim:

> Gwelet meus traou en tu all d'ar mor:
> Gwelet meus stered 'rôg 'ma bet gwelet loar,
> Gwelet meus 'n wi 'rôg 'ma bet gwelet yar,
> Gwelet meus sanket mez ba'n douar
> Rôg 'ma bet gwelet wenn zerw hag uhelvar
> Med meus ket bet gwelet biskoaz o'r zoubenn 'n eur boudenn wi!

> I have seen things on the other side of the sea:
> I have seen stars before seeing the moon,
> I have seen the egg before seeing the hen,
> I have seen planting an acorn in earth
> Before seeing oak and mistletoe
> But never did I see soup prepared in an egg-shell!

This tale I collected three weeks ago from a woman from Riec, near Quimperlé, who had learned it from her illiterate grandmother, born in 1876. It is very similar to a Welsh tale, which was published in 1830 in the *Cambrian Quarterly Magazine*, where the little rhyme of the changeling runs in exactly the same way:

> Gwelais mesen cyn gweled derwen,
> Gwelais wy cyn gweled iâr,
> Erioed ni welais ferwi bwyd i fedel
> Mewn plisgyn wy iâr.

> I have seen the acorn before seeing the oak,
> I have seen the egg before seeing the hen,
> Never did I see food being boiled for the reapers
> in the shell of a hen's egg.

This tale is known from Ireland, Scotland, the Isle of Man, Wales, and England, through to Brittany, Northern, Western and Central France, Belgium, and Switzerland, but it looks as if it focused on Brittany and Wales, the two countries that yielded the largest number of versions and the most complete.[9] It is, therefore, worth noting that we find the same comparison of the oak and the acorn in the *Vita Merlini* to assert age and experience, just as in this changeling story:

> ... In this wood stands a very old oak and I saw the fall of the acorn from which it came, so I have lived a long time!

Here again, it is the reliability of the tradition which is striking, and the innovation—which exists—lies more in the multiplicity of variants assumed by the narrative than in a real change in form, structure, or sense.

5. *Ar Falc'hon* (*The Falcon*)

I shall now turn to my last example, which never extended beyond Brittany, because of its purely local interest. It is a rebel song, which was collected in 1840 by Théodore de La Villemarqué from an old maker of wooden shoes, a man of the woods who had gone underground during the French Revolution and taken part in the fight against the revolutionaries. He gave this song to La Villemarqué as one of those they used to sing when gathered in the woods during the 1790s. Internal analysis reveals, however, a much earlier dating—three centuries before, and probably much further back for the first part of it. It goes like this:

Taget ar yar gant ar falc'hon,	The falcon strangled the hen,
Gant ar gouerez lazet ar c'hont,	The country woman killed the Count,
Lazet ar c'hont, gwasket an dud,	The Count killed, oppression came
An dud paour evel loened mud . . .	On the poor people as on brute beasts . . .
Gwasket an dud ha savet kroz:	People oppressed, a revolt aroused:
Savet yaouank ha savet koz,	Young and old, everybody rose up,
War marw eur yar hag eur falc'hon	For a hen killed and a falcon
Breiz e gwad, e tan hag e kaon!	Was Brittany in blood, in fire and in mourning!

Then the text focuses on a group of thirty country people, men and women, gathered round a fire in the mountains on Saint John's Eve, in revolt against a very heavy tax that had been laid upon them. They decide to go down the mountain to destroy the residence of the tax-collectors, the party increasing as they progress from fire to fire. From 30, they increase to 300, and when they get to Stang Rohan, their objective, they number 30,500. They then decide to pile up 30 cartloads of dry furze and set fire to it.[10]

This is a most enlightening piece to dissect for anyone interested in the composition, transmission, and evolution of this type of folk poetry. The first two verses (this enigmatic allusion to a falcon strangling a hen) refer in fact to an eleventh-century event, of which we learn from two Latin chronicles: the death of Geoffrey, Count of Rennes, from a stone thrown at him by a furious woman, whose hen had been killed by his falcon. But the other verses, from the third onwards, refer to a peasant revolt, which broke out at the very end of the fifteenth century, during the last years of Breton independence. The droll side of the situation was that this composite song, inspired by two peasant revolts against lords and landowners, was taken up by these countrymen, who were rebelling against the patriots who were supposed to bring them freedom!

It can be seen from this last example how a song is composed about an actual event and passed down from generation to generation in order to keep alive the memory of this event, with all the emotive charge and excitement it carries with it. And how it will remain in vogue as long as it retains its function as keeper of the memory of the community and guardian of its truth. For this is what makes these songs valuable for the people: they are true. La Villemarqué made this observation in 1845: when a singer wants to praise a song, whatever it is, he does not say: 'That's beautiful!', he says: 'That's true!'

Breton Folk Poetry and Breton Medieval Lays

It is remarkable to note that these two functions of this part of Breton folk poetry—that is, retaining the memory and telling the truth—are precisely the definition given to the Breton lays by those who composed or transmitted them. They all agree on that, and they insist on this double function:

> These tales they take to be true
> The Bretons who made the lay . . .
> > (Tydorel)

> Of a lay I will tell the adventure,
> Truth is what I will tell . . .
> > (Guingamor)

> The old courteous Bretons
> Made the lay to remember,
> So that nobody should forget . . .
> > (Eliduc)

> For the words to remember
> Tristan made a lay of it . . .
> > (Chèvrefeuille)

> The Bretons of Brittany
> Once by prowess used to make lays
> From the adventures they saw
> So that they should not be forgotten . . .
> > (Equitan)

I think we can take it for certain that this oral, narrative, Breton folk poetry represents the exact extension of the Breton medieval lays, as if the thread of tradition had never been broken. It is, in fact, probable that at least two of these *gwerziou* we can hear today in Breton living tradition are Breton medieval lays that never fell into decay: one is *Gwerz Skolan*, which I mentioned at the beginning of this paper; the other is *Gwerz an Aotrou Nann* (The Ballad of Lord Nann), the adventure of a nobleman who met a fairy and had to choose 'either to marry her, or to die in three days, or to lie sick in bed for seven years'. This ballad seems to have made a big impression in its time, as it spread all over Europe in oral tradition, from Brittany to Denmark, and Scotland to Spain—all through the area where Breton medieval lays appear to have extended.[11] And this, added to various arguments afforded by internal evidence and comparison of the different linguistic traditions, tends to confirm the view that the nucleus of the ballad was formed in Brittany, although it is still a debatable question, for lack of any medieval text in any language.

To conclude and gather up all our threads, from this quick survey of Breton oral literature, I would like to draw three ideas. First, of these two opposite and complementary powers influencing the content of tradition, namely conservation and innovation, the former is pre-eminent: it ensures the cohesion of the content and the permanence and durability of the ideas belonging to the social group. And we have seen that conservation works, with rather impressive results, so that in a sense we might even credit it with more confidence, give more credence to it than to written evidence, in so far as it is life opposed to fixity. It is enough to compare the emotion emerging from the singing of *Ar falc'hon* with that arising from the fifteenth-century chronicle, not to mention the fact that one comes in direct line from the rebels themselves, transmitted to us through people who were careful to serve truth, even if it was their truth and not necessarily historical, factual truth; the other—the chronicle—being written by one man, a learned one, was obviously more inclined to be in sympathy with law and order.

Secondly, if tradition holds so firm, if conservation is at times so impressive, it is because memory is its foundation-stone, a memory which is put into practice all the more as writing is more restricted, more limited in use. And it is noteworthy that this well-tried instrument, adjusted and perfected for centuries (let us think of Homer, of Greek archaic tradition with the Muses, daughters of Mnemosyne, goddess of memory, of the Breton *cantores historici* mentioned by Giraldus Cambrensis . . .) is still active in Brittany and even sprouting new growths—an aspect which, for lack of time, I have not been able to present to you in this article.

Thirdly, this durability, this permanence, of Breton oral tradition presupposes some sort of innovation. To quote J. M. Guilcher: 'La tradition non écrite est invention autant que mémoire' (unwritten tradition is as much invention as memory), in so far as it has to move to fit with the slow but unstoppable evolution of man's mentality.[12]

Breton oral tradition never stopped borrowing new words, new themes, new narratives, new melodies, which were either welcomed or finally rejected through a kind of natural process as they strengthened, settled more firmly the image of tradition, or, on the contrary, opposed it and questioned it. I borrow this Welsh proverb, quoted before on a similar occasion by Professor Proinsias Mac Cana, which sums up exactly the attitude of the Bretons towards tradition and innovation:

> Na ro' goel i newyddion oni bônt yn hen,

or to tell it in our own words:

> Newentio n'int mad da vann 'med pa int deut war gosaat,

which could be translated: 'Innovation is not a good thing except when it becomes tradition'!

Notes

1 J. C. Bouvier, *Tradition orale et identité culturelle* (Paris, CNRS, 1980).

2 L. Fleuriot, *Histoire littéraire et culturelle de la Bretagne* (Paris-Genève, Champion-Slatkine, 1988), I, pp. 7–28: 'Langue et société dans la Bretagne ancienne'; pp. 97–138: 'Histoires et légendes—lais et romans bretons'; pp. 153–72: 'Prophéties, navigations et thèmes divers'. Y. B. Piriou, *Contribution à l'histoire de la littérature bretonne perdue* (Université de Haute-Bretagne, 1982).

3 B. Merdrignac, *Recherches sur l'hagiographie armoricaine du VIème au XVème siècle* (2 vol., St Malo, 1985-6). B. Tanguy, *Les noms de lieux bretons* (Studi no. 3, Rennes, 1975). B. Tanguy, *L'hagio-onomastique bretonne* (107ème Congrès des Sociétés Savantes, Paris, 1984), II, pp. 323–40.

4 D. Laurent, 'La Gwerz de Skolan et la légende de Merlin', *Ethnologie Française*, I (1971), pp. 19–54. A. O. H. Jarman, 'Cerdd Ysgolan', *Ysgrifau Beirniadol*, X, pp. 51–78.

5 G. E. Brereton, 'A XIIIth-century list of French lays', *Modern Language Review*, XLV (1950), pp. 40–5. The author reads *Luelan lychlez* and proposes to rectify *ly chler*, an abbreviation for *ly ch(eva)l(i)er*. *Ly clerz* would be a better approximation, reminding us of the Welsh and Breton qualification of Scolan: W. *ysgolheic*, B. *kloarek*. For *chl-* = *cl-*, see *chlas* = *clas*, *chlice* = *clice* (Godefroy, *Dict. de l'ancienne langue française du IXe au XVe siècle*).

6 Y. B. Piriou, op. cit., pp. 381–405. D. Laurent, 'Enori et le Roi de Brest' in *Études sur la Bretagne et les Pays Celtiques* (Brest, CRBC, 1987), pp. 207–24. B. Tanguy, 'Le Roi de Brest' in *Études sur la Bretagne et les Pays Celtiques*, pp. 463–76. G. le Menn, 'La femme au sein d'or', *Skol-Dastum*, 1985.

7 'La légende de saint Budoc et de sainte Azénor', *Mém. de la Société d'Emulation des Côtes-du-Nord* (1866), pp. 240–8. Cf. R. Bromwich *Trioedd Ynys Prydein* (Cardiff, 1961), pp. 299–300 (Caradawc Vreichvras); pp. 512–14 (Tegau Eurvron).

8 P. Delarue et M. L. Teneze, *Le Conte populaire français*, II, pp. 221–7; Conte-type 502: 'L'homme sauvage'.

9 La Villemarqué, 'Ar bugel laec'hiet (L'enfant supposé)', *Barzaz-Breiz*, pp. 31–4. J. Rhys, *Celtic Folklore*, I, pp. 62, 259, 268–9. E. Legros, 'Trois récits de lutins et fées dans le folklore wallon', *Enquêtes du Musée de la vie wallone*, VI (Liège, 1952), pp. 129–227.

10 La Villemarqué, 'Ar Falc'hon (Le Faucon)', *Barzaz-Breiz*, pp. 130–4. D. Laurent, 'La Villemarqué et le Barzaz-Breiz: Ar Falc'hon', *Bull. de la Société archéologique du Finistère*, 1977, pp. 333–49.

11 F. J. Child, *The English and Scottish Popular Ballads*, I, 42, pp. 371–89 (Clerk Colvill).

12 J. M. Guilcher, 'Conservation et renouvellement dans la culture paysanne ancienne de Basse-Bretagne', *Arts et traditions populaires*, XV (janvier-mars, 1967), pp. 1–18.

CHAPTER VI

ARCHITECTURE IN WALES DURING THE RENAISSANCE

by Peter Smith

WHEN I was honoured by the invitation to address this Congress on the subject of architecture in Wales at the time of the Renaissance, I began to ask myself what the Renaissance was, and above all when it was. And as I pondered, I came to the conclusion that it can mean many different things to different people and that it has a very elastic time-scale. To the musician it means the music of the sixteenth century. It does not mean the revival of Greek or Roman music because no one knew, then or now, what Greek or Roman music sounded like. To the man of letters the Renaissance means the rediscovery of ancient texts and standards, and above all the rediscovery of Roman and Greek literature, and it dates, as Professor Glanmor Williams has reminded us, back to the fifteenth or even the fourteenth century. To the architect, however, it means first and foremost the rediscovery of the orders of *Roman* architecture, and the Greeks do not come into the picture. Indeed it is one of the paradoxes of the Renaissance that while the discovery of Greek literature marked its beginning, the discovery of Greek architecture marked its end. It was the *Greek* Revival about the time of the French Revolution that marked the end of the *Roman* Renaissance. The Renaissance is thus a very movable feast, and has a very movable time-scale; as we journey from Italy to England, and as we turn from literature to architecture, we travel from the fourteenth century to the eighteenth. For it was only after the Restoration and the Fire of London that the kingdom of England began to acquire in significant quantities buildings which the great Italian architects of the fifteenth and sixteenth centuries would have recognized as reflecting their ideas, and not really until the eighteenth century that our churches and country houses began to measure up to the standards of Bramante, Sangallo, and above all Palladio, whose own masterpieces date from the fifteenth and early sixteenth centuries, two hundred years earlier.

This chapter will, therefore, necessarily cover a long period in the hope that I shall cover the Renaissance as understood by as wide a segment of my listeners as possible, the architects as well as musicians and men of letters. I shall call it 'Welsh architecture during the Renaissance' rather than 'Welsh architecture of the Renaissance' because, of the architecture erected during the period of the *literary* Renaissance, i.e. the sixteenth century, comparatively little was directly inspired by the Renaissance as architects understand the term. We begin by looking at the architectural situation in Wales and in the British Isles as a whole when the bright sun of Italy was slowly beginning to illuminate Europe's grey northern shores, shall we say at the time of the Tudor seizure of power.

The historic architecture of the British Isles is characterized by the way it changes first in response to the agricultural conditions resulting from the terrain and climate and secondly in response to its distance from the Court and the centre of government in metropolitan England. Both factors can be related to an evolutionary time-scale in which ideas manifest themselves first in the south-east and appear only later in the north-west. One of the many striking contrasts which can be related to this model is evident by the accesssion of the Tudors, that between those regions to the south-east, where the usual proprietor's dwelling was likely to be a large hall-house, and those regions to the north-west, where it was much more likely to be either a first-floor hall or a tower. The hall-house zone consisted of England south of the Tees and most of Wales but not Pembrokeshire, with Glamorgan a 'grey area'. The tower-house zone consisted of the rest, the five (historic) northern counties of England, and Pembrokeshire, Scotland and Ireland (Fig. 1).

The tower-house seems to be a direct descendant of those fortified structures which had formed the dwellings of upper classes since the Normans had introduced the motte into these islands. As it represents an archaic type of building which the firm rule of the Tudors was to make obsolete in much of their kingdom, a type dating back to the early Middle Ages, it is one that might be considered first. Although more than liberally endowed with large castles, Wales itself offers only limited opportunities for the study of the tower-house. However, the Old Rectory at Angle (Pembs.) incorporates all the classic features, that is the primary accommodation at the first floor reached by an outside doorway at this level, a vaulted undercroft, a chamber over the hall and an embattled wall-walk at roof level. Another Pembrokeshire house with some of the characteristics of a tower is Eastington (Rhoscrowther, Pembs.), which again has the main accommodation at the first floor over a vaulted undercroft, the entry at first-floor level, and a castellated wall-walk. Closely related to the tower-house is the first-floor hall, again well represented in Pembrokeshire by Bishop Gower's Palace at St Davids, built just as the first stirrings of the Renaissance were being felt in Italy, and on a much smaller scale by Llandeilo Abercywyn (Carms.), which Major Francis Jones suggests could have been built as late as about 1500. A cross-section drawn through Llandeilo Abercywyn produces a building remarkably similar to Harold's hall at Bosham illustrated in the Bayeux Tapestry. The tower is represented in Glamorgan also, in Candleston Castle which has all the indicia of a small fortified dwelling including the remains of a castellated barmkin wall. This county also has some good first-floor halls, conspicuously Llanmihangel Place, mainly sixteenth century (Pl. 1), and Garnllwyd (Llancarfan). But when all the Welsh examples including the four clear instances in north Wales have been gathered together, they form but a small company compared with those to be found in Scotland and Ireland where any one of the richer Scottish and Irish counties will be found to contain more towers and first-floor halls than can be found in the entire Principality. It is evident also that they continued to be built in those countries until well on into the seventeenth century. For the Scottish laird and the Irish chieftain the tower-house formed the normal dwelling throughout the early Renaissance period, a reflection of the strength of the fortified-house tradition and the conservatism of the society which sustained it.

In contrast with the tower-house is the hall-house, the horizontally proportioned building where the central feature, the hall, stood at ground level. While halls could be (and often were) incorporated into fortified buildings, unlike the tower-house there is nothing inherently defensive about the hall-house itself. The larger halls have an unmistakable outline, H- or U-shaped in plan, the hall flanked by storeyed cross-wings (Pl. 2) while the smaller ones are in the form of an L (hall and single-storeyed cross-wing) or a simple rectangle (Pl. 3). Within the general area where the hall-houses are common are two regions which are characterized not only by the great halls of the proprietors but also by numerous halls of a class of rich tenant farmers. Such dwellings survive in large numbers in the area south-east of the limestone belt—Essex, Suffolk, Sussex and Kent, the wealth of whose yeomen has passed into legend—and also in the west Midlands, particularly the counties of Hereford, Worcester and Shropshire. This west-Midland wealth of early, quality rural architecture clearly extends into Wales, such that each of the Welsh border counties is endowed with quantities of early farmhouse hall-houses in a way the western counties of Wales and Glamorgan are not.

It is important to remember that the hall of the tenant farmer resembled that of a great landowner in all its essentials. The large, open room, with its entry by a cross-passage at one end and its dais partition against which the occupier and his family sat at the other, reflected a society in which gradations of rank were of paramount importance. It should be emphasized that a Welsh farmer's son, reared in such a hall and later completing his education at the university, would have found the arrangements in his college hall completely familiar: the fellows sitting at the high-table looking towards the undergraduates in the body of the hall, just as he and his family would have sat with their backs to the dais partition looking towards the household servants and the cross-passage beyond (Figs. 3–4).

It has not, so far, proved possible to find examples of these stately pre-Reformation hall-houses of the tenant farmers, witnesses to a now long-vanished and essentially aristocratic life-style, among the peasant houses of the other Celtic countries of the west, or indeed anywhere else in western Europe except southern and midland England of whose material culture eastern Wales is essentially a continuation. In our Anglo-centric fashion we tend to think of the south-eastern pattern being the norm, and the north-western the exception. But I wonder. A short while ago I made a tour of Normandy. All the houses of the *noblesse* built before the accession of Louis XIV appeared to be either tower-houses or tower-house derivatives. They were certainly not hall-houses. Neither were the farmhouses hall-houses as far as I could tell.

In a short chapter it is not possible to deal in great detail with all the characteristics of the hall-house. One fact to remember is that some may have been long-houses incorporating a byre at their entry end, and divided by an open partition so that the householder could see his tethered beasts from where he sat at his high table. But not all Welsh hall-houses were so designed, and some quite small halls must have housed their cattle separately (Pl. 3). Another striking feature would have been the roof, often ornamented with arch-braces and cusping. A strking feature of the Welsh scene is the way in which such ornamental roof features are found mainly to the north-east of a line drawn from Machynlleth to Abergavenny.

Three early types of roof-truss are known in Welsh domestic work, that is the simple A-frame, the cruck frame mainly found in the north-eastern half of Wales and the much less common aisle-truss and hammer-beam which are concentrated exclusively in the north-eastern half of the country. The hammer-beam is also characteristic of churches in the same area (Pl. 5).

How these remarkable distribution patterns arose is far from certain, but it is worth recalling first the evidence of place-names (not inappropriate in a conference largely devoted to philology!). A place-name map of Wales shows a scatter of English place-names, first along Offa's Dyke, and secondly, along the southern coast, which reminds us that Wales has not only a land frontier, but also a sea frontier with England. The influences which would have reached Wales by the first are very different from those which reached it by the second. Offa's Dyke separates borderland Wales from regions of England famous for their half-timbered buildings and ornate carpentry. The Bristol Channel separates Wales from an area of stone and earth-building, from a country of jointed rather than full crucks, from a country where aisled building is hardly known. In our search for origins it is also worth turning our attention to an event dated well before the beginning of the Renaissance (even by the earliest possible computation) and that is the overthrow by Edward I of the Princes of Gwynedd. The castles which Edward I constructed to consolidate his newly occupied territory are amongst the best-documented buildings we have and, thanks to the researches of Dr A. J. Taylor, we know far more about how much they cost, the architects who designed them, and the workmen who built them than many much later structures. We know that the tradesmen who built the castles of north Wales were recruited mainly from the Midland counties of England, and that they reached north Wales via Chester, while the workmen who built the castles of south Wales were recruited mainly from the Dumnonian peninsula and sailed from Bristol. Thus evidence as varied as place-names and medieval building accounts both point to close links between north Wales and the English Midlands and between south Wales and Devon and Somerset, which all studies of later architecture tend to confirm.

The strength of such links is well illustrated if we turn our attention to the architecture of the Welsh parish churches. The structure of those Welsh parish churches which are not Victorian dates, like the Welsh hall-houses, mainly from the last half-century or so before the Reformation and belongs therefore to the period of the early Renaissance. The fact that St John's Church, Cardiff, would not look out of place in a Somerset village was pointed out long ago by Sir Cyril Fox. Perhaps less well known is the great popularity of the barrel (or wagon) roof in south Wales, when a curved, panelled ceiling encloses the nave, a type that is also very popular in the west of England. Such ceilings are practically unknown over the naves in north Wales as a general roof covering, for the characteristic boarded canopy of honour over the altar rarely extends beyond the chancel in north Wales. Instead, the historic nave roof in north Wales is usually a heavily bayed structure, the trusses arch-braced with cusped apexes and wind-braces, the whole easily visible to the congregation below. The churches of Buttington (Monts.) and Llandyfalle (Brecs.) are not far from each other. The open cusped trusses of the first are in complete contrast to the barrel ceiling of the second (Pl. 4). Thus, in the mountains of mid-Wales, the carpentry style of Shropshire might be said to confront the carpentry style of Somerset. But perhaps the most remarkable of all Welsh parish church roofs are the hammer-beam roofs of the early sixteenth century. These occur extensively in north Wales but not at all in the churches of the south (Pl. 5). Other localized features of ecclesiastical architecture which characterized the Renaissance period are wooden porches (again confined to the area north-east of the diagonal Newport-Machynlleth division) and framed bell-towers which are essentially borderland. In contrast are stone vaults found mainly in the south with a major concentration in Pembrokeshire.

The Reformation marked the end of a great era of church building and, for a century or longer, architectural activity in the ecclesiastical sphere was largely limited to minor modifications or small additions—porches, lich-gates and family chapels, while rood-screens which were such a feature of the immediate pre-Reformation church ceased to be built. To this generalization there is one significant exception, and that is the very ambitious rebuilding of the nave of Llanidloes in 1542—arguably the first Protestant church in Wales—utilizing piers filched from the now ruined Abbey Cwm-hir to support a magnificent hammer-beam roof (Pl. 5). New church structures remained almost as Gothic as the nave at Llanidloes until after the Restoration. There is little indication of the Roman Renaissance about either of the additions to the parish church of Llanddwywe (Mer.), that is, the porch dated 1595 and the Vaughan Chapel dated 1616 (Pl. 8). The Gwydir Chapel, with its cusped window tracery, added to Llanrwst Church in 1633–4, is another remarkable monument to the survival of Gothic architecture in the seventeenth century, even though the memorial to the Gwydir family which it houses is Renaissance in inspiration (Pl. 6). The nearby Wynn Chapel above Gwydir, just across the Conwy, built as late as 1673, has simplified Gothic tracery in its shaped windows. It was not until the eighteenth century that churches in the classical style began to appear in the Welsh countryside, as illustrated by the parish church of March-wiel (Denbs.) or the now vanished classical temple which was built within the then ruined walls of Llandaff cathedral.

Before the eighteenth century, the impact of the Roman Renaissance on Welsh church architecture was minimal, with the one important exception of funerary monuments and memorials. In this field alone, the new style gained ground fast. One has only to compare the late Gothic of the Herbert tombs in Abergavenny Priory with the monument nearby to William Baker to see the transformation (Pl. 7). By the later sixteenth century there can be no doubt that the Roman Renaissance was the principal inspiration for funerary monuments such as the Humphrey Lloyd monument in Whitchurch, Denbigh, the Herbert monument in Montgomery (Pl. 7), that to the Vaughans in Llanddwywe (Pl. 9), or to the Bassetts and Mansels in Llantriddyd, or the Mansel tombs in Margam. These illustrations of the Roman classical style decorated the Gothic walls of our parish churches a century or more before the new style became an acceptable form of expression for the churches themselves.

But beyond the erection of memorials and family chapels the Reformation signalled a great reduction in church building, while Protestant theology discouraged expenditure on elaborate church fittings such as screens, which had been such a feature of early sixteenth-century church building.

In the domestic field, however, the Reformation did not mean any reduction of building activity. The accession of Elizabeth I—surely the greatest of all English Renaissance princes—was followed by a veritable outburst of building. This was characterized by the replacement of the medieval hall-house by the sub-medieval storeyed house as the normal dwelling of the prosperous farmer. The replacement of the hall by the sub-medieval storeyed house well illustrates the argument that phases of building which occur first in the south-east are repeated, but a generation or so later, in the north-west. The change-over to the storeyed house as the house of the typical farmer is apparent in southern England by about 1570. But it is not evident in the five northern counties of England before 1650 (Fig. 2). Eastern Wales and Glamorgan come close to the southern and Midland English timetable, while storeyed farmhouses were certainly being built in west Wales before the end of the sixteenth century. However, while in eastern Wales and Glamorgan the storeyed house rapidly became the norm for the average farmer, in the west and certainly in Snowdonia, these storeyed houses appear confined to the upper echelons among the farmers, men who could claim a measure of gentry status, while the poorer peasants continued to live in single-storeyed cottages, as they certainly did in Scotland and Ireland until at least the middle years of the nineteenth century (Fig. 2).

The new, storeyed houses, built on two floors, had of necessity to incorporate enclosed fireplaces in place of the open hearth which had previously sufficed to heat most hall-houses. It was the choice of site for the fireplace, designed to heat the now ceiled-over hall which was a decisive factor in the development of the plan (Pls. 10–11, Figs. 5–6). The most conservative was the lateral position, placing the fireplace on one of the long walls of the hall so that it interfered with neither of the traditional elements of the medieval hall interior; the cross-passage and the high table remained as before, the focal points of the room. A very good example is to be found at Plasnewydd (Llanfair Talhaearn, Denbs.), happily dated 1583 by an inscription on an exceptionally fine and still intact dais partition. The second fireplace position was on a cross wall so that it separated the hall from the passage but left the passage intact (Pl. 11). This is well illustrated by Trewalter (Llan-gors, Brecs.), again happily dated by inscription to 1653. This form of plan also characterized most long-houses of the storeyed phase of building; in these, the cross-passage had effectively been transferred from the house to the adjoining byre. The third in the series is the lobby-entry house (Pl. 11), where the fireplace stands, not against the passage, but actually in it, so the house is entered by a small lobby. This must be regarded as typologically the latest in the sub-medieval series, as one of the two key features of the hall-house, the passage, has disappeared. In our final type, the 'direct-entry', end-chimney, cross-passage house, it is the other end of the hall, the dais end which has been lost and replaced by a fireplace, which instead of the dais partition became the focal point of the hall (Pl. 10).

The numbers of the various types of sub-medieval house, built in the period 1560–1760, which housed most of the gentry and a large proportion of the more substantial tenant farmers, varied from region to region (Figs. 5–6). The earliest lateral-chimney type tends to have a peripheral distribution, exceptionally well represented in Denbighshire and Flintshire and Pembrokeshire. Elsewhere, in Anglesey, Caernarfonshire, and Merioneth, as well as in Glamorgan and Monmouthshire, this form of plan tends to be confined to the upper ranks of society. The second type, the 'hearth-passage type', having the fireplace between the hall and the passage, whether as a long-house or a free-standing dwelling, was favoured by the tenant farmers in south Wales outside Pembrokeshire. Glamorgan, Monmouthshire, and Breconshire all have exceptional numbers of houses of this type of plan. The third and, we think, the most developed type, the lobby-entry house, is, in contrast, the favoured form in the Severn Valley, eastern Merioneth, and south Denbighshire. Our final, direct-entry, end-chimney type appears to have been the earliest and commonest form of substantial farmhouse in north-west Wales, and is probably well represented in south-west Wales as well. I should like to pause for a moment in front of one such direct-entry house, Plas-du (Llanarmon, Caerns.), illustrated on Plate 10, because it was the home of a family celebrated in the history of both the Reformation and the Renaissance. It was the birthplace of John Owen, in his day more famous than Shakespeare. His Latin epigrams enjoyed a European reputation. Although born in a moderate-sized farmhouse in Caernarfonshire, he was educated at Winchester, and became headmaster of Warwick. The mere fact that a Llŷn squireen's son could be sent to Winchester to school shows us that travel in Renaissance Wales was perhaps not as difficult as the state of the roads would lead us to imagine. It also illustrates that Renaissance Wales was the scene of much 'upward mobility', as the sons of tenant farmers and minor gentry furnished with a good public school and Oxbridge education could attain high office in both Church and State. Another good instance of the process might also be illustrated by another Caernarfonshire storeyed, direct-entry house, Tŷ-mawr (Pl. 10), Gwibernant. The son of Tŷ-mawr was William Morgan, Bishop of St Asaph, who won undying fame as the first translator of the entire Bible into Welsh.

While the small hall-houses are generally confined to eastern Wales, their successors, the sub-medieval storeyed houses, are to be found right across the country, and in very large numbers in some areas, conspicuously so in Glamorgan. While it is easy to find English parallels for them, it is very difficult to find comparable farmhouses of this date in Scotland and Ireland. I think they are buildings of great significance in terms of social history as they point to the existence of a large, and quite well-to-do, rural middle class who could afford to build substantial homes. One has the general impression that not only has Welsh a richer literature than Gaelic, but also that it has so far survived more successfully. I do not think you can now hear Gaelic spoken as the natural and first language of the people (as against the consciously cultivated language of patriots and scholars) except in the western extremities of Ireland, and you cannot hear it on the Scottish mainland at all. At least you do not have to go as far as Anglesey to hear Welsh spoken naturally as the language of the people. This greater resilience of Welsh is usually attributed to religious factors, and to the determination of the Elizabethan government that, whatever language might be used to administer Wales, the people must receive their religious instruction in a language they could understand. I think the *social* factor is no less important and that it is the presence of a well-to-do middle class, of whose existence these storeyed farm-houses of the Renaissance period are tangible proof, which provided the essential basis of a thriving literary culture, without which languages wither and die (Pls. 10–11).

So far this talk has been entitled 'Architecture in Wales during the Renaissance'. I can, at this point, revert to my original title which was 'Welsh Renaissance Architecture'. Years ago, as a young Investigator, I used to travel with a senior colleague who often took rather a long time to explain to a householder why we were knocking on his door. 'I am coming to the point in a minute,' he once said after a long discussion of the state of the weather and the likely outcome of a pending by-election. Well, I have at last come to the point.

From the very beginning of the changeover from the hall to the sub-medieval storeyed house, there were indications of a much more radical change of style (Figs. 7–8). This further change can be attributed to specifically Renaissance thinking. The old hall-house was a building designed to be symmetrical about its long axis and asymmetrical about its short axis. The balancing windows on the long walls, the cross-passage with its opposed doorways, the paired openings in the dais and passage partitions, all related to an aesthetic perception limited to the interior of the dwelling, a perception which recognized only the long axis of the house. The fact that this resulted in a building which, when viewed from the exterior, was totally asymmetrical, did not seem to matter. The sub-medieval storeyed house generally followed the design conventions of the hall-house out of which it had been born, but slowly there surfaced the perception that symmetry, when viewed from without, was as important as, if not more important than, symmetry viewed from within, and that this required another sort of symmetry altogether, a symmetry concentrated on, and arranged about, not the long but the short axis of the house. This led to designs which, as one wit once put it, were 'Queen Anne at the front and Mary Anne at the back'. 'Queen Anne at the front and Mary Anne at the back' explains much of the Renaissance aesthetic as applied to architecture. One of the clearest indications of this revolution in thinking and the concentration of interest on the front elevation was the change from siting the house down the slope to siting the house across the slope. Wales, as you must by now have noticed, has a terrain which is far from horizontal, so that most dwellings stand on slopes. The traditional siting was to build the house down the slope, even if this meant that the floor and the ridge might not be level, or if they were, this had been achieved only by excavating a platform on which to build. The new thinking required the house to be built across the slope, so that it was approached from below rather than from the side. The new siting, of course, emphasized the front and created a much more impressive approach from outside; and making an impresssion externally was all part of Renaissance philosophy.

Another feature which became increasingly popular was the storeyed porch. This again emphasized the front and the short axis and was often used in an attempt to disguise the asymmetry difficult to avoid in the sub-medieval plan. Good examples of porches used to create symmetry out of asymmetry are those at Treowen (Wonastow, Mon), built shortly after 1627 (Pl. 13), and Great House (Aberthin, Glam.), built in 1658. Sometimes the sub-medieval plan was so 'tidied up' as to produce a symmetrical elevation. St Fagans 'Castle', Glamorgan, built *c*. 1580, has an impressively symmetrical elevation—symmetrical about its short axis (at least viewed externally)—but the gabled cross-wings show what the plan in any case reveals that this is not a castle but a hall-house derivative, retaining its screens, passage and its hall (Pl. 13). The service rooms between the screens and the cross wing have been designed longer than usual in order to produce a balanced elevation at each side of the porch and thus satisfy Renaissance aesthetic perceptions.

Finally, there was a tendency to produce a more compact plan, siting the service room to the rear rather than to the end of the hall. This is well illustrated by Plasauduon (Carno, Mont.) and Henblas (Llanasa, Flints.), illustrated by Figs 9–10. Such an evolution eventually led to a house built in two parallel ranges—the double pile plan—(Fig. 8) or in the house in the form of a cube, the first example of which in Wales is remarkably early, the Flemish villa which Sir Richard Clough built in 1567 in the Flintshire parish of Tremeirchion. Only the farm buildings now remain, but the drawings of this unusual structure, long demolished, tend to confirm the tradition that it was built by Flemish workmen. The date inscription in the form of iron brackets is a thoroughly Flemish but completely un-British feature.

Many of these ideas could, and often were, incorporated in houses which otherwise retained much of the sub-medieval form of plan. The dramatic change which totally changed the form of the house came with a great improvement in the design of the stair and the development of a centralized system of circulation. The sub-medieval house most characteristically had the stair tucked away in a corner in a recess alongside the fireplace. This cramped winding stair was not a prominent architectural feature; it was hidden inside, and only detectable outside by a tiny window or a slight projection. Slowly, another type of stair was developed, a well or dog-leg stair in a turret, projecting outwards, usually but not inevitably from the rear of the hall. But, by about 1650, there had been developed a type of plan in which the framed stair was placed not in a rear projection but in the body of the house itself so that it could be reached by means of an enclosed vestibule. As a result each room in the house could be approached from the stair landings, thus obviating the need for passage rooms. It was possible to combine this plan-form with an absolutely symmetrical front elevation without any difficulty, which was not the case with most other forms of plan. Thus two birds, it might be said, were killed with one stone; the Renaissance ideal of frontal symmetry had been achieved along with a perfect system of circulation. Of the older house it could be said (figuratively speaking) that the house was built first and the stair somehow fitted in afterwards. In the houses of the new look, the stair was envisaged from the beginning and the rest of the house was built round it. The Renaissance revolution was complete. The stair sited on the short axis produced not only an elevation but also a plan which was symmetrical. The advantages of the new plan were paramount; they gave privacy to all rooms, and provided living conditions suitable for an increasingly literate populace. The earliest examples of the plan-form I know of are Tŷfaenor (Abbey Cwm-hir, Rads.), probably built *c.* 1650 for Richard Fowler, High Sheriff of Radnorshire, and Plasnewydd (Llanwnnog, Mont.), probably built *c.* 1670, whose builder is unknown (Figs. 11–12). Types of plan, either single-pile or double-pile, with a central stair became the accepted basis of the eighteenth-century manor-house and the nineteenth-century farmhouse (Pl.16). For the Welsh tenanted farmhouse, 'Renaissance' and 'Victorian' are equivalent terms, an idea which calls for a considerable adjustment to the conventional nomenclature and time-scale of the literary or musical historian! During the Victorian age, Wales was being covered with symmetrical stone (or in north-east Wales, brick) boxes flanked by chimneys at the gable-ends, with the vertically proportioned windows arranged around a central door-way. By then, the increasingly literate tenant farmer required a house in which he could write a letter, or read a book, fill in a return, or do his accounts undisturbed by the through traffic inescapable in the older types of plan. This form of 'double-fronted' house plan, which all of us now take for granted, and in which many of us, including myself, were born, was in fact a comparatively recent invention made about the middle of the seventeenth century. It flourished, at least in the rural areas, until 4 August 1914. It was only after the great calamity of war that the builders and building owners of the Welsh countryside began to look beyond the simple (if effective) strait-jacket of the symmetrical, axially planned, central stair-passage house to the more freely planned houses, which spreading (as usual) down the social ladder were beginning to be adopted in the inter-war years.

My study of the development of the Renaissance plan-forms, however, has carried me far ahead of the study of Renaissance detail which I would now like briefly to consider before I conclude this chapter. The details again, like the plan-forms, can be divided into those which are characteristic of the Renaissance period, without being specifically Roman or Renaissance in inspiration, and those which arise directly from the revival of the orders of Roman architecture.

By the beginning of the sixteenth century, the most striking of all contrasts within the Principality were the east-west contrasts between those eastern regions where build-ings were normally of framed, half-timbered (black-and-white) construction and those regions where the normal wall was of mass construction, stone, or, in places, earth. A feature of the Renaissance period was a growth in brick building in the half-timbered areas, giving parts of north-eastern Wales the bright, contrasting colours—red brick and black and white—of the English Midlands, which are so different from the grey-stone and stucco finish of the remainder of the Principality. A feature of the better half-timbered building of the seventeenth century is the use of very ornate infilling patterns, lozenges, cusping and herringbone, which illustrate the love of exterior decoration of the early Renaissance. Another contrast is to be found in the north-east/ south-west division, between those regions where a tradition of ornate roof structure (inherited from the Middle Ages) was sustained in the early Renaissance phase of building, and those areas—the south-west—where roofs tend to be plain. There is also a contrast in forms of partition and fireplace construction, the counties of Cardiganshire and Carmarthenshire long retaining the plastered wickerwork for the interior wall (probably derived from lost, impermanent, all-wickerwork dwellings), while elsewhere partitions were either of stout post-and-panel construction, or half-timbered like the exterior walls of a borderland house, or again (particularly in the Vale of Glamorgan) of stonework well furnished with dressed stone doorways.

Two features with more obvious links with the Renaissance are architectural heraldry and date-inscriptions (Figs. 15–16). Both are much more in evidence in north, and in particular north-east, Wales than elsewhere. Indeed, the numbers of heraldic devices in Denbighshire houses are so high as to make it clear that the seventeenth century was certainly not the age of the common man, and that, indeed, the common man might appear to have been in danger of extinction. For, as R. T. Jenkins pointed out, 'we have a picture of a landscape so densely packed with *tai cyfrifol* . . . or gentlemen's seats . . . that we wonder where room could be found for the tenantry who provided for their upkeep'.

In the same area early date-inscriptions are also very numerous. It was passing through the Denbighshire village of Llansannan and seeing Goscombe John's monument to the great men of the Clwyd Valley, particularly to Tudur Aled and William Salesbury, that sparked off an idea in my head which sent me to consult Sir Thomas Parry's *History of Welsh Literature* and plot, not for once features of architecture, but the birthplaces of men of literary genius. The resulting labour appeared to show a remarkable concentration of men of letters and theologians associated with the very area where the heraldry and date-inscriptions are exceptionally numerous. I felt my surmise confirmed when I read in Dr Enid Pierce Roberts's essay on the Renaissance in the Vale of Clwyd: 'Most of the men of the Welsh Renaissance either belonged to the north-eastern part of the country, or to quote the words of the new prayer-book, "became its children by adoption and grace". Welsh literature and learning owes its very survival to the scholar-gentlemen of this north-east corner of Wales in the age of the Tudors.' So we can perhaps look on the Clwyd as the Arno of Wales, Ruthin as its Florence, hill-top Denbigh as its Siena, and Denbighshire as its Tuscany. For it was this fertile region that was the intellectual heart of Wales in the sixteenth century not, as today, Penglais Hill or Singleton Park.

As you can imagine, much of what has already been written goes down a lot better in north Wales than in the south, so to make amends I will return to south Wales to illustrate my final and most fundamental Renaissance theme, the movement which architecturally lay at the heart of it, and that is the revival of the orders of Roman architecture.

One must, however, at this point remember how slowly this essential part of the Renaissance movement gained acceptance in the British Isles as a whole, never mind

Wales. It was two hundred years or more after the great Italian architects had mastered the Roman style that buildings *in any quantity* were erected in these islands which were in any comprehensive sense a reflection of the revived Roman architecture. Even if one contemplates the university where most Welshmen of the Renaissance received their higher education, the advance of classical architecture was extremely slow. Indeed, a study of the buildings of Oxford is most informative and revealing: there is the progression from the irregular and thoroughly medieval sixteenth-century collegiate buildings to the symmetrical Gothic of the early seventeenth-century quadrangles, embellished with a few Roman conceits, particularly the classical centrepieces of Merton, Wadham, St Johns, and the Bodleian. But a symmetrical elevation and a centrepiece displaying the orders do not make a Roman monument measured by the standards of Palladio. Indeed it is not until after the Restoration that we find at Oxford complete buildings in a Roman Renaissance style and not until the early eighteenth century, in the building of Queen's College, do we find an entire college in that style.

So it was in Wales. Apart from tombs in churches, and small details such as screens and panelling, Welsh architecture remained more Gothic than Renaissance, at least until the Restoration. Examples of Renaissance details are, it is true, exemplified by the gatehouse at Beaupré (1586) and, even more strikingly, in the porch of 1600 (Pl. 12) embodying the orders of Roman architecture, even if a late Gothic, four-centred archway is part of the composition. Another early instance is the gatehouse at Trefalun, 1602 (Pl. 13). Classical elements are also evident in the porch at Rhiw'rperrai (Ruperra), probably built in 1626 though the remainder of the exterior of the structure is late symmetrical Gothic. The change from such houses to the types of landowner's mansion which characterize eighteenth-century Glamorgan is very striking, well illustrated by Llandaff Court of the Mathew family, rebuilt 1744–6, even if in the mind's eye one has to remove the modern eaves and restore the eighteenth-century parapets. By this time, proportions and details based on Roman Renaissance architecture had become the fashionable background to the lives of the squires. Other examples are Llanharan House, whose architect is unknown, and Penrice 'Castle' rebuilt by Thomas Mansel Talbot of Margam to the designs of Anthony Keck (Pl. 14). But perhaps the finest Renaissance building in Glamorgan is the Orangery at Margam, built to the designs of the same architect between 1787 and 1790, and reputed to be the longest, and possibly the largest, building of its kind in the British Isles (Pl. 15). It is a building where the proportions and the restrained use of the classical elements of architecture deserve all praise, and it is perhaps the appropriate point at which to bring this brief survey of Welsh Renaissance architecture to a conclusion. I like to think that as the shades of the great Italian architects who raised Roman architecture from its ashes in the late fifteenth and early sixteenth centuries and established it as the basis of all polite architecture, men such as Bramante and Serlio, Palladio and Sangallo, looked down from on high and saw the finest Orangery in the British Isles rising in West

Glamorgan, they must have noted with pleasure and approval the fact that even the Welsh in this most distant province of the Roman Empire had at last understood what the Roman Renaissance was all about, even if it had taken more than two hundred years to get the message across! What the spirits of the great Italians felt when, less than a century later, they realized that the Marquess of Bute with the help of his architect, Burges, would resurrect in Cardiff Castle and Castell Coch what Molière would have described as

> Le fade gout des monuments gothiques,
> les monstres odieux des siècles ignorants

is best left to the imagination!

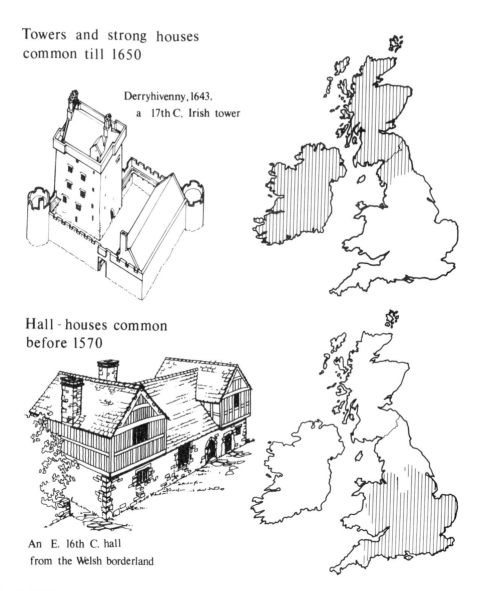

Towers and strong houses
common till 1650

Derryhivenny, 1643,
a 17th C. Irish tower

Hall - houses common
before 1570

An E. 16th C. hall
from the Welsh borderland

Fig. 1. Hall-houses and towers. In the south-east the most characteristic early dwelling is the hall, whereas in the north-west it is the tower. Many towers in the north-west represent the late survival of the fortified house which had become obsolete earlier in the south-east. In the north-west, the peasant house (represented by the hall) was slow to emerge, whereas in the south-east such peasant houses, dating from before the Reformation, survive in large numbers. The earliest peasant houses in the south-east are substantial hall-houses dating from the fifteenth century. The earliest peasant houses in the north-west are single-storeyed cottages, rarely earlier than the eighteenth century.

Single-storeyed houses common until 1850

Two-storeyed houses common after 1570

Fig. 2. Early storeyed and late single-storeyed houses. In the late sixteenth century the sub-medieval storeyed house began to replace the hall in south-eastern England a century before the first sub-medieval farmhouses appeared in the far north of England, and also before the earliest surviving single-storey farmhouses of Scotland and Ireland were built.

Fig. 3. Gloddaeth (Penrhyn, Caerns.), early sixteenth century, the hall of a great landowner looking towards the dais partition. Note the dais canopy, on which is painted the royal arms, and the handsome hammer-beam roof. The lateral fireplace is an original feature.

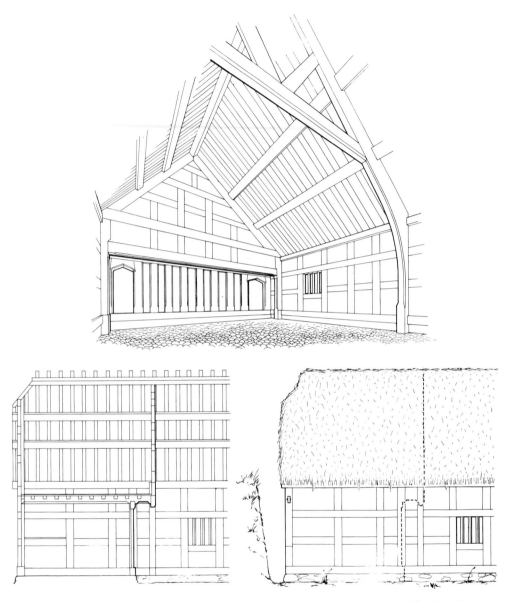

Fig. 4. Cwm Nant Meichiad (Meifod, Mont.), early sixteenth century. A cruck-framed, half-timbered, yeoman hall looking towards the dais partition, with structural details below. Note the simple dais canopy, no doubt inspired by the halls of the grandees such as Gloddaeth *opposite*. Note, however, that unlike Gloddaeth, Cwm Nant Meichiad was heated by an open hearth. The yeomen did not acquire the enclosed fireplace until after the accession of Elizabeth I, and the coming of the storeyed house.

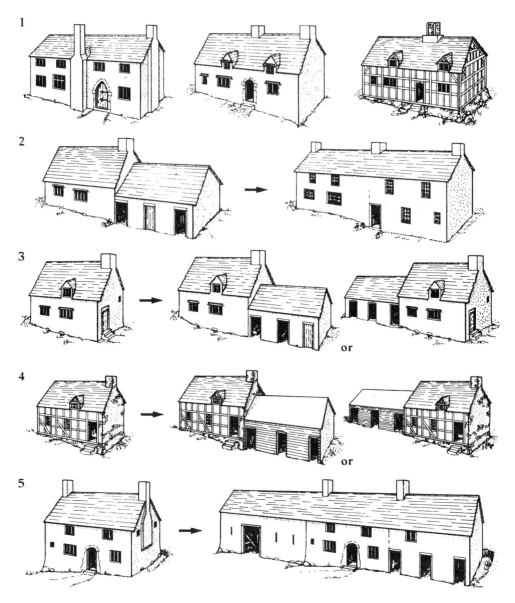

Fig. 5. The main types of sub-medieval storeyed house.

   1 Classic three-unit houses with a parlour as outer room.

   2 The long-house with byre as outer room, also showing later redevelopment.

   3, 4 and **5** Two-unit houses, often extended to have farm buildings in the same range.

Note, **1, 2, 3** and **4** have the small rooms at the dais end while in **5** these are at the passage end. Houses such as these housed a prosperous rural middle class *c.* 1550 – *c.* 1750.

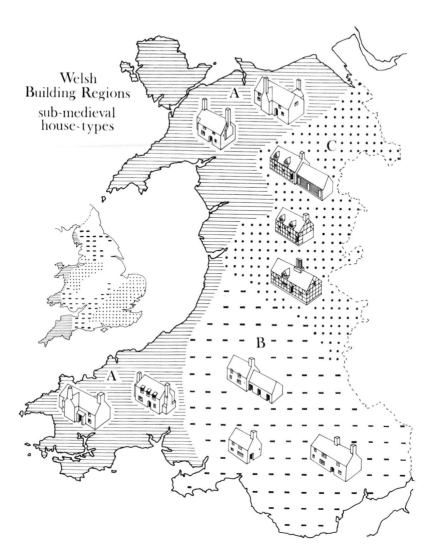

Fig. 6. Welsh building regions: sub-medieval house types. This map of the main Welsh sub-medieval house types (admittedly very much simplified) points to contrasts of some significance. The first is between the western regions, where the chimney on the outside wall predominates, and the east, where internal chimneys are more numerous. Within the eastern area there is a further significant contrast between the south-east, where the chimney is placed backing on the entry (and thus retaining the cross-passage), and the north-east, where the chimney is placed in what historically was the cross-passage, creating the lobby entry. Parts of England, particularly the south, show a clear progression of the types from east to west, lobby entry, chimney backing on the entry, and chimney on the outside wall, but the two major concentrations of lobby-entry houses, one in the south-east and one in the southern Pennine area linked with north-east Wales, pose certain problems.

119

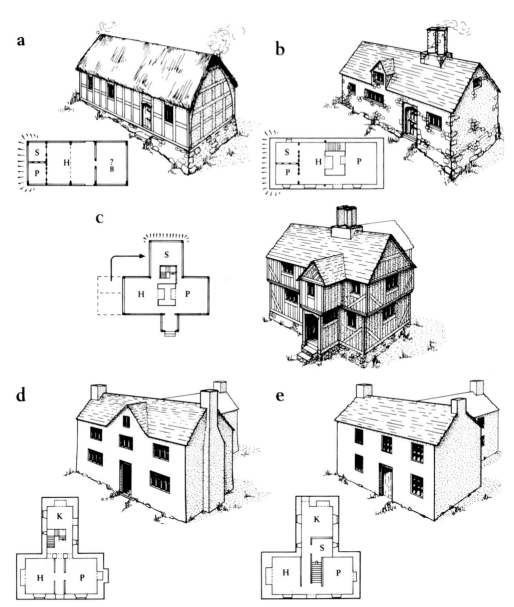

Fig. 7. Development of the farmhouse *c*. 1500–1850.

    a. *c*. 1500. Half-timbered, downhill-sited hall, outer room use uncertain, ? byre.

    b. *c*. 1600. Hall rebuilt as storeyed house; fireplace and chimney replace gable-vents; stone walls replace timber, outer room now a parlour.

    c. *c*. 1630. Early Renaissance cruciform house sited across the slope; porch to front, service-room to rear.

    d. *c*. 1680. Early centrally planned house, rear kitchen, and well stair, gable fireplaces.

    e. *c*. 1850. Late centrally planned house, rear kitchen, central stair passage, gable fireplace.

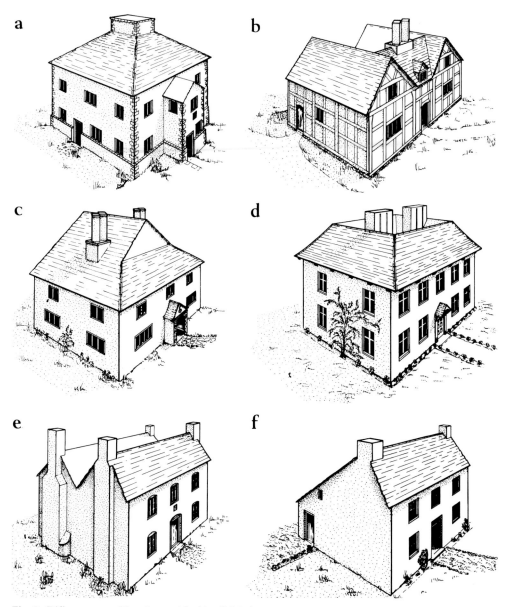

Fig. 8. Different types of Renaissance 'double-pile' design.
    a. *c.* 1650. The square house with central stack.
    b. *c.* 1670. The U plan.
    c. *c.* 1670. Square plan with spine wall, overall roof.
    d. *c.* 1670. Square plan with spine wall, double roof.
    e. *c.* 1720. The double-pile plan with double roof, gable chimneys.
    f. *c.* 1800. Single-pile main unit with lean-to and gable chimneys.

Fig. 9. A general trend was to transfer the service-room to the rear of the house. The fashion coincided with the demand for a kitchen, and as a result a kitchen at the rear tended to replace the service-room at the end. The provision of a storeyed porch at the front completed the transformation. Henblas (Llanasa, Flints.), built in 1645, embodies all these developments in a very distinguished early-Renaissance design.

Fig. 10. A house similar in conception but quite different in construction is the half-timbered Montgomeryshire house, Plasauduon (Carno). Note how the retention of the internal chimney allowed the fenestration of the gable-ends. These fenestrated end-walls are very characteristic of early seventeenth-century gentry houses and they recall the ornately glazed sterns of contemporary men-of-war.

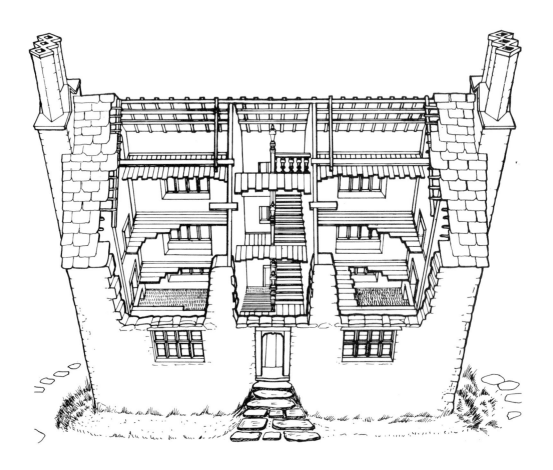

Fig. 11. Tŷfaenor (Abbey Cwm-hir, Rads.) illustrates a very early example of a house built about the central staircase, the landings of which give independent access to each room. Although the details are mid-seventeenth century, the plan looks forward to the Victorian age. The house was probably built for Richard Fowler about 1650, the year he was made High Sheriff of Radnorshire. In the nineteenth century, houses very similar to this were being built throughout Wales to house the tenant farmer and the village craftsman (see plate 16 *lower*). Thus the Renaissance fashion for a symmetrical front elevation and a centralized plan finally reached the people.

Fig. 12. Plasnewydd (Llanwnnog, Mont.) illustrates in detail an early example of a double-pile house built about a central staircase, the landings of which give independent access to all rooms, both front and rear. Here, as at Tŷfaenor (Fig. 11) the falling ground has been used to allow the complete segregation of living rooms and the kitchen, the former entered from the uphill front door, and the latter entered from the downhill rear door. Such a plan was revolutionary when it first appeared. The ovolo-moulded mullion and transom windows, stair and ceiling details suggest a date of *c*. 1670–80.

1758

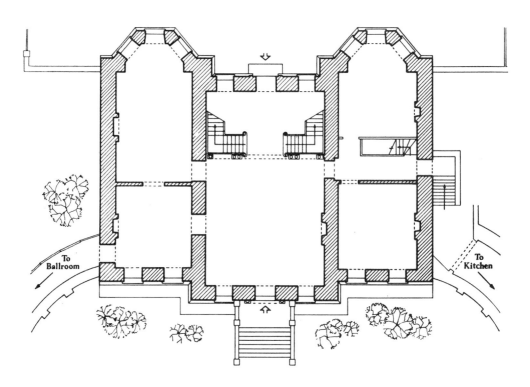

To Ballroom

To Kitchen

Fig. 13. A good example of a double-pile house incorporating a large entrance hall was Ynysymaengwyn (Tywyn, Mer.). The entrance hall and stairs are divided only by an open screen of columns *in antis*, which make a very effective design.

Fig. 14. The resulting interior is shown in the drawing above. Although the central block of Ynysymaengwyn was built (according to an inscription on the exterior) in 1758, it is likely that the interior was the result of a remodelling in the Adam style a generation later. Ynysymaengwyn was demolished in 1968 – a sad loss.

Heraldry

(before 1730)

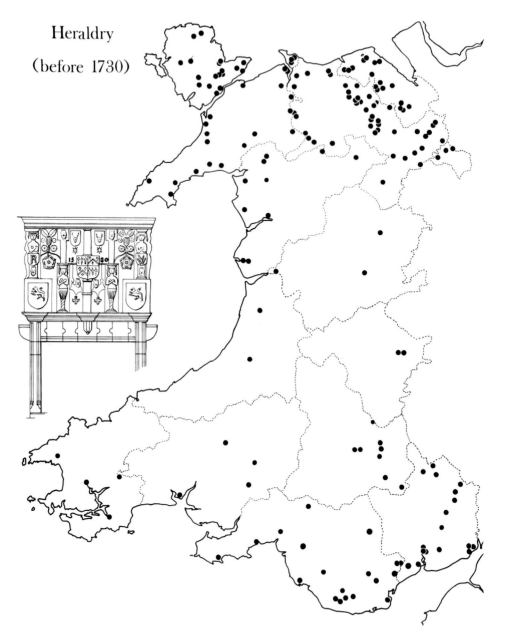

Fig. 15. Heraldry is a form of decoration which became popular in the early Renaissance period. The concentration of architectural heraldry in parts of north Wales is quite remarkable and may be related to literary traditions strong in the area.

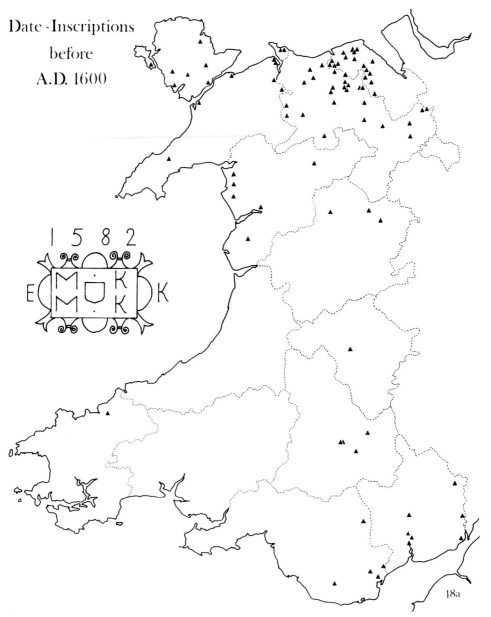

Date-Inscriptions
before
A.D. 1600

1 5 8 2

E M̤ K
 M̤ K K

18a

Fig. 16. Date-inscriptions on buildings are extremely rare in Wales (as elsewhere in Europe) before *c*. 1560, but after the middle of the sixteenth century they became increasingly common if localized. What is striking is the concentration of these early date-inscriptions in north-eastern Wales, which again suggests a link with the literary traditions of the area. In contrast, date-inscriptions in south-west Wales are rare before the nineteenth century.

Plate 1. Llanmihangel Place (Llanmihangel, Glam.), view from the south-west. Llanmihangel Place illustrates the continuation of the first-floor hall tradition in the sixteenth century. The large windows indicate the level of the primary accommodation which includes a very fine open hall over a vaulted undercroft. Note the tower elements in the design.

Plate 2. (*above*) Althrey (Bangor-on-Dee, Flints.); (*below*) Penarth (Newtown, Mont.). The **H**- or **U**-plan house, consisting of a ground floor hall flanked by gabled cross-wings, was the classic form of the large English/Welsh manor house during the sixteenth and seventeenth centuries.

Plate 3. Pit Cottage (Llanarth, Mon.), a cruck-framed peasant hall-house, probably early sixteenth century. Large numbers of such cruck-framed halls testify to the emergence of a prosperous farming class in the Welsh borderland during the early Tudor period. The interior partitions prove that this particular example could not have been a long-house. The rooms beyond the passage were evidently domestic in character.

Plate 4. (*above*) Llandyfalle parish church (Brecs.), interior showing characteristic barrel roof which extends over nave and chancel, probably the commonest type of church roof in south-east Wales. (*below*) Buttington parish church (Mont.) interior showing richly cusped open roof of a type generally characteristic of north Wales.

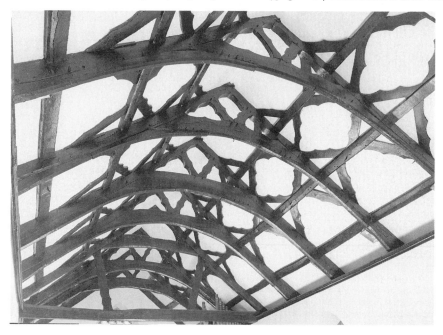

Plate 5. Llanidloes parish church (Mont.), interior showing the nave rebuilt in 1542, making it the first Protestant church in Wales, a fact expressed symbolically by the nave arcade, constructed out of material removed from the dissolved Cistercian house of Abbey Cwm-hir. Note the handsome hammer-beam roof characteristic of some of the more ambitious buildings of north Wales in the sixteenth century.

Plate 6. The Gwydir Chapel added to Llanrwst parish church in 1633–4. Note the Gothic multi-cusped window tracery flanking the almost baroque memorial to the Gwydir family.

Plate 7. Contrasting styles of monument in Abergavenny priory church; (*above*) the late Gothic tomb of Sir Richard Herbert and (*below left*) the early-Renaissance style tomb of William Baker, High Sheriff of Monmouthshire, who died in 1648; (*below right*) the monument to Richard Herbert, erected in 1600 in Montgomery parish church.

Plate 8. Family chapels: (*above*) the Vaughan chapel built against Llanddwywe (Mer.) parish church in 1615; (*below*) the interior of the chapel built in the grounds of Rug (Corwen, Mer.). Note the angel-embellished hammer-beam roof of late-medieval inspiration, although built as late as 1637.

Plate 9. The monument to Griffith Vaughan of Corsygedol, who died in 1616, incorporates elements of Roman Renaissance architecture unlike the family chapel (*opposite, above*) in which it is housed.

Plate 10. Sub-medieval storeyed houses of the 'direct-entry', end-chimney type: (*above*) Plas-du (Llanarmon, Caerns.), (*below*) Tŷ-mawr (Penmachno, Caerns.). Plas-du appears to be a house newly built in the late sixteenth century. Tŷ-mawr represents the reconstruction of an earlier cruck-framed hall-house.

Plate 11. Sub-medieval houses of the 'internal chimney' type: (*above*) Sutton (Ogmore, Glam.) is of the earlier pattern, with the entry behind the chimney; (*below*) Pant (Kerry, Mont.) follows the later lobby-entry plan. The gabled storeyed porch is characteristic of seventeenth to early eighteenth-century work and reflects the influence of Renaissance thinking.

Plate 12. The storeyed porch added to Beaupré (St Hilary, Glam.) in 1600 may instance the first use of the Roman orders as a major feature of a work of domestic architecture in Wales.

Plate 13. (*above, left*) The gatehouse at Trefalun (Allington, Denbs.), dated 1606, is another early example of Roman Renaissance detail. (*above right*) The orders applied to the porch at Treowen (Wonastow, Mon.) soon after 1627. (*below*) The main front of St Fagans Castle (St Fagans, Glam.) is a good example of a symmetrical Renaissance version of the hall and cross-wing plan previously illustrated on Plate 2. Note the strongly horizontal lines of the square headed windows although the entrance doorway is still late Gothic.

143

Plate 14. Llanharan House (Llanharan, Glam.) (*above*) and Penrice Castle (Penrice, Glam.) (*below*), built 1773–7, illustrate the formal classical style of the eighteenth century, a period regarded by architectural, in contrast with literary and musical historians, as 'late Renaissance'.

Plate 15. The Orangery at Margam designed by Anthony Keck for Thomas Mansel Talbot and built 1787–90 is perhaps the finest example of late-Renaissance architecture in Wales.

Plate 16. (*above*) The red-brick Rectory (Llanbedr, Denbs.) probably dating from *c*. 1700 is an early example of what was to become the classic eighteenth-century British manor house. Note the mullion and high transom windows soon to give way to the sliding sash window. (*below*) A typical nineteenth-century small storeyed house from west Wales illustrates the pursuit of Renaissance symmetry by the Welsh country people during the Railway Age, even if the large kitchen fireplace to the right still kept the composition a little lopsided.

SUMMARIES OF SECTIONAL PAPERS

Professor Dr Fernando ALONSO, University of Santiago (Spain)
Subject: Tradition and innovation in a Galician pilgrimage of Celtic origins

Galicia is one of the recent politically autonomous communities within Spain. This remote corner of the Iberian Peninsula was once inhabited by the Celts. Remainders of their civilization are still prevalent today in many local customs. Ethnographical studies of various aspects of the material and spiritual culture of the Galician people show their relation to the Celtic culture elsewhere in Europe. This paper deals with the origin and development of one of the oldest Galician pilgrimages and its relationship to the ancient Celtic cults and beliefs in the Underworld, principally the journey after death to a Paradise beyond the western sea and reincarnation.

Rhian ANDREWS, Yr Adran Geltaidd, Prifysgol y Frenhines, Belfast
Subject: Golwg ar y rhagenwau ategol yng nghanu'r Gogynfeirdd

Wrth drafod barddoniaeth a gyfansoddwyd cyn cyfnod y canu caeth, y duedd yw anwybyddu'r rhagenwau ategol a geir yn y llawysgrifau ar y sail nad ydynt yn cyfrif yn y mesurau. Y mae hyn yn rhagdybio nifer benodol o sillafau ymhob llinell neu gwpled; ni chyfeirir at y curiadau. Yn y papur hwn ystyrir enghreifftiau o'r rhagenwau ategol er mwyn gweld a oes arwyddocâd mydryddol neu arall i'w presenoldeb.

Leszek BEDNARCZUK, École Normale Supérieure, Cracovie/Kraków
Subject: Structural similarities between Brittonic Celtic and Western Romance languages

There are striking similarities between Brittonic Celtic and Western Romance languages. Certain of them can be explained as the influence of Vulgar Latin in Britannia on local Celtic dialects (vowel-system, stress, disappearance of nominal inflection, formation of pluperfect), while others may be interpreted as an effect of the Celtic substratum in Western Romance languages, especially in French (internal lenition, i.e. voicing and spiratization of internal stops, evolution of certain consonant groups, French *liaison*, use of enclitic pronouns, syntactic *reprise*).

To simplify, we can say that certain characteristic features of Brittonic Celtic as opposed to the Goidelic group have been formed under the influence of Vulgar Latin, whereas certain features of Western Romance, that are unknown in other Romance languages, have their source in the Celtic substratum.

Jean BERTON, Université de Bretagne Occidentale, Brest
Subject: Des conséquences de la rupture de la Vieille Alliance entre l'Écosse et la France.

Il apparait comme évident a posteriori que la Vieille Alliance toujours présente dans le coeur des Écossais en cette fin du 20ème siècle n'a jamais dépassé ni le niveau des amitiés personnelles privilégiées ni celui d'un intérêt politique immédiat dans l'esprit des Français. Ce qui est devenu une tradition sinon une légende en Écosse n'est plus qu'une péripétie depuis longtemps oubliée en France.

L'oubli est devenu aujourd'hui ignorance et cela mène à l'incompréhension de la part du francophone envers l'Écossais anglophone et surtout celtophone. Le gaélique est totalement ignoré en France et dans les universités françaises. De ce fait, un lecteur d'ouvrages composés par des auteurs écossais anglophones, qui prétendent habituellement ne pas connaître le gaélique, ne peut pas apprécier pleinement ces oeuvres parsemées de patronymes et de toponymes gaéliques, ni vraiment pénétrer la psychologie d'un personnage gaël.

Apprendre le gaélique d'Écosse en France est chose impossible. Pourtant l'étude du gaélique apporte des révélations formidables au francophone imprégné de sa civilisation occidentale américanisée, fort de sa culture latine et fier de ses origines et de son tempérament gaulois.

La langue gaélique nous offre un point de vue radicalement nouveau, ne serait-ce qu'en rapprochant le sujet de l'object, en opposant l'être à l'avoir, et le devenir au présent.

L'innovation dans les études écossaises en France serait de rétablir des liens avec l'Écosse celtophone, en un mot, de renouer avec la tradition oubliée.

Dr James J. BLAKE, Editor, *Éire-Ireland: A Journal of Irish Studies* (USA)
Subject: Liminality, clarity of perception in *Buile Suibhne*, and *Súile Shuibhne* (1983) by Cathal Ó Searcaigh

Súile Shuibhne is the first collection of poetry in book form by the Irish-Gaelic poet Cathal Ó Searcaigh. The individual poems as well as the title of the collection direct our attention to Ó Searcaigh's indebtedness to Mad Sweeney's perception and vision in *Buile Suibhne*, the medieval Irish narrative in verse and prose. Sweeney's madness makes him a figure on the edge between the claims of the group and the individual, between the Christian and the Gaelic value systems, between the rational and its opposite. Similarly, in the Modern Irish poems by Ó Searcaigh, human values have made abominable divisions that isolate not only the individual, but also Gaelic culture while consistently atomizing those insights which incorporate the physical, emotional, intellectual with the behavioural simultaneously.

Ó Searcaigh uses images and metaphoric language that clearly cut across the terrorism of systematic rationality and technocratic dominance. Like Mad Sweeney, Ó Searcaigh recreates the swirl of the non-rational, the irrational, the fantastic and the perceived. His poetry is a witness to the long-lived tradition of Gaelic literature in which the poet appears as the seer of the outer limits of actuality. Like Sweeney's lyrics, Ó Searcaigh's poems are firmly rooted in the perceptual world, the primary world for human beings. As he asserts in 'Laistiar':

> Ar an taobh cúil d'fhocail
> Tá a mhacasamhail de shaol.

(On the reverse side of words is a likeness of reality.)

Anna R. K. BOSCH, University of Chicago
Subject: Vowel–consonant syllable structure in Scottish Gaelic

Scottish Gaelic is possibly alone among languages to present a VC-type syllable, a structure which Borgstrom touched upon (1940) but which, astonishingly, has been ignored by other descriptive literature. This paper will present an examination of syllable structure in Scottish Gaelic, and parallel phonological evidence which points up this construction. Preaspiration of voiceless consonants, for one, lends emphasis to the word-initial syllable, arguing for such a division of syllables. Absence of preaspiration, voicing distinctions, and distinctions in nasality uphold this argument. The majority of phonological information is thus carried by the word-initial syllable while succeeding syllables of the same word are merely skeletal. This distribution of features motivates a revision of our understanding of Scottish Gaelic phonology; central to this understanding is the VC syllable. Finally, it should be noted, this interpretation of syllable structure is corroborated by the native speaker's intuitive articulation of syllables in careful speech.

Dr Caroline BRETT, Girton College, Cambridge
Subject: John Leland, Wales, and British history

The antiquary John Leland (d. 1552), by his attempt to write a comprehensive history of Britain based on his discoveries in monastic libraries, laid the foundation for modern historical research. He is known to have travelled extensively in Wales and to have been highly conscious of the importance of its past in British history, as of the Welsh ancestry of his patron, King Henry VIII. This paper aims, firstly, to determine by a comparison of Leland's works how large a part his 'Welsh experience' played in the development of his historical views and, secondly, to assess how much of a stimulus his work was to the growth of Welsh historiography of the Renaissance.

Andrew BREEZE, Dublin Institute for Advanced Studies
Subject: Siôn Cent, the Oldest Animals, and the Day of Life

The paper discusses two themes in the work of Siôn Cent: that of the *aetates animalium* at IGE 273, and that of the *horae diei aetates hominis* at IGE 253. A full discussion of the history of each is given, referring in the case of the first not only to previously noted parallels in Irish and Indian literature (the Book of Lismore and the *Mahabharata*), but to parallels in medieval Latin literature, where the theme is a commonplace. The theme of the *aetates animalium* is distinguished from that of the Oldest Animals proper, well known from *Culhwch ac Olwen*. An attempt is made to show that the origins of Siôn's theme are more correctly sought in classical tradition than in Celtic and oriental sources.

Discussion of the history of the *horae diei aetates hominis* draws together recent work on the poem attributed to Siôn in *A Guide to Welsh Literature*, II (1979), 178–81, 303–4 and a Middle English parallel in the Brogyntyn MS 10 at Aberystwyth. The origin for the theme is sought in commentary on the Parable of the Vineyard (Matt. 20:1–16); Origen, St Augustine, St Gregory the Great, Honorius Augustodunensis and other writers are quoted in illustration of the history of this theme. The paper concludes with some brief remarks on research on Siôn and his sources.

(The paper is published in *BBCS* XXXIV, November, 1987.)

Dr William Joseph BUCKLEY, University of Chicago
Subject: Tradition and innovation in Northern Ireland: an ethical analysis of practical reasoning about social conflict and religion in Northern Ireland

What elements of tradition and innovation inform the practical reasoning of persons in Northern Ireland when they make claims about their social conflict and religion? Contrary to many analyses of NI which disregard or marginalize the claims of parties within the conflict as ideologically distorted, this paper has three chief aims: (1) It surveys the practical moral reasoning of persons and institutions within the conflict. (2) It suggests a 'taxonomy' of ethical issues; that is, political, reactionary (paramilitaries and noncompliance), and repressive (government security measures). (3) It analyses the roles of tradition and innovation in this discourse by various parties in the conflict. In addition to these ethical 'levels' of the social conflict, I analyse and evaluate the various forms of tradition and innovation which inform the theological and religious discourse of persons and institutions in NI (i.e. the Churches). How may the pertinent aspects of tradition and innovation be sorted out from such a cacophony of voices within the seemingly intractable context of social conflict? I use a model of nonformal logic to organize and analyse the discourse of parties within social conflict. In their responses to various levels of the conflict, persons and institutions make public claims about the conflict and religion. These claims draw ideas and support from many traditional sources (e.g. political theories, theories about the just use of force or noncompliance, recurrent claims about the demonic intentions of opponents, experience, the Bible, etc.). Such responses to the conflict are also shaped by relatively modern ideas, innovative sources and uniquely contemporary technologies (e.g. economic analyses, conflict studies, the propagandistic use of modern technologies; that is media, weapons, etc.). Such discourse, like the conflict itself, is hardly reducible to theories. The author's experiences (four summers as a Peace Volunteer in NI), publications (demography and economics in *More than the Troubles: a common sense view of the Northern Ireland conflict* (Phila. New Scholars Press, 1984) and current Ph.D. research into the roles of tradition and innovation in ethical argumentation all conspire to make this contribution pertinent to your conference.

M. T. BURDETT-JONES, University of Wales (Dictionary of Welsh)
Subject: Henry Salesbury: Renaissance scholar

Henry Salesbury's wide intellectual interests, which comprehended both Welsh traditional lore and the scholarship of new learning, are assessed and a number of manuscripts in his hand or otherwise associated with him are identified. The paper closes with a discussion of his role in the debate concerning the historicity of Geoffrey of Monmouth's *Historia Regum Britanniae*.

John CAREY, Harvard University, Cambridge, Massachusetts
Subject: Fir Bolg: a native etymology revisited

T. F. O'Rahilly's derivation of the population-names *Fir Bolg* and *Belgae* from a hypothetical lightning-god **Bolgos/Belgos* still holds the field as the most recent and authoritative etymology proposed; but comparable reflexes of the relevant root seem only to be attested in the eastern dialects of Indo-European. I shall examine the possibility that **bhelgh-* 'to swell' is in fact the source of these names, discussing its descendants in Celtic and Germanic in the context of a general semantics of 'heroic tumescence' in both language families.

David CLEMENT, University of Edinburgh
Subject: Phonemic glottalization in Argyllshire Gaelic

The Gaelic dialects spoken across a major part of mainland Argyll and the islands have pairs of glotallized versus non-glottalized consonants. This applies both to dialects with and without preaspiration. It affects stops, liquids and nasals. This phenomenon has not been dealt with systematically in the literature.

Richard M. CROWE, University of Wales (Dictionary of Welsh)
Subject: Bywyd newydd i hen eiriau

Yn y papur hwn bwriedir ymdrin â'r modd y mae siaradwyr dysgedig y Gymraeg wedi ceisio ailgyflwyno hen eiriau i'r iaith er mwyn enwi gwrthrych newydd neu gysyniad newydd. Ceisir asesu methodoleg a llwyddiant yr ymdrechion hyn, yn ogystal ag ystyried cymhellion dros fabwysiadu'r dull hwn o gyfoethogi geirfa'r iaith yn hytrach na'r dulliau eraill.

Ceri DAVIES, Coleg y Brifysgol Caerdydd
Subject: Cyfieithiadau Cymraeg o'r Clasuron Groeg a Lladin

Un o ganlyniadau arhosol y pwyslais ar y clasuron Groeg a Lladin a gafwyd yn ystod y Dadeni Dysg oedd i'r arfer o gyfieithu'r clasuron i'r ieithoedd brodorol ddod yn rhan annatod o ddiwylliant gogledd a gorllewin Ewrop. Yn y papur hwn ceisir olrhain peth o hanes trosi'r clasuron i'r Gymraeg, o ddyddiau Gruffydd Robert hyd at Euros Bowen. Er nad yw'r cyfieithiadau Cymraeg yn niferus iawn, y mae iddynt arwyddocâd arbennig yn hanes ymwneud Cymru â thraddodiadau llenyddol Ewrop; manylir ar arddull rhai o'r cyfieithiadau, a chysylltir yr ymdriniaeth ag amryfal ddiddordebau llenyddol a diwylliannol cyfnod o dros bedair canrif.

Dr Sioned DAVIES, Adran y Gymraeg, Coleg y Brifysgol, Caerdydd
Subject: Y march yn y *Mabinogion*

Dadansoddiad manwl o'r modd y disgrifir meirch yn chwedlau'r *Mabinogion*, gan dynnu sylw hefyd at y disgrifiadau yn *Trioedd Y Meirch* a'r Hengerdd. Gwelir fod nodweddion arbennig yn perthyn i'r disgrifiad—pwysleisir y lliw a'r maint, ac yn aml sonnir am gyflymdra'r anifail —ac yn wahanol iawn i'r disgrifiadau o bobl, ceir fel rheol lu o epithetau i ddisgrifio'r march. Ystyrir arwyddocâd yr enwau gwahanol a roddir ar yr anifail, e.e. march, ceffyl, palffrei. Ceir peth cymharu â'r darlun o'r march yn llenyddiaeth glasurol yr hen fyd, ac yn yr oesoedd canol yn gyffredinol.

Professor Ann DOOLEY, St Michael's College, University of Toronto
Subject: The significance of the poem *M'oenurán dam ar étib* in *TBCI*
Critical readings of *TBC* have traditionally fallen into two opposing camps. On the one hand

there are the scholars such as Jackson and Dillon whose work on the Táin derives from the Chadwicks' theory of a Celtic heroic age and who view the text as reflecting an essentially archaic poetic ethos. On the other hand there is the interpretation of Carney who would see, if not the creation, then certainly the maintenance of the Táin as entirely a product of monastic learning. In taking the poem *M'oenurán dam ar étib* I should like to establish its relations to a standard medieval topos, the call to God in extremity. By thus aligning the poem alongside its Christian analogues and by examining its narrative location in *TBCI*, some conclusions emerge which are of relevance to the continuing problem of the status accorded each side in the pagan provenance/Christian redaction debate alluded to above.

Professor Dr Doris EDEL, Instituut A.G. van Hamel voor Keltische taal en letterkunde van de Rijksuniversiteit Utrecht
Subject: Tradition and innovation and the role of women

Despite the conservative character of Irish tradition—due to the 'backward-looking' attitude of its tradition-bearers—the early manuscript material contains evidence of many innovatory tendencies. Some of these concern women: (a) the role they played in society, and (b) the image society had of them.

As regards the first aspect: although the Irish jurists had a deep respect for antiquity, for the *mos maiorum*, the Old-Irish law-tracts show a progressive raising of the status of women from the earliest stratum onwards.

As regards the second aspect, I shall examine two questions: (1) women appearing as counsellors, and (2) the genre of the *aitheda*.

Ad (1): the texts have quite a lot to say about advice given by women. Not all the examples are as favourable as the one in *Aided Óenfir Aífe*, where Cú Chulainn's wife Emer openly questions the heroic code of honour of her countrymen (§8). Cú Chulainn rejects her advice (§9) and so heads for the disastrous fight in which the hopes of Ulster for a glorious future are utterly destroyed.

Ad (2): My hypothesis is that the *aithed* belongs to the innovatory tendencies mentioned above. In these love-tales women have the initiative because they are bound in a lesser degree by the traditional code of behaviour than the male members of the Irish society of those days.

Joseph F. ESKA, University of Toronto
Subject: Interpreting the Hispano-Celtic inscription of Botorrita: a progress report

This communication will report on the current state of progress in the interpretation of the Hispano-Celtic inscription of Botorrita being undertaken as a doctoral thesis at the University of Toronto. The communication will be principally concerned with:

(i) the structure of the text;
(ii) the lexicon;
(iii) morphology and syntax.

Dr James FIFE, San Diego, California
Subject: A visit to the Galapagos. Welsh Perfective Passives

Modern Welsh has a passive construction, which, though apparently a recent innovation, sheds light on passive structures going back to Proto-Indo-European. This construction, *the perfective passive*, is described and illustrated. It is grammatically and semantically distinct from other Welsh passive formations and is a later, analytical construction not partaking in its structure of any synthetic elements inherited from the PIE medio-passive. Yet the Welsh forms correspond precisely in semantics to perfective passives in several other languages, including German, French and English. These Welsh passives are therefore an important example of a semantic innovation developing in a fashion parallel to other, inherited structures in related languages. The Welsh forms provide insight into the synthetic correspondents and the widespread association of perfectivity and passivity in numerous languages.

Professor Patrick K. FORD, University of California, Los Angeles
Subject: Welsh ways with Tudor times: Elis Gruffydd in the reign of Henry VIII

Elis Gruffydd's 'Chronicle of the Six Ages of the World' is a unique document and deserving of close study for its historiography and its language. Elis was one of those thousands of Welsh who made their way into English life in the sixteenth century. He was obviously intelligent and gifted in many ways: fluent in English, and no doubt French and Latin, in addition to his native Flintshire Welsh. He was widely read in at least the historical sources of his own time, as his Chronicle shows, and he had more than a passing interest—almost a professional interest—in current affairs. In compiling his Chronicle, he was no mere copyist, although he did that too when need arose. It is clear that he attempted to use his sources critically, that he digested them and paraphrased them at times, often commenting editorially on the sources and adding further information from unnamed oral sources, hearsay, gossip, climate of opinion. That he chose to write his Chronicle in Welsh shows us that he respected the language, found it a fit vehicle for his enterprise, and felt competent enough to compose and translate in it. The present paper attempts to characterize Elis's literary product by focusing on three episodes that deal with events in England, Ireland, and Wales during the reign of Henry VIII.

Dr Helen FULTON, Centre of Advanced Welsh and Celtic Studies, Aberystwyth
Subject: Love poems to nuns in Middle Welsh

The love poetry of the fourteenth- and fifteenth-century *cywyddwyr* includes a number of poems addressed specifically to nuns. The pattern of these poems is similar enough to justify regarding them as a genre of medieval Welsh poetry. Typically, the poet attempts to make or keep an assignation with a nun, and a degree of wit and tension arises from the use of secular love imagery to address a woman in religious orders. Such a contrast is reminiscent of the practice of Continental courtly love lyric where the beloved is often synonymous with the Virgin Mary.

This paper explores the opposition between secular and religious imagery in Welsh poems to nuns, with some reference to European poetic tradition but with an emphasis on their originality. It also investigates possible reasons for the appearance of this genre in medieval Welsh poetry and its appeal for *uchelwyr* audiences.

Dr Kenneth J. GEORGE, Plymouth Polytechnic
Subject: A phonological base for Revived Cornish

Cornish died out in about 1800, and was revived 100 years later by Jenner. It is currently spoken by a small but growing band of enthusiasts. The form of the language used today is essentially that advocated by Nance and Smith during the period 1920-40. They based their reconstruction on Middle Cornish, because 86% of the extant literature dates from that phase. Nance spent many years trying to rationalize the orthography of MidC, eventually producing a system which he called Unified Cornish. He and Smith seem to have reconstructed Cornish as a written medium, and then thought out a phonological system to fit their spelling.

During the 1970s, interest grew in using Cornish as a modern spoken language, so that the question of pronunciation assumed more importance. It has been thoroughly investigated by the present author (George, 1984). In the absence of sound-recordings of traditional Cornish, it was necessary to examine the written sources. Statistical analyses were made of almost the entire corpus of extant literature, using specially developed computer programs. This work confirmed suspicions that Nance's pronunciation contains inaccuracies and anachronisms.

To remedy this situation, a phonological base is defined for Revived Cornish, approximating the pronunciation of the traditional language *c.* 1500. Details of this phonological base are presented. Its introduction has repercussions on the orthography, which needs to be revised so as to become almost completely phonemic. These improvements, at present being evaluated by the Cornish Language Board, will go a long way to dispel chronic ill-feeling between revivalists and academics, but will require the publication of new textbooks and a new dictionary in order for them to be accepted by Cornish speakers.

Dr Miranda J. GREEN, Open University of Wales
Subject: Changing traditions in pagan Celtic iconography

This paper covers the period 500 BC–AD 400, and studies traditions of Celtic cult-imagery. Before the Roman occupation of Celtic lands, Celtic religious art, far from being man-dominated, comprised mainly abstract themes. Where figural portrayals were present, they formed part of an integrated design. Roman influence introduced realistic figural imagery as an essential in iconography. The Celts adopted this method of representing their gods to an extent; thus some Celtic deities appeared in the iconographic record for the first time. But mimetic imagery was by no means the rule. The old abstract tradition continued to manifest itself in the schematic treatment of imagery. I contend that such schematism was the result of deliberate choice. The reduction of the cult-figure to its essentials may indeed have possessed a religious purpose. One may envisage a divine 'shorthand' where the very absence of realism rendered cult-images appropriate for the gods.

Dr W. P. GRIFFITH, University College of North Wales, Bangor
Subject: Wales and the English universities, 1540–1640

Wales's position in university and collegiate expansion at Oxford and Cambridge is considered by reference to the numbers (over 2,000) and proportion of Welsh students (up to 10 per cent at Oxford before 1600) and their relative distribution from within Wales. Concepts of service and of personal moral worth, as espoused by some writers, seem to have influenced decisions to send young gentlemen and others of lesser status to the universities, and their social distribution can be measured approximately. Inventories inform on individual studies, while college records reveal Welsh group presences. The question of Jesus College, Oxford, as a Welsh national seminary deserves notice, and it and other colleges' contribution to the Welsh Anglican Church is revealing. University-trained scholars, moreover, were central to the creation of vernacular religious prose, while some 2 per cent of the intake participated in the English literary scene.

Robin GWYNDAF, Welsh Folk Museum
Subject: The Welsh folk narrative tradition: continuity and adaptation

Although Wales has not seen professional storytellers with a large repertoire of *märchen*, *novelle* and heroic tales since the Middle Ages, the Welsh folk narrative tradition (with its emphasis on brief socio-historical legends, memorates, jests and anecdotes) is still a very rich one. During 1964–86 a survey of this tradition was undertaken: over 2,000 persons were interviewed, and of these 370 were recorded on tape (*c.* 600 hours). In recording, special emphasis was given to the importance of verbatim texts (the lore of the folk) and to social context (the folk of the lore). The study of social context analysed the function of the narratives, the nature of the oral transmission, passive and active tradition-bearers, individual and collective tradition, and the informal and unconscious nature of the storytelling activity—the importance of studying narratives not so much as static items of folklore, but as narrative in action, narration as performance and a communicative process.

The present paper seeks to show how the Welsh folk narrative tradition has exhibited a remarkable continuity, and how it has adapted itself to changing social circumstances. To illustrate the shift from the *märchen* tale of wonder to the *sagen* local legend and memorate, and from the *novelle* to the joke, anecdote and local gossip, reference is made to modern Welsh versions of an international popular tale combining types A.T. 922 and A.T. 924 B ('The King and the Bishop' and 'Sign Language Misunderstood').

Professor Eric P. HAMP, University of Chicago
Subject: Tradition and innovation in modern Celtic languages

Language provides a useful and transparent sample of human culture. The Celtic languages have undergone notable changes in surface structure since Indo-European, even since Common Celtic. Yet their most innovative aspects can be shown to encompass and exemplify remarkable archaisms, i.e. continuities of tradition. Examples are drawn from modern and dialectal Scottish Gaelic, Breton and Welsh.

Scottish Gaelic conserves with fidelity Archaic Irish syllable count, including hiatus, *svarabhakti*, and consonant (resonant) strength, as well as much IE syllabic information; yet its neutralizations in non-initial syllables form a phonetic wonder for all Europe, and a total restructuring. In Vannetais drastic phonetic change makes it so that ironically consonants inform us on vowel content and vice versa; and archaic suppletives form new systems. Welsh plurals and singulatives conserve most IE noun stem information (even the semantax of collectives) in a new grammatical economy.

Tradition and innovation are aspects of continuity, never totalities.

Dr Leigh J. HANSEN, Marlborough School, Los Angeles
Subject: The poet in a changing society

Dafydd ap Gwilym was a classically trained bard, skilled in the traditional style of Welsh poetry, but as he saw his country's centuries-old way of life crumbling about him, he developed a need to escape from the formulaic eulogies and courtly love poems which no longer reflected reality. Innovative in style, subject, and form, his work spans the gap between the traditional Welsh society and the political and economic changes imposed by the English on the threshold of the Renaissance.

Although Dafydd has most often been compared to Ovid for this nature and love poetry, the parallel with Catullus is even more striking. Both were skilled poetic craftsmen who responded to a disintegrating system of values by abandoning older topics and forms of poetry and inventing a new, individualistic method of expression.

This paper points out similarities between the two in style, outlook and theme, and attempts to place each in the context of his changing society. Perhaps we can draw some conclusion from this comparison as to the poet's role at a time of change.

Dr Anthony HARVEY, Royal Irish Academy
Subject: The Ogam inscriptions and their geminate consonant symbols

A striking feature of the Irish Ogam inscriptions is the frequency with which consonantal symbols are doubled, and for nearly a century scholars have been suggesting tentatively that this phenomenon is in some way linked with the representation of lenition. To date, however, no rigorous statistical analysis has been carried out to evaluate this claim. The present paper offers such an analysis, based on a large sample of the Ogam corpus. The material is described, the method briefly outlined, and the findings explained. These are that a significant connection between orthographic gemination and phonological lenition is indeed implicated but that it is the opposite of what has conventionally been suggested, since gemination correlates with non-lenitability rather than with lenitability. This spelling feature and others (to be described) align the Ogam tradition firmly with early Irish Latinity, and the conclusion is put forward that a strongly cultural continuity seems likely to have existed between the two. Interestingly, this position is almost identical to that reached recently by Dr Damian McManus (*Ériu* 37) on entirely separate grounds.

John S. HENNESSEY, Jr., Anthropology Department, Columbia University
Subject: Spirantization to lenition in Kerauzern Breton: interpretation of morphophonological
      variability

This paper addresses the interpretation of variable dialect phenomena and the dangers inherent in sociological explanations of the same without understanding the recent grammatical history of the speech area. A series of changes has occurred in the morphophonology of Kerauzern (Ploubezre, C-du-N) Breton such that lenition now variably occurs in environments where the spirant mutation is historically 'expected': following the numerals 3, 4 and 9, and the possessive /ma/ ('my'). Younger speakers are progressive relative to older speakers, particularly with regard to leniting /ma/.

Similar Breton dialect data have been interpreted as evidence of grammatical simplification and declining speaker competence in a decaying speech community. Such an analysis does not account for the facts at Kerauzern.

Internal evidence and data from the ALBB indicate that the replacement of spirantization by lenition is largely recent in the area, and is an active change process. Older speakers are themselves 'progressive' as regards the changes, and younger speech shows an orderly extension of a tendency present throughout the speech community.

Phonological process complexity is unchanged, since all previous alternations still occur in some environments. Morphophonological pattern complexity is increased, since lenition in the new environments affects only radicals which could be spirantized.

Dr Máire HERBERT, University College, Cork
Subject: The Middle-Irish Prefaces to *Amra Coluim Cille*

Amra Coluim Cille is probably our earliest datable piece of Irish verse, composed around the time of the death of its subject, St Columba, in the year 597. Our surviving texts of the poem, however, date from the eleventh century onward. In its Middle-Irish redactions, the ancient poem not only is heavily glossed, but it also acquires a substantial amount of prefatory material. This links the circumstances of the poem's composition with events surrounding the historical 'Convention of Druim Cet' in the year 575. Does this material contain any shred of historical evidence or is it purely literary in origin? A re-examination of the texts seeks to address the problem.

Steve HEWITT, ENSTBr, Brest, Brittany
Subject: The pragmatics of Breton word order

This paper proposes an initial exploration of the hitherto unexplored problem of word order in Breton. The traditional dictum that the first word in the sentence is that to which the speaker wishes to draw attention means very little, and furthermore is simply not true. Using the pragmatic functions of functional sentence perspective theme, rheme, topic, focus, etc., two neutral orders are set up, VSO and SVO/TV . . . Expressive orders with initial focus seem to impose certain constraints on which arguments of the verb may subsequently be expressed, and these constraints are not always observed in the literary language as practised by non-native-speakers. The pragmatic role of the passive is considered and the existence of dialect variation is noted in the distribution of certain initial constructions: '*mañ* . . ., *bez*', '*e skriv* . . ., *h-an da lared*' . . .'

Humphrey Lloyd HUMPHREYS, St David's University College, Lampeter
Subject: Reflections on the verb-systems of contemporary Breton and Welsh

On the basis of readily available publications, it is extremely difficult for the outsider to arrive at a proper appreciation of the synchronic organization of the modern Brittonic verb. This is largely because the grammatical traditions of both languages are dominated by a prescriptivism which often ignores, and not infrequently contradicts, the reality of spoken usage, too often assumed to be globally inferior in quality. Adequate documentation will be provided in a handout, while the oral communication will comment on some salient characteristics and contrasts. Among these will be the marking of person and the role of compound tenses.

Dr Colin A. IRELAND, Dublin Institute for Advanced Studies
Subject: Aldfrith/Flann Fína: the Irish legacy of an Anglo-Saxon monarch

The Anglo-Saxon King Aldfrith/Flann Fína has a number of works in Irish attributed to him. He ruled Northumbria from 685 to 705. His father, King Oswy (ruled 642–70), had been educated among the Irish at Iona during Edwin's reign (617–33). His mother, Fín, was daughter of the northern Uí Néill High King Colmán Rímid. Aldfrith, like his father before him, was educated by the Irish at Iona. Two learned contemporaries, Adomnán of Iona and Aldhelm of Malmesbury, presented him with copies of their works. Bede described Aldfrith as a *vir in scripturis doctissimus*. At least four works in Irish are attributed to this exceptional, literate Anglo-Saxon king, yet there is not even a suggestion that he wrote anything in Old English. By examining those texts ascribed to him this paper will attempt to assess the influence this Anglo-Saxon monarch had on early Irish letters.

Dr Christine JAMES, University College, Swansea
Subject: Tradition and innovation in some later medieval Welsh lawbooks

Cyfraith Hywel is the traditional name given to native Welsh law, after the tenth-century king who was the purported instigator of those laws. While it is quite probable that Hywel Dda actually played a significant role in the development of Welsh law, the term *Cyfraith Hywel* is somewhat misleading since the earliest extant lawbooks in both Welsh and Latin are 'patch-works', containing much material which was already archaic in the tenth century, other material which we might easily believe to be contemporary with Hywel Dda, and yet further material which is demonstrably later than that period.

Although the defeat of Llywelyn in 1282 effectively heralded the demise of native Welsh law in Gwynedd, in certain parts of south Wales it remained a real and developing force until the second quarter of the sixteenth century. The south Wales lawbooks compiled during the fourteenth and fifteenth centuries include not only a basic recension of *Cyfraith Hywel* but also long and illuminating appendices of legal material of varying age, type and significance.

In this paper I propose to examine the construction of these later texts, paying particular attention to the 'appended' material.

Dr Elizabeth JEREM, Archaeological Institute of the Hungarian Academy of Sciences
Subject: Tradition and innovation in the Eastern Celtic culture

We would like to focus on two decisive periods of the late Iron Age in the Carpathian Basin. Above all, our aim is to endeavour to pursue the emergence of the La Tène culture in our area, to demonstrate the first appearance of Celtic stylistic elements in the archaeological material, and to indicate the direction of its influences.

For instance, there is a certain group of grave goods which can prove the mergence of local/native tradition into the characteristic assemblages of subsequent newcomers. Brisk trading contacts complete the finds-spectrum.

The next part of the paper examines the late development of the Celtic civilization, especially their workshops, pottery and metal production, their coinage, and organization of industry.

We then trace, with the help of new evidence, the increasing signs which support former convictions that the Celts preserved their own culture and actually survived for many centuries after the Roman conquest. One can even see nowadays that geographical names record relevant tradition among non-Celtic speakers up to the present day.

Dr David R. JOHNSTON, Adran y Gymraeg, Coleg y Brifysgol, Caerdydd
Subject: 'Henynt o le ni hunir'

Ymdrinnir ag awdl Llywelyn Goch ap Meurig Hen i Rydderch ab Ieuan Llwyd a Llywelyn Fychan, a geir yn Llyfr Coch Hergest, col. 1308-9. Yn gyntaf, eglurir cefndir hanesyddol y gerdd yng nghyd-destun traddodiad llenyddol Glyn Aeron yn yr Oesoedd Canol diweddar, gan roi sylw arbennig i Lywelyn Fychan a'i deulu. Ac yna trafodir rhai enghreifftiau o chwarae geiriol Llywelyn Goch, gyda sylwadau ar ffurf geiriau cyfansawdd y beirdd.

Professor Bedwyr Lewis JONES, Department of Welsh, University College of North Wales, Bangor
Subject: Henry Perri and the art of fine speech

Henry Perri's *Egluryn Phraethineb* (1595) is one of the most revealing works of the sixteenth-century 'humanists' in Wales. It is the fullest treatise on rhetoric in Welsh and the only one to be published in book form. The paper will outline how Perri gathered material for his book from an earlier Welsh rhetorical treatise by William Salesbury, from contemporary handbooks on rhetoric in English—especially the 1593 edition of Peacham's *Garden of Eloquence*, from manuscripts of Welsh poetry, etc. It will go on to argue that Perri then reorganized the material for presentation according to new principles of rhetorical theory laid down by Petrus Ramus. In this respect the paper will differ from G. J. Williams's introduction to the 1930 re-edition of *Egluryn Phraethineb*. Finally, a brief attempt will be made to place Perri's Ramist work in its context amongst tracts on rhetoric in Welsh and to assess its influence.

Nerys Ann JONES, Y Ganolfan Uwchefrydiau Cymreig a Cheltaidd, Aberystwyth
Subject: Breintiau a Gwelygorddau Cynddelw—'Propaganda'r Prydydd'?

Mae Gwelygorddau Powys a Breintiau Gwŷr Powys gan Gynddelw Brydydd Mawr yn ddwy gerdd sy'n sefyll ar wahân i holl waith y Gogynfeirdd. Yn y papur hwn bwriadaf gynnig cyd-destun hanesyddol iddynt yng ngwleidyddiaeth y ddeuddegfed ganrif a cheisio dangos sut y maent yn unigryw o ran cynnwys, arddull a mesur.

Yr Athro R. M. JONES, Adran y Gymraeg, Coleg Prifysgol Cymru, Aberystwyth
Subject: Traddodiad yr Ymddiddan

Diffinnir yr Ymddiddan yn ffurfiol. Dangosir fod yna draddodiad helaeth o Ymddiddan o gyfnod y Canu Cynnar hyd at J.R. a Brutus yn y ganrif ddiwethaf. Eithr parhad catastroffig ydyw, parhad a geir nid oherwydd dylanwad uniongyrchol un gwaith ar waith arall, eithr oherwydd fod pob gwaith yn ei dro yn llenwi anghenion y ffurf. Y patrwm ffurfiol yn y meddwl a dros-glwyddir ac sy'n rhoi i'r Ymddiddan ei sefydlogrwydd. Ond pan ymyrra nodweddion ffurfiol y ddrama aeddfed, y cilia'r Ymddiddan.

Dr K. JONGELING, Department of Hebrew, State University of Leiden, Netherlands
Subject: Similarities between Welsh and Hebrew, typological remarks

Similarities between Welsh and Hebrew have attracted scholarly attention for a long time, sometimes to such an extent that a historical, genetic relationship of the two languages was postulated (with a broader view this was done for Insular Celtic and Hamito-Semitic by Pokorny and Wagner, using the substratum theory). We are not convinced of this direct historical relation, but the similarities between Welsh and Hebrew remain and they are interesting from a typological point of view. Many striking similarities are to be found in syntactical constructions, e.g. the expression of the 'genitive' relation combining two nouns (and the use of the article in this case) both in Welsh and Hebrew by juxtaposition of the two nouns; the order noun-adjective-adverb; the existence of conjugated prepositions in both languages; the combination of personal forms of verbs or prepositions with longer forms of the pronouns; the use of the infinitive to describe a circumstance or something like it; the 'replacement' of a finite verb by an infinitive in a series of co-ordinate statements; the order verb-subject-object in many sentence types; comparable construction of several types of subordinate clauses, etc. The similarities thus found may be useful in several ways: (a) on a very practical level, description of one language may profit from insights gained in the study of the other one, (b) typological similarities may supply means to assess relations connecting different grammatical features (as e.g. the probable relation between the noun-adjective-adverb order, and the verb-subject-object order)—comparisons with other languages are necessary in this case, (c) something more definite may be said on the theory historically linking Welsh and Hebrew by taking into account the probability of typological similarities.

Professor Fergus KELLY, Dublin Institute for Advanced Studies
Subject: Early Irish crops

In this lecture, I discuss what the written sources (mainly seventh- to eighth-century law texts) tell us about the crops grown by the Early Irish. Most of the information relates to the types of cereal which were grown, but there is also reference to the cultivation of peas, beans, other vegetables, medicinal herbs, fruit-trees, dye-plants and flax. I discuss the soil preparation, planting, harvesting, processing and storage of these crops.

P. R. KITSON, Department of English, University of Birmingham
Subject: On the voicing or otherwise of Brittonic final voiceless stops under lenition

Standard doctrine (Jackson LHEB 552–3 etc.) is that final, like, medial, lenited, voiceless stops were uniformly pronounced voiced in OWCB. This necessitates explaining away substantial evidence in OE borrowings from 'Prw' that they were voiced medially but not finally. The purpose of this paper is to show that explaining away (LHEB 555 etc.) rests on a misunderstanding by Ekwall of English dialect developments, and is untenable. There is also positive reason, in the position of the accent in OWCB, why the voicing of final stops should not have been general until the Middle period, and positive evidence from Cornish and elsewhere that the voiceless variant survived until then.

Dr John T. KOCH, Harvard University
Subject: Manawydan, Mandubracios

A detailed correspondence can be demonstrated between the characters Caswallawn and Manawydan of the medieval Welsh Mabinogi on the one hand and Cassivellaunos and Mandubracios (as they figured in Caesar's British campaign of 54 BC) on the other. Implications proceed concerning the mythological 'deep structure' of *Manawydan* and the Four Branches generally. An examination of other reflexes of the historical events (as per, e.g., Orosius, Bede, Nennius, Geoffrey, and the Triads) points towards an independent native witness subsumed into the Welsh versions. The tentative theory advanced is of an underlying saga of gods and heroes that glorified the anti-Roman Catuvellauni and cast the philo-Roman Mandubracios (Manawydan) as a quintessential Celtic 'un-king' who—like the Irish *anflaith* Lugaid Mac Con—shirked battle, handled mice, and presided over a blighted wasteland.

Dr Heidi Ann LAZAR-MEYN, University of Pennsylvania
Subject: The historical development of the common Celtic colour system

Comparative linguistic evidence establishes that common Celtic had four basic colour terms, i.e. colours that could not be described as 'shades of another colour', represented in Goidelic and Brythonic respectively by O.Ir. *dub*, W. *du* (black), O.Ir. *find*, W. *gwyn* (white), O.Ir. *ruad*, W. *rhudd* (red), and O.Ir. and W. *glas* (green). Although both groups in the historical period are five-colour systems, O.Ir. *buide*, W. *melyn* (yellow) are linguistically unrelated and appear to be marginal members of the system. Both groups include the cognate O.Ir. *liath*, W. *llwyd* (grey), but this term is not part of the basic system of either group.

This paper will analyse the usage of these and other non-basic colour terms in early Irish and Welsh literature, with comparative data from the other Celtic languages. It will trace the integration of 'yellow' into the four-colour system, the relegation of *find* and *ruad* to subsidiary terms in the Goidelic languages in favour of *bán* and *derg* respectively, leading to parallel non-basic systems, and the coexistence of *rhudd* and *coch* in the Brythonic languages. Of particular interest are compound colour-words, composed of two terms which may be either both basic, both non-basic, or one of each, as they establish where the boundaries of colour terms and systems meet. If time permits, I will remark on colour-term usage in Celtic-language translations of the Old Testament, as compared both with other Celtic languages and with the original Hebrew, which has an identical five-colour system: ʃáxór (black), *láván* (white), *ádom* (red), *jǎrók* (green), and *tsáhóv* (yellow) (marginal).

Dr Wendy J. LEWIS, Harvard University
Subject: Another look at the *-éba* future in Middle Irish

Among the more interesting verb forms which arise in Middle Irish are future forms in *-éb-*, e.g. *ní aidlébthai* BDD 709. Thurneysen, and later Marstrander, proposed that these forms resulted from a misanalysis of the future stem of GAB-compounds, e.g. *turcéba* (*torcbaid*), *faicéba* (*fácbaid*). This paper proposes instead that the *-éba* future forms are part of a more general Middle Irish phenomenon: 'hybrid' forms.

Hybrid forms are defined as forms which combine elements of different stem formations, e.g. future *rirfes* SR 1073 (reduplication and *-f-* suffix), preterite *-mertsam* SR 3029 (*-t-* and *-s-* suffixes). It is shown that such forms are characterized by very specific criteria. Based on this discussion, it is argued that the -*éba* futures can be explained formally as examples of hybrid forms combining elements of the -*é*- and -*f*- futures. Furthermore, -*éba* futures meet the criteria characteristic of other hybrids.

Ceridwen LLOYD-MORGAN, National Library of Wales, Aberystwyth
Subject: Elis Gruffudd's Arthurian history and its sources

The Arthurian section of Elis Gruffudd's *Chronicle* is compiled, like the rest of that work, from a variety of sources. For his account of the history of Arthur's reign, Elis Gruffudd turned to a variety of Latin, French and Welsh texts. Comparison of this material with the chronicler's narrative sheds light upon his methods of selection, editing and presentation, and suggests that whilst he shared some of the characteristics of contemporary chroniclers outside Wales, he also has strong affinities with the traditions and practices of Welsh redactors of the later Middle Ages.

Peredur LYNCH, Y Ganolfan Uwchefrydiau Cymreig a Cheltaidd, Aberystwyth
Subject: Goronwy Owen a'r Gogynfeirdd

Darlun digon annelwig, yn ôl ein safonau ni o leiaf, oedd gan Gymry'r ddeunawfed ganrif o orffennol llenyddol eu gwlad. Hyd y mae hynny'n bosibl, fe grynhoïr eu syniadau a'u gwybodaeth hwy am y Gogynfeirdd fel rhan o gefndir y papur.

Yn Walton, a chan hynny ar ôl y cyfnod tra chynhyrchiol hwnnw yn Donnington, y cyflwynwyd Goronwy i waith y Gogynfeirdd. Ofer felly i raddau helaeth yw sôn am ddylanwad uniongyrchol y Gogynfeirdd ar ei gerddi cynnar pwysig, ond cawn drafod paham y credai fod gwaith y Gogynfeirdd yn gydnaws â'i syniadau ef ei hunan ynglŷn â barddoniaeth. Cawn holi hefyd a oes rhywbeth yn natur y prif ddylanwadau llenyddol a fu arno sy'n egluro paham y gwirionodd i'r fath raddau ar eu gwaith.

Pa mor gywir mewn gwirionedd oedd adnabyddiaeth Goronwy o'r Gogynfeirdd? Ai'r un nodweddion a welai ef yn eu gwaith ag a welwn ni heddiw? Beth yn y pen draw oedd natur ei ddiddordeb ynddynt? Dyna rai o'r cwestiynau y gobeithir eu hateb yn y papur hwn.

Donald MACAULAY, Department of Celtic, University of Aberdeen
Subject: Tradition or innovation? Some linguistic similarities between Scottish Gaelic and Welsh

The paper will present some typological similarities between Scottish Gaelic and Welsh concentrating on cases where Scottish Gaelic is divergent from Irish.

Syntactic similarities (for example, in the expression of aspectual differences) and morphophonemic similarities (for example, the exponents of nasal mutation in dialects such as that of the Island of Lewis) will be looked at particularly, but not exclusively.

The implications of these typological similarities will be discussed: whether they represent conservation; whether they represent inter-P- and Q-Celtic interference (for example, the influence on Gaelic of contact with P-Celtic varieties in Scotland); whether they represent a natural structural convergence, given the common elements with the languages, under outside pressure; or whether they are a function of serendipity.

Uáitéar MAC GEARAILT, St Patrick's College, Drumcondra, Dublin 9
Subject: The date of composition of some later Ulster Cycle tales

In his *Die irische Helden- und Königssage*, Thurneysen assigned the late versions of *Cath Ruis na Ríg* and *Aided Con Culainn* to a fifteenth-century *Modernisator*. In his view they are based to one degree or another on the twelfth-century Book of Leinster texts of those tales. E. J. Gwynn, the editor of the metrical *Dindsenchas*, considered the tale *Cath Cumair* to be a late composition based on Cúán úa Lothcháin's (ob. 1024) topographical poem *Druim Criaich*. In this paper the author re-examines the views of Thurneysen and Gwynn and considers the evidence in favour of late dates of composition.

Caoimhín MAC GIOLLA LÉITH, University of Edinburgh
Subject: Oidheadh Chloinne Uisneach: innovation and modification in the transmission of a Gaelic romance

It is not uncommon for editors of Early Modern Gaelic texts to dismiss as 'corrupt', 'degenerate' and consequently unworthy of attention all but a handful of early MS versions of a given text. This practice has the unfortunate consequence that much that is of interest in the development of these texts in the MS and oral tradition of Gaelic Ireland and Scotland is neglected or obscured.

This paper proposes to take as a case study one of the most popular of the medieval romances, *Oidheadh Chloinne Uisneach* (OCU), and discuss its development and transmission from the earliest extant MS, the (early sixteenth-century?) 'Glenmasan MS', unfortunately incomplete, down to the paper MSS of the nineteenth century. The relationship of OCU to the earlier *Longes Mac nUislenn* and the influence of the version of these events recounted in Keating's *History of Ireland* on the development of OCU is discussed. An attempt is made to sketch a rough taxonomy of change and innovation in the transmission of this text which, it is hoped, may contribute to an understanding of the nature of the transmission of Early Modern Gaelic narrative in general.

Dr Kenneth MacKINNON, The Hatfield Polytechnic Lesser-Used Languages Research Unit
Subject: Language maintenance and viability in contemporary Gaelic-speaking communities: Skye and the Western Isles today

Language-shift in the Scottish Gaidhealtachd has contracted the strongly Gaelic-speaking area to the Western Isles and parts of the Inner Hebrides. The language is moribund over most of its traditional Highlands area, yet three-quarters of its speakers live outside the 'Gaelic areas'.

The 1984 Montgomery Report on Scottish Island Areas asked whether Gaelic had prospects of continuation and viability. A current ESRC-funded survey attempts an answer.

Recent censuses have indicated some aspects of viability and even regeneration of Gaelic. The survey seeks to identify social and individual factors which are associated with language retention, intergenerational transmission, everyday usage and language loyalty.

Skye provides an interesting contrast between areas which have been urbanized, penetrated by incomers and increasingly anglicized, and areas which demonstrate viability of the Gaelic population and high incidence of speakers amongst all age-groups. Analysis of usage patterns and attitude levels with social identity can help to identify factors promoting maintenance and decline.

Professor Gordon W. MACLENNAN, University of Ottawa, Canada
Subject: Linguistic notes on the Irish of Donegal

Le cupla bliain anuas tá mé ag obair ar stór béaloidis Aine Nic Ghrianna, nach maireann, as Rann na Feirste, Tir Chonaill, á athscriobh, ag cur eagair air, agus á dheánamh réidh le foilisiú. Tá an chuid is mó den ábhar i dtaisce i láimhscríbhinni Roinn an Bhéaloidis, Coláiste na hOllscoile, Baile Atha Cliath, ach thaifead mé féin cuid dó. Beidh mé ag caint sa pháipéar seo ar chuid do na rudai suimiúla a thug mé fá dear i gcanúint Aine i dtaca le foghraíocht, deilbhíocht, comhréir, foclóir, agus cora cainte.

Dr Liam MAC MATHÚNA, Coláiste Phádraig, Baile Átha Cliath/St Patrick's College, Dublin
Subject: On the semantics of Irish words derived from IE *g^{u}her-* 'hot'

The study of the origin and history of individual items of the vocabulary of the Irish language has been increasingly supplemented in recent years by the application of methodology grounded in lexical field theory. Words belonging to particular lexical sets have been investigated, their synchronic, semantic interrelationship observed and parallels in their diachronic development from disparate roots traced. Semantic affinity has been the point of analytical departure. This paper adopts the contrary approach with regard to the IE root *g^{u}her-* 'hot', which has been quite productive in Irish and yielded reflexes of special interest. The Irish words derived from this one IE root are subjected to a case-study, as it were, in order to examine the interaction of morphological and semantic change. In conclusion, any perceived general implications of etymon-derivatives study for conventional lexical field research in Irish will be discussed.

Dr A. T. E. MATONIS, Temple University, Philadelphia, Pennsylvania, USA
Subject: The conservative impulse of the Welsh bardic grammars

My paper will argue first that, if we fail to appreciate the importance of grammatical tracts in the Middle Ages or to see the Welsh grammars as part of this tradition, we miss a major source for understanding the intellectual history of the period. However, rather than playing an innovative role (as did the speculative grammars), the Welsh grammars represent an earlier tradition which ties the study of grammar closely to the analysis of literary forms. Here comparisons can be made with the speculative grammars, which disdained all attempts at descriptive formulation of patterns and rules, and which, basing their study on extra-linguistic premises, ushered in a dialectical preoccupation with metaphysics and logic. Thus the very nature and objectives of the speculative grammars distinguish them from the Welsh texts—though here recognizing that the aim of the Welsh grammars is debatable. The Welsh grammars will then be compared to Geoffrey of Vinsauf's *Poetria nova* and Dante's *De Vulgari Eloquentia* with particular attention to the traditional and innovative features of each.

Professor Catherine A. McKENNA, Queens College and Graduate Center, City University of New York
Subject: Hagiographic and panegyric traditions in Llywelyn Fardd's *Canu i Gadfan*

John Lloyd-Jones and J. E. Caerwyn Williams, among others, have noted that the *Canu i Gadfan*, like other *Gogynfeirdd* poems in honour of saints, is as much a poem about Cadfan's church in Tywyn as it is a poem about the saint himself. Nevertheless, the poem is one of our primary sources of traditions connected with Cadfan.

I would argue that the content of the *Canu i Gadfan* is a function of the conventions of the *Gogynfeirdd molawd*: the biographical patterning of the saint's *vita* or *actae* has no place in such a poem, whether religious or secular. This paper will discuss the differences between two kinds of celebratory text, hagiography and panegyric, and will examine the traditions concerning Cadfan that can be elicited from the poem when it is read in the context of bardic conventions.

Professor Daniel F. MELIA, University of California, Berkeley
Subject: Irish saints' lives as historical sources

In his recent survey titled *Medieval Households* (Cambridge, Mass.: Harvard University Press, 1975), David Herlihy devotes a section of the chapter 'The Household in Late Barbarian Antiquity' to Irish households in the period 800–1200. Admittedly an outsider with respect to Celtic scholarship, he is nevertheless able to draw up a coherent picture of certain aspects of medieval Irish family life based on material he extracts from a variety of Irish hagiographical material—some in Latin, and some translated from Irish into English. I think that there will be agreement among social historians of the Celts that Herlihy is correct about some things and incorrect about others. What I wish to discuss here, however, is the validity of using material selected from a rather varied corpus of pseudo-historical and pietistic literature to draw historical conclusions. I argue that the means are available to develop principles of selection more powerful than Herlihy's (what seems plausible to him as a social historian of other cultures) for testing the likelihood of the correct depiction of certain customs. Knowledge of the apparent political and social aims of the authors of the saints' lives (e.g. the status of women, and fines for their abuse, proposed in *Cáin Adamnáin* by a legally trained cleric) can provide systematic rather than impressionistic evidence. Close reading with an eye to the author's relationship to his primary intended audience can indicate which details are part of the argument and which are incidental. The evident stylistic overlap among hagiographical, legal and saga material gives further clues as to which elements are fanciful and which credible.

Professor Joseph Falaky NAGY, University of California, Los Angeles
Subject: Compositional concerns in the *Acallam na Senórach*

There has been little scholarly consideration in the past of the relationship between the form and the content of the redactions of the medieval Irish work *Acallam na Senórach* ('Colloquy of the Ancients'). In this paper an attempt is made to establish from the text what were the main criteria used by the author(s) for their selection and arrangement of Fenian (and some non-Fenian) lore, and to determine the thematic connections, if any, between the inserted materials and the framing premise of the *Acallam* (i.e., Patrick's encounter and discourse with the Fenian survivors). What we learn from such an investigation puts us in a better position to understand the possible functions and meanings of the *Acallam* within the medieval literary tradition.

Professor Kenneth E. NILSEN, St Francis Xavier University, Antigonish, Nova Scotia
Subject: Gaelic in mainland Nova Scotia

The Gaelic of mainland Nova Scotia has received little attention from scholars in recent years. This paper will provide a brief sketch of the history and present state of Gaelic in mainland Nova Scotia. Based partially on recently collected oral material, the paper will describe several vibrant Gaelic-speaking communities which persisted on the Nova Scotia mainland until the early decades of this century. Notable features of the dialect will be discussed and their relation to similar phenomena in the Gaelic dialects of Scotland will be treated.

Elizabeth O'BRIEN, Dundrum, Dublin
Subject: Tradition and innovation—a review of burial practices in late prehistoric to early historic Ireland

A significant amount of information regarding the culture, customs and economy of a people at particular periods in time can be gleaned from reliably dated literary sources. The value of such information is further enhanced when it can be compared with the archaeological record. Using this interdisciplinary approach it is possible to comment (1) on lingering traditional Iron Age burial practices in Early Christian Ireland, and (2) on the introduction of Roman-derived burial practices. This combination of literary and archaeological evidence can also help ascertain when, and for what reasons, burial in formal Christian cemeteries superseded pagan burial practices in Ireland.

Máirtín Ó BRIAIN, Department of Modern Irish, National University of Ireland
Subject: Tradition and innovation in eighteenth-century Ossianic poetry: 'Oisín in the Land of the Young'

'Laoidh Oisín ar Thír na nÓg', which is attributed to an eighteenth-century Clare poet, Micheál Coimín, comes towards the end of a long tradition of Ossianic lays. It tells of Oisín's enticement to Tír na nÓg (The Land of the Young) and how, having spent more than 300 years there, he met St Patrick when he returned to Ireland. The lay fills an important gap in the Ossianic tradition since no explanation of Oisín's longevity had hitherto been furnished in the corpus of Ossianic lays. Its author has combined traditional literary and folk elements in order to remedy this defect. This paper traces some of Coimín's sources and examines his use of them and explains how his version of the story has gained universal acceptance and has been recognized as the standard and definitive one.

Dr Ailbhe Ó CORRÁIN, Uppsala University, Sweden
Subject: The syntax and semantics of repetition in Irish

One of the most characteristic features of the Irish language in both its written and spoken varieties is the frequent occurrence of various forms of repetition. However, this phenomenon has received surprisingly little scholarly attention and, as yet, no detailed examination of the basic syntactic patterns and functions of verbal (as opposed to thematic) repetition has been made. This paper will concentrate on the modern language and attempt to distinguish and classify the most important types of verbal or phrasal repetition.

The material will be codified according to various criteria and three overall categories of repetition distinguished. The word classes which most frequently undergo reiteration will be dealt with in turn and the syntactic patterns within each category delineated. The functions of the various types of repetition will also be examined.

Professor Donnchadh Ó CORRAIN, Department of Irish History, University College, Cork, Ireland
Subject: Women and the law: some legal aspects of *pica* and other female conditions in early Irish law

An outline of the paper would be as follows: (1) to establish the occurrence of *pica* as a socially recognized condition (this can be done from the Patrician hagiography and the law texts); (2) to outline the legal responsibility of the husband if he failed to meet his wife's need in this respect; and (3) to discuss the legal responsibility of the woman suffering from *pica* in respect of property and in respect of her pregnancy. This would entail a discussion of *Corpus Iuris Hibernici*, 270–1, 940–1, 1256–7 and related materials. Reference would also be made to other legal materials bearing on pregnancy and related conditions.

Diarmuid Ó LAOGHAIRE, Institute of Theology and Philosophy, Dublin
Subject: Common prayer tradition of Ireland and Scotland; native and European roots

There is a common heritage of traditional prayer, mostly in verse, in Ireland and Scotland. The great Scottish collection, *Carmina Gadelica*, and the various Irish collections often show even verbal identity. Since the two countries effectively ceased to have cultural relations after the mid-eighteenth century at latest, these prayers, many of them still current, can be dated back to at least the seventeenth century. A good number of the prayers belong to the common pre-Reformation, European tradition, while others are of native or common Celtic origin.

Dr Damien Ó MUIRÍ, St Patrick's College, Maynooth
Subject: Neuter gender in Old Irish

Old Irish, unlike Middle and Modern Irish, had three genders, masculine, feminine and neuter, the disappearance of the latter being an inevitable consequence of the loss of phonemic contrast in unstressed vowels, which occurred at the end of the early period. Notwithstanding the survival of neuter inflection in countless phrases for several hundred years and the persistence of a few old neuters in calcified words or phrases down to the present day, it seems likely, however, that neuter gender was far from being productive, even during the Classical Old Irish period. Given this fact, together with the extended period covered by the *Contributions to a Dictionary of the Irish Language*, our corpus, admittedly, is doubtless incomplete, yet it is hoped that, based on the evidence provided by the extant examples and the predictability of patterns generally, a hypothetical reconstruction of the probable rules determining the assignment of neuter gender to nouns can be achieved.

Morfydd E. OWEN, The Centre for Advanced Welsh and Celtic Studies
Subject: Dr John Davies and the *Gogynfeirdd*

The Renaissance scholar, Dr John Davies of Mallwyd, like many of his contemporaries throughout Europe, was a key figure in the history of the transmission of the texts of the Middle Ages to later times. His *Liber A*, BL Add MS 14869, and *Liber B*, NLW MS 4973B, are the fruits of his attempt to compile a full corpus of *Gogynfeirdd* poetry. These manuscripts are revealing, not only with regard to John Davies's editorial methods, but also for the light they throw on the medieval sources for *Gogynfeirdd* poetry available at the time of the Renaissance.

Dr Meirion PENNAR, Coleg Prifysgol Dewi Sant, Llanbedr Pont Steffan
Subject: Morgan Llwyd a'r Chwyldro

Ceisir mynd i'r afael â rhan Morgan Llwyd yn y gwaith o greu ac o lunio'r Chwyldro Piwritanaidd yn ystod y ddau brif gyfnod 1641–7 a 1648–56.

Pwysir ar ei gerddi, ei lythyron a'i weithiau printiedig yn Gymraeg ac yn Saesneg wrth geisio trafod ei osgo syniadol, yn grefyddol ac yn wleidyddol. Olrheinir hefyd ddatblygiad ei feddwl effro hyd at ei farwolaeth yn 1659.

Dr Erich POPPE, Philipps-Universität Marburg
Subject: A functional approach to Middle Welsh word-order

One peculiar feature of MW syntax is the fact that the statistically 'normal' word-order in a positive statement is 'abnormal', at least in current grammatical terminology, but also when compared to the regular order verb-subject-object in Old and Modern Welsh. In a MW positive statement, (at least) one sentence constituent (subject, object, or adverbial expression) normally precedes the verb; exceptions are rare. The approach advanced here attempts to explain the choice of fronted constituents in terms of their function for the information-structure of a sentence within its context. It is suggested that a fronted constituent normally acts as topic, i.e. it delineates what the sentence is about. It thus constitutes the starting-point for the display of the information contained in the sentence. A number of examples will be discussed in detail to show the application of the theory. Particular attention will be paid to the explanation of the position of temporal adverbials which function as sentential and scene-setting when fronted. The problem whether MW had a fixed word-order will be considered briefly.

Dr Huw PRYCE, History Department, University College of North Wales, Bangor
Subject: Trefeglwys and the 'Celtic charter-tradition' in twelfth-century Wales

The two earliest charters relating to St Michael's Church, Trefeglwys (Arwystli), record grants made in the second third of the twelfth century by Madog ap Maredudd, King of Powys, and Hywel ap Ieuaf, King of Arwystli. These grants predate the transfer of Trefeglwys to Haughmond Abbey, Shropshire. Both documents are of particular interest in that they exhibit a significant number of features associated with the 'Celtic' tradition of charter-writing to which Professor Wendy Davies has drawn attention. This paper opens with a brief discussion of the authenticity of the charters, before proceeding to a diplomatic analysis of their structure and formulae, paying particular attention to the question of how far these represent native practices of charter-writing; in conclusion, it assesses the importance of these documents as sources for the relations between churches and native rulers in twelfth-century Wales.

Professor Joan N. RADNER, American University, Washington, DC
Subject: Interpreting irony in medieval Celtic narrative: the case of *Culhwch ac Olwen*

Whether they have emphasized its relation to oral or to literary tradition, scholars have tended to regard *Culhwch ac Olwen* with some frustration, and most have explicitly or implicitly assumed—considering the pervasive anomalies of structure and tone—that the author of the tale was to some degree incompetent. It has been easier for scholars to quarry *Culhwch ac Olwen* for the ore of early Arthurian tradition than to interpret it as a fully realized work in its own right.

An ironic interpretation of *Culhwch ac Olwen*, however, allows the text to be seen as a competent and coherent literary production directed strategically at a particular audience. In addition, such an approach suggests that *Culhwch ac Olwen* be treated more cautiously than formerly as a source of information about Arthurian origins. Finally, ironic interpretation is offered as a fruitful strategy for dealing with aspects of other medieval Celtic narratives which have so far proved intractable to contemporary scholarship.

Jan Erik REKDAL, Keltisk Institutt, Blindern, Oslo
Subject: Approaching a description of the sixteenth-century *Life of Columcille* (*Betha Colaim Chille*)—the text and its traditions

In his description of this *Life of Columcille* Joseph Szövérffy, the folklorist and medievalist, implicitly defines the two traditions which it conflates: 'Written at the threshold of the Middle Ages and the modern world, . . . it is indeed a bridge between medieval Irish tradition and modern folklore' (*Éigse* 8:108). This differentiation by Szövérffy, of medieval Irish tradition on one side and modern folklore on the other, does not hold good if we are to accept the opinion (most distinctly formulated by Professor Mac Cana) that medieval Irish literature is characterized by the interaction of a monastic (written and Christian) tradition and a native (oral and pagan) one. Our description of this Life depends on how we define the medieval Irish literary tradition and terms such as 'tradition' and 'innovation'. Only then may we arrive at an understanding of the concept of genre underlying this text and an appreciation that will refute the misapprehension of this Life as indicated once by Joseph Vendryès: 'Les défauts du genre y apparaissant même d'autant plus qu'elle est de dimensions plus étendues . . . Malheureusement il (Manus O'Donnell) manquait de critique, et par suite il n'échappe pas aux reproches que méritent les hagiographes plus anciens dont il s'est inspiré' (*Revue Celtique* 39:88).

Robert G. RHYS, Adran y Gymraeg, Coleg y Brifysgol, Abertawe
Subject: Dieithrio'r Cyfarwydd: traddodiad a newydd-deb yng ngwaith Gwyn Thomas

Edrychir ar y berthynas gyfoethog rhwng traddodiad a newydd-deb ym marddoniaeth Gwyn Thomas. Er iddo gael ei gydnabod yn un o feirdd mwyaf gwreiddiol a ffres ei genhedlaeth, eto nid mabwysiadu dyfeisiau ymwybodol 'arbrofol' a wnaeth, nac ychwaith impio ffasiynau cyfoes ar gnewyllyn traddodiadol: yr hyn a wnaeth yn hytrach oedd rhoi swyddogaeth a chyd-destun newydd i ddyfeisiau traddodiadol gan adfer iddynt lawer o'u grym cysefin. Sylwir yn arbennig ar y defnydd helaeth a wna o ffigurau traddodiadol fel haul, gaeaf, nos, niwl ac ati ac ar ei ymdrechion i ddieithrio ymateb y darllenydd i'r ffigurau confensiynol hyn. Cyfeirir hefyd at y swyddogaethau a rydd i odl a chytseinedd a dadleuir fod modd canfod yr allwedd i rym y farddoniaeth yn aml trwy sylwi ar absenoldeb dyfeisiau barddonol poblogaidd.

R. J. ROBERTS, Bodleian Library, Oxford
Subject: John Dee and the matter of Britain

John Dee as a Renaissance collector of books and manuscripts amassed a great deal of material on British and Welsh history, and recorded the whereabouts of 'monuments' in the hands of others. He does not seem to have taken much interest either in those or in his Welsh ancestry in the first forty years of his long life, but contacts with his 'cousins' (who included Thomas Jones of Tregaron and John Prise) seem to have increased after 1567 and particularly after about 1570; perhaps under the influence of the antiquarian publishing of Matthew Parker and his circle, and the posthumous publication of Prise's *Defensio* and Llwyd's *Commentarioli*, Dee visited Wales in 1574 and seems to have picked up some documents on his journey. Several of his texts of Geoffrey of Monmouth (manuscript and printed), and of Gildas, have survived with heavy annotations, as have some of his Welsh manuscripts where the notes show he could understand some of the contents. His obsessive interest in Arthur underpinned the imperialist 'Art of Navigation' in 1577 and provided justification for *British* claims on the New World. Dee's industry also produced versions of his own pedigree. After the disastrous Continental journey of 1583–9 Dee's 'British' interest declined, but he was still supplied with food by his Welsh cousins in his later years.

Dr John SHAW, Glendale, Nova Scotia, Boe, Canada
Subject: Gaelic songs from Cape Breton and Scotland: a cultural comparison

Among researchers on both sides of the Atlantic there has been an active interest in comparing the traditions of Gaelic Scotland with those of Cape Breton Island, Nova Scotia, North America's only remaining Gaelic-speaking region. One area in which the two Gaelic communities contrast noticeably is in the songs—particularly those dealing with social commentary, nature, immigration and the politics of Gaeldom—composed since the time of emigration and the settlement of Cape Breton in the early nineteenth century. Such a contrast is of considerable interest in view of the role played by songs in providing the main internal historical and social record of Gaeldom. Songs from Cape Breton bards, drawn from printed sources and field recordings, will be compared with published collections and studies of their nineteenth-century counterparts in Scotland and the implications with regard to outlook, underlying causes and cultural evolution will be discussed.

Professor Edgar M. SLOTKIN, University of Cincinnati
Subject: Fabula, story, and text in *Breuddwyd Rhonabwy*

Breuddwyd Rhonabwy is unique among medieval dream visions in that the sequential ordering of the text's dream runs backwards. This anachronous nature of the dream story has a number of implications: (1) we are forced to consider the dream seriously as a dream and not merely as a convention or a parody of a convention; (2) the expected effects from the causes narrated do not occur but lead only to further causes. Employing a narratological analysis, I shall suggest that these 'incoherent' features of *Breuddwyd Rhonabwy* have a coherent purpose in which satire plays only one part. Those scholars who have noted the contrast between the dream and the frame story have been on the right track as was Mary Giffin in her dating of the text.

Professor Nancy STENSON, University of Minnesota
Subject: Initial mutation of loanwords: some Irish evidence

In his 1983 study of the interaction of loanwords with initial mutations in Scottish Gaelic, Watson called for additional studies of as many dialects as possible in order to help clarify the patterns of initial mutations as applied to loanwords in the Gaelic languages. This paper answers that call with an examination of the behaviour of loanwords in mutation environments for an Irish dialect. Although certain consonants seem to undergo the appropriate mutations quite regularly and unexceptionally, others exhibit considerable variation in their behaviour, both cross-dialectally and within dialects. This variation will be examined for the speech of Ráth Cairn, Co. Meath. The occurrence of mutations with the various consonants will be tabulated and compared with Watson's data and that available from other dialects of Irish. Segments will be classified according to level of susceptibility to mutations, so that generalizations can be made characterizing specific consonant groups with shared behaviour patterns. Watson's proposal to explain the variation in terms of preservation of the identity of the radical consonant will be examined and refined in light of the new data.

   Reference: Watson Seosamh (1983), 'Loan-words and Initial Mutations in a Gaelic Dialect', *Scottish Gaelic Studies* 14:100–13.

Dr Janig STEPHENS
Subject: Non-finite construction in Breton

In this paper I propose to examine a number of non-finite clauses, some of which are complement clauses, in which case the question arises as to whether they are VPs or Ss with a PRO subject. Breton has also non-finite constructions of a more independent nature as in:

'KARO,' EME KAOURINTIN, HAG INT O TIJUNIN ER GAMBR.
'Karo,' said Kaourintin, and they Prog. breakfasting in the bedroom.
'Karo,' said Kaourintin while they were having breakfast in the bedroom.

Sentences like this raise the question of order of constituents. Breton has a basic VSO order, but here the subject is in initial position. Is SVO the basic order in non-finite clauses and do we have a two-order system in Breton?

Dr Marie SURRIDGE, Queen's University, Kingston, Ontario, Canada
Subject: Linguistic factors governing gender assignment in Welsh

The assignment of grammatical gender to Welsh words has received little attention in the recent past either from diachronic or from synchronic linguists. This paper addresses both the proportions of masculine, feminine and variable gender words and the influence of linguistic factors which allow gender to be predicted with a considerable degree of accuracy.

   Stratified sampling indicates that the percentage of feminines in Welsh is below 30 per cent and that of variables below 3 per cent. Furthermore, it will be shown that the gender of a high proportion of the feminines is assigned according to relatively simple rules.

   Gender assignment in Welsh, as in other Indo-European languages, is influenced by sexui-semblance (the identification of male with masculine and female with feminine), the association of a given suffixal morpheme with one or other gender, and various aspects of other derivational processes. Some phonetic endings are strongly linked with masculine or feminine. Certain initial phonemes or phoneme groups probably also favour one or other of the genders. The origin of loanwords is an additional factor, varying in its role according to the source language and its connection with Welsh. The relationship of these influences to one another will be examined and an attempt will be made to set up a tentative hierarchy of application.

From the theoretical point of view, it is important to add information about Welsh gender to the growing body of knowledge about the phenomenon in the Indo-European languages as a whole. In addition, the problem presented by grammatical gender to learners of Welsh can certainly be reduced by systematic presentation based on findings of this kind.

Dr Dorothy Dilts SWARTZ, Harvard University
Subject: Significant parallels between the style of LL *TBC* and twelfth-century classical rhetoric

The widely admired Book of Leinster *Taín Bó Cúalnge* (LL *TBC*) contains close parallels with at least thirty-three rhetorical techniques, of which seven appear to be particularly significant of a direct relationship between the LL version and the twelfth-century European Renaissance of classical learning including rhetoric, although most of the devices have simpler antecedents in earlier Irish tradition. The redactor uses these techniques consistently and in a style that becomes increasingly highly developed, markedly so in comparison with the earlier version in *Lebor na Huidre* (TBC I). The most significant devices consist of two forms of repetition (interlacement or *complexio* and classical *climax*), personal description (*ecphrasis*), and three forms of comparison (balance, *similitudo*, and *conlatio*) and 'the rhetorical question'. The stylistic indications of a relationship are reinforced by minor indications, several of which were brought to attention by Thurneysen, who also left the challenge of drawing a psychological portrait of the redactor, who left tell-tale signs of his personality in his great masterpiece.

Professor Eve SWEETSER, Department of Linguistics, University of California, Berkeley
Subject: Changing metrical structures in medieval Welsh verse

In Klar and Sweetser (1986), a view of medieval Welsh metrics was put forward which strove to give continuity to the development of the Welsh poetic tradition. It was suggested that many standard patterns of later syllabic Welsh metrics could be seen as natural formal developments from earlier stress-metrical patterns such as those found in *Canu Aneirin* (cf. Sweetser, in press) or *Canu Taliesin* (cf. Haycock, in press).

This paper examines a much broader corpus of medieval Welsh verse, both *cynfeirdd* and *gogynfeirdd* verse, showing in detail how regular stress patterns and syllabic regularity often coexisted in the same poetic works. The object is to establish a likely means for the change in metrical structure, since it seems that there was no sudden break in the Welsh metrical tradition. Changes in line-length, or redefinition of lines, of course interact with rhyme-scheme, and so internal and final rhyme-patterns will also be discussed.

Beth THOMAS, Welsh Folk Museum, St Fagans, Cardiff
Subject: Dialect shift: tradition and innovation in the spoken Welsh of Pont-rhyd-y-fen

This paper will consider the process of shifting from traditional dialect in a south Wales industrial village. It will be shown that variables characteristic of the dialect are being gradually lost in the community, but that for each of them the pattern of change is different. Linguistic innovation in each case appears to be linked to patterns of social interaction and to the domains in which Welsh is used by different groups within the community.

Dr Stephen N. TRANTER, English Seminar, Freiburg University, W. Germany
Subject: Brian Boru, warrior-hero or saint?

The Battle of Clontarf figures in two literary works central to their respective countries' traditions, 'Cogadh Gaedhed re Gallaibh' and 'Njáls saga'. It illustrates the adaptation of historical portrayal for pragmatic purposes.

The two works arose in comparable political climates, the Sturlung Age in Iceland and twelfth-century Ireland. In both countries, extreme turbulence in internal affairs paved the way for an invasion by a foreign power. Also, each work is arguably a reflection of the age of writing. Nonetheless there is a clear divergence in the use of the same historical theme.

It is the nature of this divergence, and its possible significance as an aid in evaluating the roles of the two accounts within their respective traditions, that this paper attempts to clarify.

Hildegard L. C. TRISTRAM, Englisches Seminar, Universität Freiburg
Subject: Tradition and innovation in the *Táin Bó Cuailnge*

The topic of this paper arises out of the research on the *Táin Bó Cuailnge* complex of texts, currently under study in the Freiburg (FRG) research project 'Orality and literacy in Early Irish literature'. Each redaction and/or version is viewed as a special kind of verbal innovation founded on the textual tradition. It is the transformation undergone by the story-line at successive stages that defines 'tradition' as the continuation of basic story matter in the deep-structure (to borrow a linguistic metaphor). Each transformation is understood to be conditioned by specific socio-cultural needs.

The talk will also take issue with such matters as editing Old and Middle Irish texts, the theory of book-prose versus free prose, and the traditional stemma model of source and manuscript relationships.

Professor Maria TYMOCZKO, University of Massachusetts, Amherst
Subject: The lost Welsh Arthurian cycle

On the basis of evidence from extant Welsh Arthurian materials and allusions to lost Arthurian stories, a reconstruction of the lost Welsh Arthurian Cycle will be proposed. Comparative evidence from Irish material and from later Romance materials about Arthur will be used to draw conclusions about the ideology of the lost Welsh cycle as well as about the poetics of the cycle. Ideological aspects to be addressed will include values, mores, and functions of the cycle; the discussion of poetics will include plotting, tale types, characterization, tone, narrative devices, and form. There will be a statistical evaluation of the size of the lost cycle *c.* 1050–1225. The implications of these conclusions for our understanding of the development of the genre of Arthurian romance will be addressed.

Dr R. L. VALENTE, Cornell University, Department of English
Subject: Gwydion and Aranrhod: crossing the borders of gender in the Fourth Branch

The codes of behaviour governing male–female interactions in Middle Welsh society are outlined in the first three Branches of the Mabinogi, providing the structure and motivation for events in those three narratives. In the Fourth Branch, these codes are consistently violated, leading to the instability—if not the destruction—of the social contracts between men and women. Events in this Branch which can be classified as legal violations are the rape of Goewin, Aranrhod's false assertion of virginity, and Blodeuwedd's and Gronw's adultery. These violations are woven into a narrative concerning the interactions between Gwydion and Aranrhod: their desires and powers are paralleled in the narrative through their relationship as siblings, and their competitive contention symbolizes the traditional war between the sexes. This paper will analyse the passages in which the two appear together—Aranrhod's test as Math's footholder and Gwydion's attempts to overcome Aranrhod's prohibitions against Lleu—showing that legal violations are brought about when either of the pair attempts to challenge or take on a power or right which is traditionally assigned to the opposite gender.

Professor Charlotte WARD, University of Minnesota, Minneapolis, USA
Subject: Einion Offeiriad's poetical treatise as a Renaissance phenomenon

The fourteenth-century Welsh treatise traditionally ascribed to Einion Offeiriad has frequently been dismissed as a forced application of Latin grammatical principles to the Welsh language and a prescriptive listing of metres not necessarily indicative of actual Welsh bardic practice. Yet it stands in favourable comparison with poetical treatises written in Latin and Provençal from the twelfth to the fourteenth centuries and proves that Welsh poetry of the time cannot be accurately described as the 'Celtic Fringe'. The critical stance is in keeping with the consciousness of what Haskins named the 'Twelfth-Century Renaissance', and the application of universals to language theory is a European-wide phenomenon in the later full-blown Renaissance period. Einion's treatise is in many ways ahead of its time; twentieth-century linguistic theory based on 'deep structures' would discover much sophistication here. Though not mentioned in the G. J. Williams and E. J. Jones edition of 1934, many of the poetical extracts can be specifically identified with *Gogynfeirdd* poets, and the intensive editing now under way on this period through the auspices of the newly opened Centre for Advanced Welsh and Celtic Studies should reveal how useful a map Einion's treatise is to this flowering of native tradition stimulated by contact with European poetry as a whole, thus fitting the characteristics of 'Renaissance' as described by Eric Auerbach.

Dr Gruffydd Aled WILLIAMS, Coleg Prifysgol Gogledd Cymru, Bangor
Subject: Psalmae Wiliam Midleton

Cytunir yn gyffredinol mai methiant llenyddol oedd *Psalmae y Brenhinol Brophwyd Dafydh*, mydryddiad Wiliam Midleton o'r Salmau a orffennwyd yn Escudo, Panama, ym 1596 ac a gyhoeddwyd yn Llundain ym 1603. Yn y papur hwn dadleuir i'r gwaith weithiau gael ei feirniadu ar gam ac y perthyn iddo ddiddordeb na chafodd ei lwyr amgyffred gan haneswyr llenyddol. Maentumir mai camgymeriad fu cyplysu'r gwaith â mydryddiadau o'r Salmau a fwriadwyd yn unswydd ar gyfer canu cynulleidfaol, megis 'Salmau Cân' Edmwnd Prys. Dylid ei gymharu'n hytrach â mydryddiadau o'r Salmau gan feirdd llys fel Clément Marot yn Ffrainc a Syr Philip Sidney yn Lloegr, fersiynau a ysgogwyd gan gymhellion celfyddydol yn ogystal â rhai crefyddol.

O gofio i Midleton dreulio cyfnod yng ngwasanaeth brawd-yng-nghyfraith Sidney, Henry Herbert, Iarll Penfro, ystyrir hefyd y posibilrwydd ddarfod i Salmau Sidney ei ysgogi'n uniongyrchol.

Dr Penny WILLIS
Subject: Phonological rules and true mutations in Breton

In Breton, there are several phonological rules which resemble the initial consonant mutations, and which have been erroneously treated as mutations or extensions of them. One example is fricative voicing which has often been identified with lenition. However, while true lenition is morphologically conditioned in modern Celtic, fricative voicing is still phonologically conditioned. There is not only a failure to distinguish between the two types of rule mutations, but also a reduction of insight into the way in which linguistic history appears to be repeating itself in Breton.

A related problem is phonological rules which modify, or reverse, the outcome of mutation rules. Examples are provective *sandhi* and velar palatalization (in V and eastern K dialects). The interaction of these rules with the mutations seems to be poorly understood; the result is needless complication in the description of the true mutations in Breton.

Dr Juliette WOOD, University College of North Wales, Bangor
Subject: Constructing a type and motif index for Welsh folk narratives

Since the pioneering work of Stith Thompson and Antti Aarne, the similarities and distribution of folk stories have been of great interest to students of traditional literature. A number of national indexes have been produced following the models developed by Thompson and Aarne, but none has, so far, been attempted for Wales.

The Welsh Folk Museum collection contains about 15,000 oral stories plus manuscript and printed material, and it was decided that this material could and should be organised as a Type and Motif Index. As such, it would be a useful tool to researchers, both Welsh-speaking and not, and would be of particular use for students of folklore who did not have direct access to the Welsh Folk Museum collection.

This paper is intended as an introduction to this project. Among the important aspects of compiling such an index, a major requirement is to adapt the material to the existing Aarne-Thompson format. As Welsh contains a great deal of narrative material not covered by existing indexes, it has been necessary to extend the system and often to create completely new categories. The compilers of the Welsh index have attempted to do this in such a way that new categories will be compatible with the old ones, and not present future users with unnecessary difficulties. A second important aspect to be considered is the reasoning behind choosing this rather traditional format of a type/motif index. The third and final aspect is the contribution of new technology to such a project. Although the end result will be in book form, computers have proved useful in creating the data base and due consideration must be given to the role of computers in long-term projects such as this one.

Dr Steffan ZIMMER, Freie Universität, Berlin
Subject: Bahuvrihi in Welsh

Unlike many other IE languages, Welsh has retained the possibility of forming exocentric nominal compounds. After a short discussion of the historical background (IE origins, CC formations) and some remarks on the history of the type in Welsh (e.g. its frequency in the Four Branches), the paper outlines its present state in Modern Welsh (with the exclusion of poetical language). Among others, answers to the following questions will be proposed: What kind of words are possible as first and second members? Are there any semantic restrictions? Which sub-types are productive today? The problem of the so-called reversed *Bahuvrihi* is given due attention.

MEMBERS OF THE CONGRESS

Alqvist, Dr Anders, Room 512, Tower 1, University College, Galway, Ireland.

Alonso, Professor Fernando, Facultad de Filologia, Universidad de Santiago, Spain.

Alonso, Mrs Fernando.

Andrews, Rhian, The Queen's University of Belfast, Belfast, BT7 1NN, Northern Ireland.

Anthony, Ilid E., Inglenook, 194 Merthyr Road, Cardiff, CF4 1DL, Wales.

Arnell, J., Castell Gorfod, Crosswell, Brynberian, Dyfed, Wales.

Awberry, Dr Gwen, Yr Amgueddfa Werin, Sain Ffagan, Caerdydd, Cymru.

Badone, Louise and Donalda, 34 Avondale Avenue, Willosdale, Ont., M2N 2T9, Canada.

Ball, Dr Martin, Department of Behavioural and Communication Studies, Polytechnic of Wales, Pontypridd, Wales.

Berton, J. A., Université de Bretagne Occidentale, Brest, France.

Bednarczuk, Leszek, 31–118 Krakow, ul. Grabowskiego 5–5, Poland.

de Bhaldraithe, Professor Thomas, An Tealta, 4B Temple Villas, Rathmines, Dublin 6, Ireland.

de Bhaldraithe, Mrs T.

Bijlmer-Adriaanse, L. W., Schubertstraat 41, 1077 Gr Amsterdam, Netherlands.

Blake, Professor James J., Apartment 9p, 230 East 15 Street, New York 10003, USA.

Blankenhorn, V. S., Department of Irish Studies, New University of Ulster, Coleraine, Co. Londonderry, BT52 1SA, Northern Ireland.

Bosch, Anna R. K., Linguistics Department, Classics Building, University of Chicago, Chicago, Il 60637, USA.

Bowen, Yr Athro D. J., Adran y Gymraeg, Coleg y Brifysgol, Aberystwyth, Dyfed, Cymru.

Bowen, Dr Geraint, Yr Hen Reithordy, Tal-y-llyn, Tywyn, LL36 9AJ, Gwynedd, Cymru.

Bowen, Mrs Zonia.

Bowen, Roderic, London House, Cilgerran, Aberteifi, Dyfed, Wales.

Breatnach, Liam, Department of Irish, Trinity College, Dublin, Ireland.

Breatnach, Dr Padraig A., Department of Irish, University College, Dublin 4, Ireland.

Breeze, Andrew, Dublin Institute for Advanced Studies, 10 Burlington Road, Dublin 4, Ireland.

Brett, Dr Caroline, Girton College, Cambridge, England.

Broderick, Dr George, Universität Mannheim, D6800 Mannheim, Schloss E.W.294, Germany.

Bromwich, Dr Rachel, 11 Sea View Place, Aberystwyth, Dyfed, Wales.

Bruford, Dr Alan J., School of Scottish Studies, University of Edinburgh, 27 George Square, Edinburgh, Scotland.

Bruford, Mrs Alan J.

Buckley, William J., 4940 South Woodlawn, Chicago, Illinois 60615, USA.

Burdett-Jones, M. T., Geiriadur Prifysgol Cymru, Llyfrgell Genedlaethol Cymru, Aberystwyth, Dyfed, Wales.

Byrne, C., Co-ordinator, Irish Studies, St Mary's University, Halifax, Nova Scotia, Canada.

Campbell, Cefin, 34 Nesta Road, Canton, Cardiff, Wales.

Carey, Dr John, Department of Celtic Languages and Literatures, Harvard University, 61 Kirkland Street, Cambridge, Massachusetts 02138, USA.

Clas, Arnaud, University College, Dublin 4, Ireland.

Clement, R. D., Linguistic Survey of Scotland, University of Edinburgh, 27 George Square, Edinburgh, EH8 9LD, Scotland.

Coe, Paula Pwers, 1322 N. Beverly Glen, Los Angeles, CA 90077, USA.

Crowe, Richard, Geiriadur Prifysgol Cymru, Llyfrgell Genedlaethol Cymru, Aberystwyth, Dyfed, Wales.

Davies, Ceri, Classics Department, University College, PO Box 78, Cardiff, CF1 1XL, Wales.

Davies, Dr Sioned, Adran y Gymraeg, Coleg y Brifysgol, Caerdydd, CF1 1XL, Cymru.

Davis, Daniel R., Jesus College, Oxford, OX1 3DW, England.

Dery, Robert, St John's College, Cambridge, CB2 1TP, England.

Dooley, Professor Ann, Department of Celtic Studies, St Michael's College, University of Toronto, 81 St Mary's Street, Toronto, M5S 1J4, Canada.

Edel, Professor Dr Doris, Witte de Withlaan, 14, 3941 WS Doorn, Netherlands.

Edwards, Dr Nancy, Adran Hanes, Coleg y Brifysgol, Bangor, Gwynedd, Cymru.

Eska, Joseph F., Centre for Medieval Studies, University of Toronto, 39 Queen's Park Crescent East, Toronto, M55 1A1, Canada.

Evans, Alun, Y Gofrestrfa, Coleg y Brifysgol, Parc Singleton, Abertawe, Cymru (Treasurer).

Evans, Yr Athro D. Ellis Evans, Coleg Iesu, Rhydychen.

Evans, Dr Dafydd Huw, Adran y Gymraeg, Coleg Prifysgol Dewi Sant, Llanbedr Pont Steffan, Dyfed, Cymru.

Evans, Yr Athro D. Simon, Adran y Gymraeg, Coleg Prifysgol Dewi Sant, Llanbedr Pont Steffan, Dyfed, Cymru.

Evans, Geraint, Pencefn, Capel Seion, Aberystwyth, Dyfed, Cymru.

Fife, James, 740 Archer Street, San Diego, California 92109, USA.

Findon, J., 46 Pritchard Avenue, Toronto, Ontario, M6N 1T3, Canada.

Fissore, Professor Valerio, Dipartimento di Scienze del Linguaggio, Universita di Torino, Via S. Ottavio, 20, 10124 Torino, Italy.

Franzinetti, Professor Joan Rees, Dipartimento Di Scienze del Linguaggio, Universita di Torino, Via S. Ottavio, 20, 10124 Torino, Italy.

Fulton, Dr Helen, Y Ganolfan Uwchefrydiau Cymreig a Cheltaidd, Coleg y Brifysgol, Aberystwyth, Dyfed, Cymru.

George, Dr K. J., Bospren, Keveral Lane, Seaton, Torpoint, Cornwall.

Gerriets, Marilyn, St Francis Xavier University, Antigonish, Nova Scotia, B2G 1CO, Canada.

Gillies, Professor William, Department of Celtic, David Hume Tower, George Square, Edinburgh, EH8 9JX, Scotland.

Gleasure, James W., Department of Celtic, The University, Glasgow, G12 8QQ, Scotland.

Gorini, Giovanni, Instituto di Archeologia-Universita di Padova, Italy.

Grant, William, 29a Drummond Place, Edinburgh, EH3 6PN, Scotland.

Green, Dr Miranda J., The Open University of Wales, 24 Cathedral Road, Cardiff, Wales.

Griffiths, Professor R. A., Department of History, University College of Swansea, Singleton Park, Swansea, Wales.

Griffith, Dr W. P., Adran Hanes Cymru, Coleg Prifysgol Gogledd Cymru, Bangor, Gwynedd, Cymru.

Grooms, Chris, Adran y Gymraeg, Coleg Prifysgol Cymru, Aberystwyth, Dyfed, Cymru.

Gruffydd, Yr Athro R. Geraint, Canolfan Uwchefrydiau Cymreig a Cheltaidd, Coleg y Brifysgol, Aberystwyth, Dyfed, Cymru.

Gwyndaf, Robin, Amgueddfa Werin Cymru, Sain Ffagan, Caerdydd, Cymru.

Hamp, Professor Eric P., Department of Linguistics, The University of Chicago, 1010 East 59th Street, Chicago, Illinois 60637, USA.

Hamp, Mrs Eric P.

Hannaher, Liam, 6626 Tunlaw Court, Alexandria, Virginia 22312, USA.

Hansen, Dr Leigh, 722 Copeland Street, Apt. 4, Santa Monica, CA 90405, USA.

Harries, W. Gerallt, Adran y Gymraeg, Coleg y Brifysgol, Parc Singleton, Abertawe, Cymru.

Harrison, Dr Alan, Department of Modern Irish, University College, Dublin, Ireland.

Harvey, Dr Anthony, Royal Irish Academy, 19 Dawson Street, Dublin 2, Ireland.

Hawke, Andrew, Geiriadur Prifysgol Cymru, Llyfrgell Genedlaethol Cymru, Aberystwyth, Dyfed, Cymru.

Haycock, Dr Marged, Adran y Gymraeg, Coleg Prifysgol Cymru, Aberystwyth, Cymru.

Hedlund, Mary E., 2010 27th Avenue, N.E., Minneapolis, MN 55418, USA.

Heffley, Sylvia P., 323 Mulberry Road, Mansfield Center, Conn. 06250, USA.

Henken, Elissa, 728 E. Hunter, Bloomington, Indiana 47401, USA.

Hennessey, John Jr., 1500–7th Street 6B, Sacramento, CA 95814, USA.

Herbert, Dr Maire, Department of Early and Medieval Irish, University College, Cork, Ireland.

Herity, Professor Michael, Dean of Faculty of Celtic Studies, University College, Dublin 4, Ireland.

Hewitt, Steve, Ar Veroudeg, Ar C'houerc'had, 22420 Plouared, Llydaw, Ffrainc.

Hirashima, Naoichiro, Kartäuserstr. 28, 7800 Freiburgh im Breisgau, West Germany.

Hofman, Dr R. H. F., Ameland 109, 3527 Am Utrecht, Netherlands.

Humphreys, Humphrey Lloyd, Adran Ffrangeg, Coleg Prifysgol Dewi Sant, Llanbedr Pont Steffan, Dyfed, Cymru.

Hunter, Jerry, 2 Portland Street, Aberystwyth, Dyfed, Wales.

Ireland, Dr Colin A., Dublin Institute for Advanced Studies, 10 Burlington Road, Dublin, Ireland.

Ireland, Mrs Colin A.

James, Dr Christine, Adran y Gymraeg, Coleg y Brifysgol, Parc Singleton, Abertawe, Cymru.

Jarman, Yr Athro A. O. H., 4 Henllys Road, Cyncoed, Caerdydd, Cymru.

Jarman, Mrs A. O. H.

Jefferiss, Paul, Dunster G–21, Harvard University, Cambridge, MA 02138, USA.

Jenkins, Yr Athro Emeritws Dafydd, 17 Min y Bryn, Aberystwyth, Cymru.

Jenkins, Manon, Coleg Sant Ioan, Caergrawnt, CB2 1TP, Lloegr.

Jerem, Dr Elisabeth, Archaeological Institute of the Hungarian Academy of Sciences, I., Uriutca 49, 1250 Budapest, Hungary.

Johnston, Dr David R., Adran y Gymraeg, Coleg y Brifysgol, Caerdydd, Cymru.

Jones, Yr Athro Bedwyr Lewis Jones, Adran y Gymraeg, Coleg Prifysgol Gogledd Cymru, Bangor, Gwynedd, Cymru.

Jones, Alun, Y Llyfrgell Genedlaethol, Aberystwyth, Dyfed, Cymru.

Jones, Dr Dafydd Glyn, Adran y Gymraeg, Coleg Prifysgol Gogledd Cymru, Bangor, Gwynedd, Cymru.

Jones, Gina, 47 Heol Iscoed, Rhiwbeina, Caerdydd, Cymru.

Jones, Dr J. Gwynfor Jones, 1 Westminster Drive, Cyncoed, Caerdydd, CF2 6RD, Cymru.

Jones, Nerys Ann, Y Ganolfan Uwchefrydiau Cymreig a Cheltaidd, Coleg Prifysgol Cymru, Aberystwyth, Dyfed, Cymru.

Jones, Yr Athro R. M. Jones, Adran y Gymraeg, Coleg Prifysgol Cymru, Aberystwyth, Dyfed, Cymru.

Jones, Dr Robert Owen Jones, Adran y Gymraeg, Coleg y Brifysgol, Parc Singleton, Abertawe, Cymru (Organizing Secretary).

Jongeling, Dr K. Vakgroup Hebreeuwse, Aramese en Ugaritische taal-en letterkund, Matthias de Vrieshof 4, 2311 BZ Leiden, Netherlands.

Kalyguine, Victor P., Institute of Linguistics, Academy of Sciences, Moscow, USSR.

Kelly, Professor Fergus, Dublin Institute of Advanced Studies, 10 Burlington Road, Dublin 4, Ireland.

Kelly, Dr Patricia, Institut fur Anglistik, Universität Innsbruck, Innrain 52, A-6010, Innsbruck, Austria.

Kitson, P. R., Department of English, The University, Birmingham.

Kobus, Isabel, Werderring 15, D. 7800 Freiburg, West Germany.

Koch, Dr John T., Department of Celtic Languages and Literatures, Harvard University, 61 Kirkland St., Cambridge, Mass. 02138, USA.

Korolyov, Andrey A., Institute of Ling., Academy of Sciences, Moscow, USSR.

Lambert, P. Y., 212 rue de Vaugirard, 75015 Paris, France.

Lambkin, Brian, 57 Candahar Street, Ballynafeigh, Belfast 7, Northern Ireland.

Laurent, Dr Donatien, 12 rue de Lorient, 29200 Brest, France.

Lazar-Meyn, Heidi Ann, 9321 Cedar Lane, Bethesda, Maryland 20814 USA.

Lewis, Richard Llewellyn, Manteg, 4 Tonna Uchaf, Tonna, Castell Nedd, Cymru.

Le Duc, Professor G., 4 rue de la Lane-Varques, La Trinité-Surzur, 56190 Muzillac, France.

Lewis, Dr Wendy, 34551 A Via Espinoza, Capistrano Beach, California 92624, USA.

Leyshon, Alysia, 3 Ruthin Gardens, Cathays, Caerdydd, Cymru.

Lloyd, Dr Nesta, Adran y Gymraeg, Coleg y Brifysgol, Parc Singleton, Abertawe, Cymru.

Loesch, Dr Katharine T., 2129 North Sedgewick St., Chicago, Illinois, 60614, USA.

Lorenz, Kathryn M., 1719 Wilmington Drive, Loveland, Ohio 45140, USA.

Lynch, Peredur, Y Ganolfan Uwchefrydiau Cymreig a Cheltaidd, Aberystwyth, Cymru.

MacCaulay, Cathlin, 192 Wilton Street, Glasgow, G2O 6BW, Scotland.

Macaulay, Donald, Department of Celtic, University of Aberdeen, Aberdeen, AB9 AUB, Scotland.

Macaulay, Mrs Donald.

Mac Cana, Professor Proinsias, Dublin Institute for Advanced Studies, 10 Burlington Road, Dublin 4, Ireland.

Mac Craith, Mícheál, Roinn na Nua-Ghaeilge, Colaiste na hOllscoile, Gaillimh, Eire.

MacDonald, Donald A., School of Scottish Studies, 27 George Square, Edinburgh, Scotland.

MacDonald, Kenneth D., Department of Celtic, University of Glasgow, Glasgow, Scotland G12.

Mac Eoin, Professor Gearoid, Department of Old and Middle Irish, University College, Galway, Ireland.

Mac Eoin, Mrs G.

Mac Gearailt, Uaitear, St Patrick's College, Drumcondra, Dublin 9, Ireland.

Mac Giolla Leith, Caoimhin, Department of Celtic, David Hume Tower, University of Edinburgh, George Square, Edinburgh, EH8 9JX, Scotland.

MacInnes, Dr John, 114 Braid Road, Edinburgh, EH10 6AS, Scotland.

MacKinnon, Dr Kenneth, Ivy Cottage, Ryefield, The Black Isle, by Conon Bridge, Ross-shire, IV7 8HX, Scotland.

Maclennan, Professor Gordon W., Department of Modern Languages, Tabaret Hall, University of Ottawa, Ottawa, Ontario, Canada.

Macleod, Morag, School of Scottish Studies, 27 George Square, Edinburgh, EH8 9LD, Scotland.

Mac Mathuna, Dr Liam, St Patrick's College, Drumcondra, Dublin 9, Ireland.

MacQueen, Professor John, 12 Orchard Toll, Edinburgh, EH4 3JF, Scotland.

MacQueen, Mrs John.

Mahon, William J., Department of Celtic, Harvard University, 61 Kirkland St, Cambridge, MA 02138, USA.

Matheson, Paul, Top Flat Right, 187 Bruntsfield Place, Edinburgh, EH10 4DQ, Scotland.

Matonis, Professor A. T. E., 7312 Emlen Street, Philadelphia PA19119, USA.

McKendry, Dr Eugene, St Mary's College, 191 Falls Road, Belfast, BT12 6FE, N. Ireland.

McKenna, Professor C., 182 Sackett St, Brooklyn, New York 11231, USA.

Meid, Professor Wolfgang, Institut für Sprachwissenschaft, Universität Innsbruck, Innrain 52, A-6020 Innsbruck, Austria.

Melia, Professor Daniel F., Department of Rhetoric, University of California, Berkeley, CA 94720, USA.

Merkt, Gisela, Universität Bonn, Fischweiher 37, 43 Essen 13, West Germany.

Morgan, Dr Ceridwen Lloyd, Adran Llawysgrifau, Llyfrgell Genedlaethol Cymru, Aberystwyth, Dyfed, Cymru.

Morgan, Dr Prys T. J., Department of History, University College of Swansea, Singleton Park, Swansea, Wales.

Muir, Dr Kay, 57 Candahar Street, Belfast 7, Northern Ireland.

Müller, Nicole, Sprachwissenschafteichen Institut der Universität, An der Schlosskirche 2, D-5300, Bonn 1, West Germany.

Mulligan, Dr Raymond A., 6901 Big Bear Drive, Tucson, Arizona, USA.

Mulligan, Mrs Raymond A.

Nagai, Ichiro, 3–6, Sengawa-machi, Chofu-shi, Tokyo 182, Japan.

Nagy, Dr Joseph Falaky, Department of English, University of California, Los Angeles, CA 90024, USA.

Ní Chatháin, Dr Poinseas, Department of Early Irish, University College, Dublin 4, Ireland.

Ni DhOmhnaill, Dr Cáit, Baile Ard Bearna, Co. na Gaillimh, Eire.

Ni Laoire, Siobhan, Roinn na Nua-Ghaeilge, University College, Belfield, Dublin 4, Ireland.

Ni ChOnghaile, Noirin, Kappler Str. 57/3258, D-7800 Freiburg 1 Br., West Germany.

Ni Mhaonaigh, Maíre, D.I.A.S., 10 Burlington Road, Dublin 4, Ireland.

Nilsen, Professor Kenneth, Department of Celtic, St Francis Xavier University, Antigonish, Nova Scotia, Canada.

O'Briain, Máirtín, Roinn na Gaeilge, Colaiste na hOllscoile, Gaillimh, Eire.

O'Brien, Elizabeth, 121 Barton Road East, Dundrum, Dublin 4, Ireland.

O'Cathasaigh, Professor Tomás, 14 Wilfield Road, Sandymount, Dublin 4, Ireland.

O Cleirigh, Professor Conn R., Linguistics Department, University College, Dublin 4, Ireland.

O Conchuir, Padraig,

O'Connell, N.,

O Corráin, Professor Donnchadh, Department of Irish History, University College, Cork, Ireland.

Ó Corráin, Dr Ailbhe, Uppsala Universitet, Department of English, Celtic Section, Box 513 S 751 20 Uppsala, Sweden.

Ó Cuív, Professor Brian, Dublin Institute for Advanced Studies, 10 Burlington Road, Dublin 4, Ireland.

Ó Cuív, Mrs Brian.

Ó Dubhthaigh, Dr Bearnárd, Department of Education, Hawkins House XI, Dublin 2, Ireland.

O Flaithearta, Míchéal, Englisches Seminar der Universität, Löwenstr. 16, D7800 Freiburg, West Germany.

O hAodha, Dr Donncha, Department of Old Irish, University College, Galway, Ireland.

Ó Laoghaire, Revd Diarmuid, Pairc Bhaile an Mhuilinn, Baile Atha Cliath 6, Eire.

O Madagáin, Professor Breandan, Dept of Modern Irish, University College, Galway, Ireland.

Ó Máille, Tomas S., Cuilleann, An Bothar Ard, Gaillimh, Eire.

Ó Máille, Mrs T. S.

O Maoláin, Peadar, 7 Sráid Cormac, Tulach Mor, Co. Uibh Failí, Eire.

Ó Maolfabhail, Art, 10 Achadh Feá, Caislean Cnucha, Baile Atha Cliath, Eire.

O Muiri, Dr Damien, Department of Modern Irish, St Patrick's College, Maynooth, Co. Kildare, Irish Republic.

O Muiri, Mrs Damien.

O'Sullivan, Helen, 13 Eardley Road, Sevenoaks, Kent, TN13 1XX, England.

O'Sullivan, William, Harbourne, Torquay Road, Foxrock, Co. Dublin, Ireland.

Owen, Ann Parry, Y Ganolfan Uwchefrydiau Cymreig a Cheltaidd, Coleg y Brifysgol, Aberystwyth, Dyfed, Cymru.

Owen, Leslie, Department of Old Irish, University College, Galway, Ireland.

Owen, Morfydd E., Y Ganolfan Uwchefrydiau Cymreig a Cheltaidd, Coleg y Brifysgol, Aberystwyth, Cymru.

Owen, Trefor M., Meillionydd, 27 Tal y Cae, Tregarth, Bangor, Gwynedd, Cymru.

Padel, O. J., Institute of Cornish Studies, Trevenson House, Pool, Redruth, Cornwall.

Patton, Laurie L., 1100E 55th St, Chicago, Il 60615, USA.

Pennar, Dr Meirion, Adran y Gymraeg, Coleg Prifysgol Dewi Sant, Llanbedr Pont Steffan, Dyfed, Cymru.

Poppe, Dr Erich, Beethovenstr. 10, D-6250 Limburg I, West Germany.

Powell, Nia M., Adran Hanes Cymru, Coleg Prifysgol Gogledd Cymru, Bangor, Gwynedd, Cymru.

Pryce, Dr Huw, Adran Hanes, Coleg Prifysgol Gogledd Cymru, Bangor, Gwynedd, Cymru.

Radner, Professor J., Department of Literature, College of Arts and Sciences, The American University, Washington DC20016, USA.

Ragland, Amy, Adran Allanol, Coleg Prifysgol Cymru, Aberystwyth, Dyfed, Cymru.

Reaves, Anne, University of Texas at Austin, 806 Keasbey St, Austin, TX78751, USA.

Rees, Siwan Non, Coleg Iesu, Rhydychen/Oxford, OX1 3DW, England.

Rhys, John, Cyfarwyddwr, Gwasg Prifysgol Cymru, 6 Stryd Gwennyth, Caerdydd, Cymru.

Rhys, Robert G., Adran y Gymraeg, Coleg y Brifysgol, Parc Singleton, Abertawe, Cymru.

Riley, Ann Dobbs, 10317, Morning Avenue, Downey, CA 90241, USA.

Roberts, Dr Brynley F., Y Llyfrgellydd, Llyfrgell Genedlaethol Cymru, Aberystwyth, Dyfed, Cymru.

Roberts, Mrs Brynley F.

Roberts, R. J., Keeper of Printed Books, Bodleian Library, Oxford, England.

Rockel, Dr Martin, D.D.R. 1110 Berlin, Grabbeallee 75, German Democratic Republic.

Ross, Bianca, Pfaffenberg 7, 3550 Marburg-Elnhausen, West Germany.

Rossi, Andrea, 121 Ox Yoke Drive, Wethersfield, CT 06109, USA.

Rowland, Dr Jenny, Adran y Gymraeg, Coleg y Brifysgol, Dulyn/Dublin, Iwerddon/Ireland.

Ryan, Revd John, St Mary's College, Rhos on Sea, Colwyn Bay, LL28 4NR, Cymru.

Ruddock, Gilbert, Adran y Gymraeg, Coleg y Brifysgol, Parc Cathays, Caerdydd, Cymru.

Ryan, John Vincent, 27 Lothian Road South, London N4 1EN, England.

Ryan, Kathleen, 6 St Leger Place, Tramore, Co. Waterford, Ireland.

Russel, Dr Paul, 4 Church Walk, Oxford, England.

Saari, Peggy M., University of Cincinnati, Department of English and Comparative Literature, 220 McMicken Hall (ML 69), Cincinnati, Ohio 45221-0069, USA.

Sannomiya-Ikegami, Ikuko, Department of English, College of Gen. Education, Kyushu University, Ropponmatsu, Fukuoka, Japan.

Shaw, Dr John, RR1 West Bay Road, Glendale, Nova Scotia, Canada.

Sims-Williams, Dr Patrick, 7 Corporation Street, Aberystwyth, Dyfed, Cymru.

Slotkin, Professor Edgar M., Department of English and Comparative Literature, 248–9 McMicken Hall, University of Cincinnati, Cincinnati, Ohio 45221, USA.

Smith, Yr Athro Beverly, Adran Hanes Cymru, Coleg Prifysgol Cymru, Aberystwyth, Dyfed, Cymru.

Smith, Peter, Royal Commission on Ancient and Historical Monuments in Wales, Edleston House, Queen's Road, Aberystwyth, Dyfed, Wales.

Stempel, Dr Reinhard, Sprachwissenschaftliches Institut der Universität Bonn, An der Schlosskirche 2, D-5300 Bonn 1, West Germany.

Stempel, Mrs R.

Stenson, Professor Nancy, Department of Linguistics, University of Minnesota, 142 Klaeber Ct., 320 SE 16th Ave., Minneapolis, Mn 554455, USA.

Stephens, Dr Janig, Pen y Bryn, Llanfaes, Llanilltud Fawr, CF6 9XR, Cymru.

Stewart, James, 5 Maunsell's Road, Galway, Ireland.

Stuart, P., St Mary's College, 191 Falls Road, Belfast BT12 6FE, Northern Ireland.

Surridge, Dr Marie, Department of French, Queen's University, Kingston, Ontario, Canada K7L 3N6.

Swartz, Herman S., 19 Highland Avenue, Lexington, Mass. 02173, USA.

Swartz, Dr Dorothy.

Sweetser, Professor Eve, Department of Linguistics, University of California, Berkeley, California 94720, USA.

Ternes, Professor Dr Elmar, Papenmoorweg 36e, D2083, Halsten Bek, West Germany.

Thomas, Beth, Amgueddfa Werin Cymru, Sain Ffagan, Caerdydd, Cymru.

Thomas, Dr Ceinwen H., 4 Cae Delyn Road, Whitchurch, Caerdydd, Cymru.

Thomson, Professor Derrick S., Department of Celtic, The University, Glasgow G12 8QQ, Scotland.

Thomson, Robert L., 35 Friary Park, Ballabeg, Castletown, Isle of Man.

Thorne, Dr David A., Adran y Gymraeg, Coleg Prifysgol Dewi Sant, Llanbedr Pont Steffan, Cymru.

Toorians, Dr L.G.M.C., Griegstraat 417, 5011, Hk Tilburg, Netherlands.

Tranter, Dr S. N., Englisches Seminar, Der Albert Ludwigs Universität, D-7800 Freiburg, I.B.R. den Lowenstrasse 16, West Germany.

Tristram, Dr Hildegard, L. C., Englisches Seminar der Universität Postfach, D-7800 Freiburg, Germany.

Tymoczko, Professor Maria, 28 Pomeroy Terrace, Northampton, MA 01060, USA.

Uhlich, Jürgen, Dublin Institute for Advanced Studies, 10 Burlington Road, Dublin 4, Ireland.

Valente, Dr Roberta, Department of English, Cornell University, Ithaca, NY 14850, USA.

Wailes, Bernard, 6 St Leger Place, Tramore, Co. Waterford, Ireland.

Walsh, Kevin, Dublin Institute for Advanced Studies, 10 Burlington Road, Dublin 4, Ireland.

Walter, Barbara, Karl Barth Strasse 71, 53 Bonn 1, West Germany.

Ward, Professor M. Charlotte, Assistant Professor, Department of English, University of Minnesota, Minneapolis 55455, USA.

Watkins, Professor T. Arwyn, Department of Welsh, University College, Belfield, Dublin 4, Ireland.

Williams, Yr Athro Glanmor (Chairman), 11 Grosvenor Road, Sgeti, Abertawe, Cymru.

Williams, Dr G. Aled, Adran y Gymraeg, Coleg Prifysgol Gogledd Cymru, Bangor, Gwynedd, Cymru.

Williams, Yr Athro J. Gwynn, Adran Hanes Cymru, Coleg Prifysgol Gogledd Cymru, Bangor, Gwynedd, Cymru.

Williams, Margaretta, Adran y Gymraeg, Coleg Prifysgol Cymru, Aberystwyth, Dyfed, Cymru.

Willis, Dr Penny, 48–26 196 St, Flushing, New York 11365, USA.

Wood, Dr Juliette, Amgueddfa Werin Cymru, Sain Ffagan, Caerdydd, Cymru.

Wooding, Jonathan, Department of History, University of Sydney, 2006 NSW, Australia.

Wringe, Mark, Department of Modern Irish, University College, Galway, Ireland.

Zimmer, Dr Stefan, Fabechstr 7, Freie Universität Berlin, D-1000 Berlin 33, Germany.